Experiences in Movement

with Music, Activities, and Theory

**Rae
Pica**

Delmar Publishers Inc.

I(T)P An International Thomson Publishing Company

Albany · Bonn · Boston · Cincinnati · Detroit · London · Madrid · Melbourne
Mexico City · New York · Pacific Grove · Paris · San Francisco · Singapore · Tokyo
Toronto · Washington

DEDICATION

To my friends at Human Kinetics, my first publishing family, and my husband, Richard Gardzina, for all they have made possible in my life.

Cover Illustration: Alexander Piejko
Cover Design: Bob Clarke
Illustrations: Dawn Bates

Delmar Staff
Acquisitions Editor: Jay Whitney
Developmental Editor: Christopher Anzalone
Project Editor: Eugenia Orlandi

Production Coordinator: Jennifer Gaines
Art & Design Coordinator: Douglas Hyldelund

COPYRIGHT © 1995
By Delmar Publisher
a division of International Thomson Publishing Inc.

The ITP logo is a trademark under license
Printed in the United States of America

For more information, contact:

Delmar Publishers
3 Columbia Circle, Box 15015
Albany, New York 12212-5015

International Thomson Publishing Europe
Berkshire House 168-173
High Holborn
London WC1V 7AA
England

Thomas Nelson Australia
102 Dodds Street
South Melbourne, 3205
Victoria, Australia

Nelson Canada
1120 Birchmount Road
Scarborough, Ontario
Canada M1K 5G4

International Thomson Editores
Campos Eliseos 385, Piso 7
Col Polanco
11560 Mexico D F Mexico

International Thomson Publishing GmbH
Königswinterer Strasse 418
53227 Bonn
Germany

International Thomson Publishing Asia
221 Henderson Road
#05 - 10 Henderson Building
Singapore 0315

International Thomson Publishing - Japan
Hirakawacho Kyowa Building, 3F
2-2-1 Hirakawacho
Chiyoda-ku, Tokyo 102
Japan

1 2 3 4 5 6 7 8 9 10 XXX 01 00 99 98 97 96 95

Library of Congress Cataloging-in-Publication Data

Pica, Rae, 1953–
    Experiences in movement with music, activities, and theory / Rae Pica.
        p. cm.
    Includes index.
    ISBN 0-8273-6478-4
    1. Movement education.   I. Title.
GV452.P515 1995
372.86—dc20   94-33269
                                                          CIP

Contents

28.95

CHAPTER **11**

Bringing Movement Education Outdoors 303

APPENDIX **1**

Developmentally Appropriate Practice in Movement Programs for Young Children Ages 3–5 323

APPENDIX **2**

Sources and Resources 336

PREFACE

*O*ccasionally, it takes an extra long time for an idea to take hold—for the "light bulb" to switch on.

I have been conducting movement workshops since 1981, during which time I have provided information to thousands of women and men working and studying to work with young children. During these many years, I have spent a lot of money and hours preparing handouts so participants would not have to take copious notes or try to remember everything I said in a 2-, 3-, or 6-hour workshop.

Throughout this period, I have also taught continuing education courses to pre- and in-service early childhood and physical education professionals. For the past 5 years, I have taught movement fundamentals to physical education majors at the University of New Hampshire. And every time I filled out forms for required texts for these classes, I was reminded there was no one book that offered the information I felt my students needed.

Still, in spite of the opportunities these situations provided—and despite the fact that I had already written several movement activity books—it never occurred to me I should simply write my own movement textbook.

Finally, a chance conversation with a professor teaching movement to early childhood majors switched on my light bulb. We were lamenting that there was no just-right book that addressed the hows, whats, and whys of movement education for young children. Physical education texts were mainly written for those planning to teach K–6 and thus offered too much—and mostly inappropriate—material. Movement books written for early childhood professionals offered too *little,* often treating movement as something extra for young children to enjoy, rather than a necessary and integral part of the child's education. Movement activity books were fine for providing ideas but failed to explain the how-to, should readers opt to go beyond the ideas presented. Creative dance and educational gymnastics texts informed readers of just two possible aspects of movement education. And a large number of books, in these categories, indicated much equipment would have to be made or purchased for a movement program to take place.

Thus, the idea for *Experiences in Movement with Music, Activities, and Theory* was born. Offering information regarding both theory and practice, the text is written with the belief the child's body is the only equipment absolutely needed for movement. It is written for anyone who realizes the potential value of movement in young children's lives and wishes to know more, and do more, about movement. It has been written for those who are, or plan to be,

- early childhood professionals in public or private preschools, kindergartens, or child-care centers;
- physical education specialists whose job descriptions now include preschoolers as well as kindergarteners;
- movement specialists who go wherever their services are required—early childhood settings, recreation and gymnastic centers, YM- and YWCAs, and dance studios;
- early childhood and early elementary music educators; and
- primary-level classroom teachers.

Although this may seem like a diverse group, all these professionals share two common traits: They work with children ages 2 to 8, and they know children of this age need to move to develop physically, emotionally, socially, and cognitively!

Written in a simple, straightforward manner, *Experiences in Movement with Music, Activities and Theory* begins by attempting to answer the question I am *so often* required to answer: What exactly is movement education? Following this, the principal content of the book is divided into four sections.

In Part One the basics of movement education are covered, with Chapter 1 outlining some of the many reasons why movement must be part of children's lives. Chapter 2 looks at the cognitive, affective, and motor development of toddlers, preschoolers, early elementary children, and children with special needs, and at how the movement program has an impact on these various ages and stages of development. Chapter 3 defines the ingredients that should comprise an early childhood movement curriculum.

Part Two: Planning for Movement and Music deals with such practical considerations as planning and scheduling lessons, group size, and the use of space and available equipment. Because music makes such a significant contribution to movement education—and movement to music education—Chapter 6 offers detailed suggestions for choosing and using music. Strategies are given to help readers provide for rich and varied music-and-movement experiences.

Part Three: Facilitating Movement Experiences, offers recommendations that can help ensure success for both teachers and children. Chapter 7 focuses on the three teaching methods most often used in movement education, and Chapter 8 covers the topic that is frequently the teacher's primary concern: managing a room full of moving children.

Finally, because movement should not be a segregated part of the curriculum, Part Four explores some of the ways in which movement experiences can be used to enrich other curricula areas: art, language arts, math, science, and social studies. Chapter 10: Using Movement and Music for Transitions, explains how to make daily transitions more manageable and more relevant to the curriculum as a whole.

Chapter 11 explores how movement exploration can contribute to playground experiences.

At the end of each chapter, key points are highlighted for study and discussion, and suggestions are made for assignments that elicit answers to thought-provoking questions and require students to conduct additional research and gain hands-on experience. Throughout the book, numerous sample activities are presented to clarify points made, provide examples for the children to enjoy, and stimulate the reader's own ideas. Also, anecdotes—my own and those of others with stories to share—highlight some of the humor, frustrations, and joys related to simultaneously working in two exciting, rewarding, and important fields: early childhood and movement education.

Acknowledgments

I want to offer my sincere thanks to everyone who helped make this book possible: Carol Hammett and Rhonda Clements, for their thoughtful suggestions and dedication to the field; Dawn Bates, my friend and illustrator through ten books; Patti Page, whose love and encouragement helped get me through the project; and Collin who, through the struggles and celebrations, is always there when I need him.

My reviewers, for their time, effort, and contributions: Sara Jane Anderson, Mount Ida College, Mass.; Suzanne T. Berry, Ph.D., Eastern New Mexico University, N.M.; Rhonda Clements, Ph.D., Hofstra University, N.Y.; Dorothy Conteh, Fort Valley State College, Ga.; Lou Gerardy, Amarillo College, Texas; Carol Hammett, Curriculum Specialist, Ore.; Mara Maislen, Capital Community–Technical College, Conn.; Mary Jo Pollman, Metropolitan State College of Denver, Colo.; Lynda Roberts, Cerritos College, Calif.; Ann Schmidt, Champlain College, Vt.

My deepest appreciation, also, to the children and teachers from the following schools and centers, who appear in my photos:

- Barnstead Elementary School, Barnstead, N.H.;
- Calvary Nursery School, Merrick, N.Y.;
- Concord Community Music School, Concord, N.H.;
- Nashua Child Learning Center, Nashua, N.H.; and
- The Diane Lindner-Goldberg Child Care Institute at Hofstra University, Hempstead, N.Y.

Special thanks to Christine Hagerty, for her support and her commitment to movement education.

INTRODUCTION

*I*nevitably, when I am on an airplane en route to conduct a workshop or deliver a speech, the person in the seat beside me will ask, innocently enough, what I do for a living. I realize this is a common question and, for most people, the answer is simple. But I have learned to wish he or she would not ask.

"I'm a movement education specialist," I respond. And their eyes go blank because they have absolutely no idea what movement education is. So, naturally, I have to try to explain it to them.

The problem is that I have never, in all these years, managed to devise a perfect one- or two-sentence definition of movement education. When I am tired, or I have a briefcase stuffed with work, I have been known to take the lazy way out and say simply, "Movement education is creative movement." But that term does not begin to do justice to what is a multifaceted and important subject, so I end up feeling guilty that I did not take the opportunity to better inform someone.

Now, of course, there is no easy way out; a textbook about movement education must define the topic. But after more than 15 years in the field, defining it is still not an easy task for me. (Like a word we use as a regular part of our vocabulary, we *know* what it means; it is just describing it to somebody else that is a problem.)

Movement education's historical origins provide some insight. Rudolf Laban is generally considered the father of movement education. A dancer, choreographer, dance educator, and director of modern dance and ballet companies, Laban studied movement in its many forms. But it was not until Hitler's regime made it impossible for him to remain in Germany and he had immigrated to England that his work began to gain recognition. In England, he developed a system of analyzing movement through what he termed the elements of time, weight, space, and flow (the elements described in Chapter 3 are adapted from these). He also determined experimentation should be used as a teaching method (the origin of the indirect teaching styles described in Chapter 7).

Laban and his associates developed his work in the English schools, and gradually his methods extended to Western Europe and then to the United States, where movement education has had its highs and lows but has never stopped evolving.

Of course, movement education's ever-changing state is one of the reasons it is difficult to nail down a definition. Recently, when preparing a keynote address for an early childhood movement conference, the solution seemed to be to describe what movement education is *not*.

Movement education incorporates creative movement and even creative dance, but it cannot accurately be called by either name. Both are concerned primarily with expressive movement, or the communication of ideas. Although Laban's work dealt more with the expressive than the functional—movement that "fulfills a purpose in work, sports, or activities of life" (Brown & Sommer, 1969, p.44)[1]—movement education today values both the expressive *and* the functional.

Although movement education is *physical* education in that learning takes place primarily through the physical domain, it is not physical education as many of us remember it. In other words, it is not the subject where

- the teacher stands in front of the students and tells them exactly what to do and how to do it (jumping jacks and push-ups always surface in my recollections);
- there is a *right* way and a *wrong* way to do everything (remember trying to climb the rope and staring down at the "horse" waiting to be jumped?); or
- only the physical domain is considered (my repeated failures wreaked havoc with my affective domain).

Rather, movement education

- uses less direct approaches to instruction that are more child-centered;
- allows students to experience success almost every time; and
- involves the *whole* child.

In fairness, many physical education programs also do the same these days. But they also include activities that do not fall under the heading of movement education, like soccer and square dancing.

So what *is* movement education? Well, one of the best definitions I have ever read is from Moran and Kalakian (1974, p. 111).[2] They describe it as *basic movement,* which "is the foundation upon which the complex movements for all activity areas of physical education are built," and implementing *movement exploration,* which they call "the problem-solving approach to the teaching of physical education." Although many of us take movement a bit beyond the basic and use more than one instructional method, basic movement and exploration are indeed the essence of movement education. But Moran and Kalakian's description of the *purpose* of movement education hits the proverbial nail on the head. They write:

---

1 Brown, M. C., & Sommer, B. K. (1969). *Movement education: its evolution and a modern approach.* Reading, Mass., Addison-Wesley.
2 Moran, J. M. & Kalakian, L. H. (1974). *Movement experiences for the mentally retarded or emotionally disturbed child.* Minneapolis: Burgess.

The intent of the program is to help the child become aware of his own potentials for moving efficiently and effectively in all aspects of living, including motor tasks involved in daily activities for play, work, and creative expression. Through movement education the child develops his general capacity for movement and learns the fundamentals necessary to facilitate his subsequent skill development. . . . Movement education incorporates the child's natural inclination to move freely, to be creative, and to test his own abilities. (p. 112)

Of course, after studying this text and conducting movement sessions with children, you will probably find your own definition. And as the years pass and you find yourself adapting your movement activities to suit varying situations and different children, your definition will probably change, too. And that is as it should be. But there is one thing I hope you will discover in the very beginning as you read the following chapters, and that will *never* change: Movement education is fun!

I suppose if I were to condense all the above into just *one* sentence, I could say movement education is a success-oriented, child-centered, noncompetitive form of physical education emphasizing fundamental movements and the discovery of their variations, which can later be used in games, sports, dance, gymnastics, and life itself.

Now, if I can commit that definition to memory, I just might get some work done on those planes!

PART ONE

The Basics of
Movement Education

CHAPTER 1

Benefits of Movement Education

Figure 1-1
The development of movement skills is perhaps the most important reason children should be encouraged to move.

*C*hildren love to move! And there are many valid reasons—in addition to enjoyment—why they should be given ample opportunity to do so. Among them is the increasing evidence that children use movement to learn about themselves and the world around them.

But perhaps the simplest and most important reason children should be allowed and encouraged to move is to develop movement skills.

Although it is commonly believed children automatically develop motor skills as their bodies develop, maturation only means the child will be able to execute most movement skills at a low performance level. Continuous practice and instruction are required if the child's performance level and movement repertoire are to increase (Cleland & Gallahue, 1993; Gallahue, 1993; Seefeldt, 1984). A developmentally appropriate movement curriculum can give students the practice and instruction necessary to refine their movement skills and expand their movement vocabularies. And this is critical because their ability to move well promotes feelings of self-confidence and competence and will affect them socially, emotionally, and physically (Bunker, 1991; Poest et al., 1990).

Furthermore, a developmentally appropriate movement curriculum can help develop physical fitness, provide a well-rounded introduction to music, foster social development, stimulate cognitive development, and enhance creativity, as this chapter will show.

Physical Fitness and the Young Child

Although children love to move—and adults tend to think of them as constantly in motion—there is some concern that children today may be leading much more sedentary lives than their predecessors. Children 2 to 5 spend an average of $25\frac{1}{2}$ hours a week watching television, and 6- to 11-year-olds spend almost 23 hours a week in front of the set (Groves, 1988). During a year, that is as much time as children spend in school. The advent of computers and video games, though beneficial in many ways, may also contribute to a decline in

CAUTION: CHILDREN NOT AT PLAY.

Once, children spent their time running and playing. Today they're more likely to be found in front of the TV. Encourage children to be more active. Fighting heart disease may be as simple as child's play. To learn more, contact your nearest American Heart Association, 7272 Greenville Avenue, Box 36, Dallas, TX 75231-4596.

You can help prevent heart disease and stroke. We can tell you how.

American Heart Association

This space provided as a public service.   ©1992, American Heart Association

Figure 1-2
Reproduced with permission. Winter/Spring 1992 Magazine Ad Kit. Copyright American Heart Association.

activity. Some studies show up to 50 percent of American children are not getting enough exercise (Taras, 1992).

To further compound the problem, Westerners have yet to completely accept the unity of mind and body—so we insist on training minds in classrooms and bodies in physical education classes, which are practically nonexistent in preschools and child-care centers and are increasingly disappearing in elementary schools due to budget cuts. When available, these classes still too often stress competition and elimination. And then what happens to the child's love of movement?

Does this mean our children are unfit? Currently, this issue generates much debate. Pangrazi and Corbin (1993) assert results of studies in the early 1950s (which were based on skill-related fitness test items, as opposed to health-related test items)—and the ensuing media hype—have reinforced the notion that American children are unfit. They state when determining fitness is based on the results of health-related tests, the majority of children and youth are considered fit.

We do know, however, 40 percent of 5- to 8-year-olds show at least one heart disease risk factor, including such risk factors as hypertension and obesity, which is rising (Berenson, 1980; Ross et al., 1987). Studies by the Institute for Aerobic Research (1987) also indicate the first signs of arteriosclerosis are appearing at about age 5.

Unfortunately, at present, little research suggests whether childhood physical activity has an impact on childhood health. It is believed, however, individuals who are physically active as children are likely to remain physically active in adulthood; therefore, physical activity in childhood may indeed have an impact on adult health

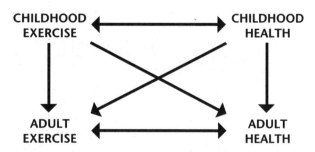

Figure 1-3
Conceptual model of how childhood exercise habits may affect health throughout life. Arrows indicate possible relationships. From David R. Lamb & Carl V. Gisolfi, *Perspectives in Exercise Science and Sports Medicine, Volume 2: Youth, Exercise, and Sport.* Copyright © 1989 by Benchmark Press, Inc. Reprinted by permission of William C. Brown Communications, Inc., Dubuque, Iowa. All Rights Reserved.

(Blair, 1992; Blair et al., 1989). Sedentary habits among adults are a major health problem in the United States, with an estimated 250,000 deaths a year due to low levels of activity and fitness (Hahn et al., as cited in Blair, 1992).

FUTURE IMPLICATIONS

The implications are clear—and frightening. Obese children tend to become obese adults (Shapiro et al., 1984). Children with high blood pressure are likely to become adults with high blood pressure (Parker et al., 1984). These facts, combined with evidence of arteriosclerosis in young children—and a society that places less and less value on recreation—could mean future generations in which cardiovascular disease becomes an even greater threat than it is at present.

Physical Best (1989), developed by the American Alliance for Health, Physical Education, Recreation, and Dance (AAHPERD), defines physical fitness as "a physical state of well-being that allows people to (1) perform daily activities with vigor, (2) reduce their risk of health problems relative to lack of exercise, and (3) establish a fitness base for participation in a variety of physical activities."

If this definition of physical fitness is to become a reality for the children of today, they must be taught physical activity is just as important throughout life as good hygiene and a proper diet (Taras, 1992). Parents and teachers must encourage, praise, and validate physical activity at every opportunity.

Yes, the competition with television and video games is steep, but children will never be as motivated to be physically active as they are during the early years. And children who are physically active and experience success in movement tasks show higher levels of self-esteem and a greater sense of accomplishment (Bunker, 1991; Seefeldt, 1980). So parents and early childhood professionals are not without weapons in their war against sedentary lifestyles.

THE ROLE OF MOVEMENT

The role of movement is evident: Physical activity promotes fitness, and physical activity *is* movement. However, there are two different points of view to consider in terms of promoting physical fitness in early childhood. The first has to do with movement itself; the second concerns movement *education*.

Regarding the former, caregivers and teachers of young children have a definite advantage over most elementary education teachers.

THE PHYSICALLY EDUCATED PERSON This five-part definition of the physically educated person was created by the National Association for Sport and Physical Education (NASPE) Outcomes Committee and published in 1992. Although parts of the definition are beyond the range of the young child's developmental levels, the early childhood and elementary professional can still do much to help ensure the children in their care will eventually be physically educated individuals.

According to the document, the physically education person

- Has learned skills necessary to perform a variety of physical activities . . .
    1. moves using concepts of body awareness, space awareness, effort and relationships.
    2. demonstrates competence in a variety of manipulative, locomotor and nonlocomotor skills.
    3. demonstrates competence in combinations of manipulative, locomotor and nonlocomotor skills performed individually and with others.
    4. demonstrates competence in many different forms of physical activity.
    5. demonstrates proficiency in a few forms of physical activity.
    6. has learned how to learn new skills.

- Is physically fit . . .
    7. assesses, achieves and maintains physical fitness.
    8. designs safe, personal fitness programs in accordance with principles of training and conditioning.

- Does participate regularly in physical activity
    9. participates in health enhancing physical activity at least three times a week
    10. selects and regularly participates in lifetime physical activities.

- Knows the implications of and the benefits from involvement in physical activities . . .
    11. identifies the benefits, costs and obligations associated with regular participation in physical activity.
    12. recognizes the risk and safety factors associated with regular participation in physical activity.
    13. applies concepts and principles to the development of motor skills.
    14. understands that wellness involves more than being physically fit.

15. knows the rules, strategies and appropriate behaviors for selected physical activities.
16. recognizes that participation in physical activity can lead to multicultural and international understanding.
17. understands that physical activity provides the opportunity for enjoyment, self-expression and communication.

- Values physical activity and its contributions to a healthful lifestyle . . .
18. appreciates the relationships with others that result from participation in physical activity.
19. respects the role that regular physical activity plays in the pursuit of life-long health and well-being.
20. cherishes the feelings that result from regular participation in physical activity.

The Institute of Aerobic Research (1987) has stated children need to exercise aerobically at least three times a week to reduce arteriosclerosis. Further, if cardiovascular fitness is to be improved, the physical activity must be continuous. Although most elementary physical education specialists are seeing their time with the children significantly reduced—and elementary classroom teachers are constrained by lack of time or space—many early childhood professionals do see their young charges at least three times a week. So they have the perfect opportunity to make certain regular physical activity is a vital part of the children's weekly schedule.

Teachers who do not see students at least three times a week can still make a meaningful impression by encouraging exercise outside of school and providing developmentally appropriate information regarding fitness and exercise. The activity itself is not the only important facet of fitness education (Pangrazi & Corbin, 1993).

The significance of movement education (i.e., a developmentally appropriate movement curriculum) is that it offers the children frequent opportunities to experience success in movement. Everyone—young and old—enjoys experiencing success. And when an experience is enjoyable, people are likely to want to repeat it often. Garnet (1982, p. 11) wrote: "Our biological need for movement is ensured by the sensation of pleasure in movement."

In other words, if a child's early encounters with movement are successful, confidence-building, and fun, that child is much more

Figure 1-4
Early childhood professionals must ensure the children do not lose their love
for movement.

likely to want to keep moving throughout his or her life. So the early childhood professional's most vital role in creating physically fit adults may simply be ensuring that her children do not lose their love for movement.

SAMPLE ACTIVITIES

Physical activity, like everything else in children's lives, should be appropriate for their level of development. Calisthenics and structured exercise regimens are not developmentally appropriate for young children (Poest & Leszynski, 1988) and are not likely to contribute to a lifelong desire to keep moving. In fact, the no-pain-no-gain approach to exercise so often adopted by adults is not only incomprehensible to young children but can create an early dislike for any movement.

Pangrazi and Corbin (1993, p. 17) report most children are involved in low-intensity, high-volume (long duration) activity during a day and "this naturally occurring activity is consistent with the developmental levels of children." Therefore, teachers need not be overly concerned with the type or intensity of the activity, as long as regular activity remains a part of the child's life. If fitness activities are not naturally occurring or if more are desired, teachers can incorporate a daily walk or creative movement activities performed to moderate- to fast-paced music into the program.

The following are more specific suggestions:

Marching. An energetic march around the room is a great fitness activity. You can provide an accompanying drumbeat or play a recording of a John Phillip Sousa composition, a march from Hap Palmer's *Mod Marches* or *Patriotic and Morning Time Songs,* or from Dennis Buck's *Patriotic Songs and Marches,* available from Kimbo and Educational Record Center (see Appendix 2). Challenge the children to swing their arms and raise their knees while keeping the rest of their bodies straight and tall. What role do they want to play in the parade? Flag bearer? Baton twirler? Perhaps they would like to pretend to play a musical instrument found in a marching band. Which one?

The Track Meet. Running is great aerobic exercise, and a lively piece of music in a steady 4/4 meter can help motivate the children. Ask them to pretend they are in an Olympic long-distance race. That means they must pace themselves if they are to make it to the finish line (the end of the song or a predetermined number of times around the room or playground).

With primary-grade children, you can challenge them to race across the country, plotting their daily progress on a U.S. map, thereby integrating physical fitness with geography and math lessons. Once around the room might, for instance, equal a mile on the map. With preschoolers, you might use a puzzle map instead. Every day they run around the gym or playground or for the length of a favorite recording, another state is placed on the puzzle to show their progress.

Rabbits and 'Roos. Children love to pretend to be animals. Ask them to jump like rabbits and kangaroos, alternating from one to the other. Which is the larger of the two animals? Which would jump the heavier?

"Pop Goes the Weasel."   Ask the children to walk to this familiar melody, jumping into the air each time they hear the "pop." You can hum or sing the song or play a recording of it. This popular piece is found in Pica (1990a & b) from the Moving & Learning Series (see Appendix 2); on *Children's All-Star Rhythm Hits* by Jack Capon and Rosemary Hallum, available from Educational Activities (see Appendix 2); on Ella Jenkins' *Early Early Childhood Songs;* and on *The Hokey Pokey, Rhythm Band Time,* and *Froggy Went A' Courtin',* available from Melody House (see Appendix 2). Once they have mastered the challenge to jump on the "pop," ask them to jump and change direction, too.

Giddy-up.   If there are children in your group who cannot yet gallop, challenge the class to move like horses. Those children who can gallop will likely do so, and those who cannot will simply pretend to be horses, still meeting your challenge and thus experiencing success.

In essence, any locomotor skill can be an aerobic activity if it is performed continuously. Begin slowly and gradually increase the length of the activities, challenging the children to push themselves a bit further each time (Poest et al., 1990).

Music and the Young Child

Why is music important to young children? Although many teachers and caregivers remain unaware of why they make it part of the curriculum, other than that children really enjoy it, music is frequently a principal ingredient in early childhood programs.

The reasons why children should have many and varied musical experiences are numerous. Among them is the belief children exposed to music have a greater motivation to communicate with the world, perhaps because music provides their first exposure to the existence and richness of their own culture, as well as the heritage and cultures of other people and regions. Perhaps it is because music is a nonverbal form of communication and, therefore, can bridge the gaps among people of differing backgrounds.

Music is also vital to the development of language and listening skills. Music and the language arts both consist of symbols and, when used in combination, abstract concepts become more concrete. Further, music activities can help improve attention span and memory and expand vocabulary (Bayless & Ramsey, 1991).

Isenberg and Jalongo (1993, p. 106) tell us:

The child who learns to sing "This Old Man," for instance, has learned to focus on a task, sequence material, and link words with actions. Musical experiences, such as creating a tune at a keyboard, can develop all the higher-level thinking skills of application, analysis, synthesis, and evaluation.

Music is also mood-altering (see Music and Moods). Whether a teacher/caregiver is trying to bring peace to overstimulated children, make routine activities more enjoyable, or provide a little extra energy to a low point in the day, music is the key.

Finally, McDonald and Simons (1989, p. 2) believe the most important role of music in education may be what it offers the children

MUSIC AND MOODS More and more research is being conducted on the power of music to alter moods and even restore and maintain health. But even without the benefit of research studies, most of us can state unequivocally that music does indeed have the ability to energize, soothe, and change moods.

Personally, I have all the evidence I require. Should I ever feel the need of the emotional release of a good cry and a sad movie is not on television, all I have to do is put on a recording of Samuel Barber's "Adagio for Strings." On the other hand, if my mood is in serious need of improving, in goes my tape of the Boston Pops performing Strauss waltzes. It does not seem to matter how grumpy I was feeling; in a matter of moments I'm pirouetting around the house!

Many teachers have related stories to me about the effect of music on young children's painting techniques. They have found playing slow classical music during painting sessions results in long, smooth brush strokes, while livelier pieces of music result in short, punctuated jabs.

Listening in on a staff meeting prior to a workshop one evening, I was fascinated by the teachers' discussion regarding behavior management. They talked about what was working and what was not and what had been overused. They then turned to one teacher who had not contributed to the conversation.

"You!" one of them said, pointing at her. "You have the best behaved class in the school—you and your Handel's *Water Music!*"

They all laughed good-naturedly, but they did not seem to realize they had actually discovered the solution to their behavior management dilemma: the calming effect of certain music.

aesthetically: "the development of sensitivity for the feelings, impressions, and images that music can convey." By helping children develop their aesthetic senses, we can significantly enrich their lives.

FUTURE IMPLICATIONS

Plato said:

> [Music] is a moral law. It gives a soul to the universe, wings to the mind, flight to the imagination, a charm to sadness, gaiety and life to everything. It is the essence of order and leads to all that is good, just, and beautiful, of which it is the invisible, but nevertheless dazzling, passionate, and eternal form.

He may have gotten a bit carried away with his estimation. But music does have much to offer humankind; and if children receive a rich variety of musical experiences, music will continue to serve them into adulthood. Though many will never become professional—or even amateur—musicians, they will know they can rely on music to offer peace, enjoyment, or a little extra energy. They can turn to music when they wish to learn more about a region or a culture. And if their early experiences with music have indeed heightened their sensitivities, how much better for the world in general.

THE ROLE OF MOVEMENT

It is impossible to think of music and movement as completely separate entities. Music educator Carl Orff based his approach on the belief music, movement, and speech are interrelated. Jaques-Dalcroze (1931, p. 115) felt traditional methods of training musicians concentrated too heavily on the intellect, thereby neglecting the senses. To him, "the most potent element in music and the nearest related to life is rhythmic movement."

Not only did educators like Dalcroze and Orff consider music and movement inseparable, but children do, too. For young children, experiencing music is simply not limited to the auditory sense (Isenberg & Jalongo, 1993; Haines & Gerber, 1992; Bayless & Ramsey, 1991), as evidenced by even infants' "whole-body" response to music.

Unfortunately, still too often a child's musical ability is judged by an ability to sing or play an instrument (Driver, 1936). Even if a child possesses such talent, if his exposure to music is limited to one of these two avenues, he is not experiencing music to the fullest. And

Figure 1-5
For young children, experiencing music is not limited to the auditory sense.

what of the child who shows no interest in or aptitude for singing or playing an instrument?

If all children are to fully experience music, they should explore it as a whole, being given opportunities to listen, sing, play, create, and *move*. When a child tiptoes to soft music, stamps her feet to loud music, moves in slow motion to Bach's "Air on the G String" and then rapidly to Rimsky-Korsakov's "Flight of the Bumblebee," sways to a 3/4 meter and skips to a piece in 6/8, she is experiencing the music on many levels. Not only is she listening, but she is using her body, mind, and spirit to express and create. And, because she is using a multimodal approach, what she learns will make a lasting impression.

SAMPLE ACTIVITIES

Although the information in Chapter 6 will provide more information—and, thus, more ideas—for choosing and using music, the following are several activities for exploring some music basics (excerpted from Pica, 1990a):*

Clapping Rhythms. Clap a small group of beats, which the children attempt to repeat. You can choose any beat groupings you like, but this would be a good time to introduce the most commonly used meters in Western music.

The first of these is 2/4—two quarter-notes in each measure (or you count to two before beginning again). A quarter-note can be likened to a walking step—it takes approximately the same time to complete. So you will simply clap and count 1–2, 1–2, and so on, at a moderate tempo.

Next is 3/4, or three quarter-notes to the measure (clap and count 1–2–3, 1–2–3, with the accent on the 1). In 4/4 time, there are four quarter-notes to the measure (clap and count 1–2–3–4). Finally, in 6/8 time, there are six eighth-notes to the measure. An eighth-note is twice as fast as a quarter-note (more like a running step), so you will clap 1–2–3–4–5–6 at a brisker pace, again with the accent on 1.

Once the children are comfortable clapping these meters, ask them to stand and try stepping in place to each count. You may

Figure 1-6
Sample measures.

---

* Note: From, *Preschoolers moving & learning,* 2nd ed. (p. 29). Rae Pica, Champaign, Ill.: Human Kinetics.Copyright 1990 by Rae Pica. Reprinted by permission.

have to count more slowly here, and you may find that 6/8 is too difficult at first.

Exploring Common Meters.   Having introduced the children to the above-mentioned common meters, the next step is to select pieces of music in each of these four meters, encouraging the children to try your suggested movements for each. The following are some possibilities:

For pieces in 2/4
    clapping 1–2   stamping feet
    marching   jumping or hopping
For pieces in 3/4
    clapping 1–2–3   swaying
    swinging bodies or body parts
For pieces in 4/4
    clapping 1–2–3–4   stamping feet
    jogging   bouncing
For pieces in 6/8
    clapping 1–2   rocking
    marching   moving head from side to side

Statues.   Asking children to move in the way the music makes them feel is bound to be an intimidating request to many of them. But making a game out of putting movement to music can free children of inhibitions. Statues is a great game for this purpose, and it develops listening skills and helps children differentiate between sound and silence.

Instruct the children to move in any way they like while the music is playing. When the music stops (you press the pause button on the tape player or lift the needle off the record), they must freeze into statues and stay that way until the music begins again.

To take the children by surprise and inspire a variety of responses, vary the time you allow the children to move before stopping the music. Do not always stop it at the end of a musical phrase (unless, of course, the object is to teach them about musical phrases).

To expose your children to a variety of musical styles and rhythms, use a song with a different feel (a march, a waltz, rock and roll) each time you play Statues. (See Chapter 6 for more on providing musical variety.)

Props are also wonderful for alleviating self-consciousness (the focus is on the prop and not the child). Give your children light-weight scarves, streamers, hula-hoops, foam balls, or rhythm sticks (depending on what you have available and the song you will be playing) and ask them to show you how the music makes them feel like moving the *prop*.

Figure 1-7
Providing the children with props can help alleviate self-consciousness.

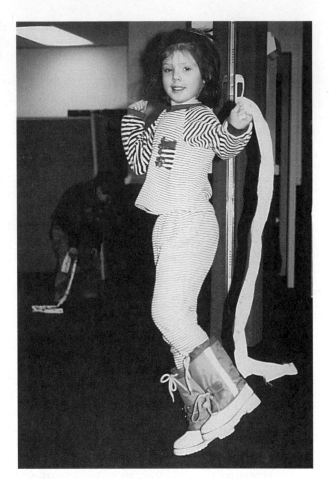

Social Development and the Young Child

The term *social development* can encompass many interpretations, meaning different things to different people. To some early childhood professionals, it brings to mind *social play,* the ability of children to interact with each other (Isenberg & Jalongo, 1993). To others, it connotes *social studies* that Mayesky (1995, p. 383) states "are designed to develop intelligent, responsible, self-directing individuals who can function as members of groups—family, community, and world—with which they become identified." Erik Erikson used the term *psy-cho*social development to refer to development of the personality, including one's self-concept.

In the context of this book, social development will encompass all the above and include the development of a sense of personal and social responsibility, which Greenberg (1992, p. 17) tells us

- is activated by an urge to contribute something to someone—a person, a group, or one's own best "self";
- is an outgrowth of self-esteem, which in turn is an outgrowth of independence, competence, and initiative; and
- grows out of an ability to see other people's viewpoints and feel concern for them (empathy).

Regardless of how the term is specifically interpreted, social development is a long and continuous process that begins with self-discovery and results in the ability to interact with others. *How well* individuals learn to function among others can greatly depend on their early childhood experiences, especially in light of Bloom's (1964) contention that 90 percent of a person's habits and attitudes are established by age 12.

FUTURE IMPLICATIONS

Imagine a world in which cooperation is valued more highly than competition; a world in which all people have such healthy self-concepts they are able to *respect* one another's differences. Can you envision a world in which everyone is able to feel empathy with everyone (and everything) else?

In such a world, there would be fewer crimes and fewer wars (and possibly no crime or war). There would be greater respect for *all* the world's creatures and for the planet itself. And when a problem arose, people would know how to work together to solve it.

Such a world might well be considered utopia and beyond the range of possibility. But is not a perfect world what everyone wishes for the children of the future? If that is what we truly desire, then we must believe in its possibility. And we must do our part to help make it a reality—beginning with the social development of the children in our care.

THE ROLE OF MOVEMENT

Frostig (1970, pp. 9, 10) wrote:

Movement education can help a child to adjust socially and emotionally because it can provide him with successful experiences and permit interrelationships with other children in groups and with a partner. Movement education requires that a child be aware of others in [activities] in which he shares space . . . he has to take turns and to cooperate. He thus develops social awareness and achieves satisfaction through peer relationships and group play.

These are fairly obvious ways in which movement can affect children socially. But educators can also make important choices with regard to curriculum content and teaching methods that can help ensure the movement curriculum has a positive impact on the children's social development.

First, they can choose to incorporate activities specifically emphasizing cooperation (cooperative activity books are listed in Chapter 2). Too many physical activities in children's lives pit them against one another, supposedly in preparation for a dog-eat-dog world. But when students are given opportunities to work together toward a solution or common goal—achieving a balance, creating a shape, planning a movement sequence, or crowding together on the one remaining seat in a game of *cooperative* musical chairs—they know they each contribute to the success of the venture. Each child knows she or he plays a vital role in the outcome, and each accepts the responsibility of fulfilling that role. The children also learn to become tolerant of others' ideas and to accept the similarities and differences of other children.

Second, curriculum planners can choose a balance between child-directed and teacher-directed learning experiences. Child-directed activities automatically place more responsibility on the children. As a result, they learn to account for their behavior and performance (Morris, 1980).

Also, a creative problem-solving approach to instruction (discussed in Chapter 7) lends itself to success because it allows students to respond to challenges at their own developmental levels and rates (Pica, 1993). This approach increases the children's self-confidence (and, thus, their self-esteem) as they see their choices being accepted and praised. And, according to Mosston and Ashworth (1990, p. 259), two important results of problem solving are the "development of patience with peers and the enhancement of respect for other people's ideas."

SAMPLE ACTIVITIES

Activities that emphasize multicultural education (such as using the music or learning the dances of other cultures and countries) or that enhance a respect for the environment or the world's creatures can have a significant impact on young children. For such activities to do so, the imagination must play a large role. To feel empathy, one must be able to imagine what it is like to be someone or something else.

Three specific activities can encourage children to pretend. Whether they realize it or not, they will be putting themselves in someone (or some*thing*) else's shoes. The final activity, Touch and Move, is performed most successfully with older preschoolers and early elementary children who are developmentally ready to handle the respect and cooperation involved.

"It's Their World, Too."   Poems and songs about animals lend themselves to movement experiences that help develop empathy. By giving children opportunities to imagine what it is like to *be* the animals, we are perhaps ensuring they will never be able to imagine a world *without* the animals. You can use the lyrics to "It's Their World, Too" (Pica & Gardzina, 1990) as a poem.

Can you imagine
A world without dogs
Or rabbits or horses or sheep?
A world that had no playful kittens
Or singing birds
Or baby chickens that peep?

Can you imagine
What life would be like
If we knew we never would see
A groundhog poking up from his hole
A dolphin swim
Or a squirrel in a tree?

How quiet, how still
The forests would grow
And the jungles and barnyards, too
If, by chance, we had no animals
To share the world
With humans like me and you.

How sad it would be
If the day should come
When the eagles no longer soared
When elephants ceased swinging their trunks
Seals didn't play
And lions no longer roared.

The world is theirs, too
And it's up to us
To see that they always will be
Allowed to live their lives as they should
Life without fear
Safe and happy and free.

Oh, it's their world, too
Yes, it's their world, too
It's a world large enough to share
With all creatures great and small
Living in peace, living in peace
It can happen if we care!

More Nature Activities. A similar activity is one in which the children explore movements related to various aspects of weather (e.g., rain and wind of varying forces, lightning, thunder, snow, heat, and cold). The children might also be asked to move like a spider weaving a web, a bee flying from flower to flower, an ant carrying food to the nest, a caterpillar crawling, and a butterfly floating through the air (Pica, 1991a).

Not only will the children explore a variety of movement skills and concepts through such activities, but also they will develop a greater awareness of nature. For example, by pretending to be the insects cited above, the children will develop a heightened awareness of insects and will be less inclined to take them for granted. Chances are they will later be more responsive to lessons learned in science class and will give greater consideration to insects' role in the environment.

Occupations. Ask the children to demonstrate movements associated with the work of people of varying occupations. Possibilities might include a police officer, a firefighter, a chef, a hairstylist, a teacher, a musician, a secretary, and a homemaker.

This activity allows the children to consider the important societal roles played by each of these occupations. But the children will also be alerted that they have all these options available to them in life—regardless of gender. So simply by exploring movement possibilities and having fun, the children can be introduced to some images of a world in which men and women are equal!

Touch and Move. This activity challenges partners to connect various body parts, which you designate, and then to remain connected as they discover how many ways they can move. After the children have selected partners, ask them to connect right or left hands, right or left elbows, one or both knees, right or left feet, and backs.

Cognitive Development and the Young Child

Confucius said, "What I hear, I forget. What I see, I remember. What I do, I know." Since then, we have discovered the majority of people are more likely to really *know* what they have a chance to *do*. In fact, the more senses involved in the learning process, the greater the impression it makes and the longer it stays with us. Fauth (1990, p. 160) tells us we retain

- 10 percent of what we read;
- 20 percent of what we hear;
- 30 percent of what we see;
- 50 percent of what we hear and see at the same time;
- 70 percent of what we hear, see, and say; and
- 90 percent of what we hear, see, say, and *do* (acting out, dramatizing, dancing, painting, drawing, constructing).

Studies of how young children learn have proven they especially acquire knowledge experientially—through play, experimentation, exploration, and discovery. More recently, a great deal of research has been done on learning styles, with studies showing children acquire knowledge using different modalities and individuals possess varying degrees of strength in each of them.

The four modalities are visual (information is obtained through the sense of sight), auditory (learning takes place primarily through what is heard), tactile (sometimes called tactual; the sense of touch provides the greatest amount of information), and kinesthetic (*doing* and *moving* stimulate learning). Reiff (1992) reports a Barbe and Milone study concludes approximately 25 to 30 percent of students in a classroom are visual learners, 25 to 30 percent auditory, and 15 percent tactile/kinesthetic. Flaherty (1992) reports about 40 percent of students in K–12 consider themselves visual learners, 20 percent believe they are auditory, and 40 percent say they are tactile or kinesthetic learners.

Whatever the exact numbers, increasing evidence indicates, although some students have strengths and weaknesses in certain modalities, most students learn with all their modalities; and many who are doing poorly in school are primarily tactile or kinesthetic learners (Reiff, 1992).

For the past three years, Corso (1993) has conducted research on how body/space awareness transfers to paper/space awareness. For example, if you ask 3- to 8-year-old children to touch their shoulders, some touch only one shoulder. Similarly, some children, when asked to jump and touch the ceiling, reach with only one hand. When requesting samples of the children's papers, Corso discovered the quadrant of paper not used in writing and coloring is the same quadrant of body space not used. Her other findings include the following:

- Children who cannot cross midline tend to focus on the vertical of the paper, sometimes writing or drawing down the vertical center of the page and sometimes changing the pencil to the other hand at the midpoint of the paper.
- Children who have trouble finding a personal space or who line up too closely to the person in front or back of them usually write their letters in a similar pattern.
- Children who cannot cross midline tend to stop reading at the middle of the page.
- The omission of gross motor instruction may be especially devastating to children who are predominantly kinesthetic learners.

All this information causes one to imagine a major revolution in the educational system. Sadly, there has been no revolution. Most elementary school children are still expected to sit for long periods and to learn by memorization and rote. Kinesthetic learners are still too often labeled hyperactive. And the recent clamor for accountability has placed more pressure on school systems to test, test, test.

In early childhood programs, many teachers are torn between what they know about how young children learn and preparing children for first-grade academics. And in elementary schools, even recess is in danger of extinction as administrators attempt to offer students more "learning" time.

FUTURE IMPLICATIONS

With the information we now have about how children (how most people, in fact) learn, it is frightening to imagine how much potential has been lost due to methods aimed at teaching subject matter rather than children. But that trend need not continue.

According to Klein (1990, p. 27), teachers must think in terms of educating children for the future as well as the present. She insists:

If we want them to be healthy, active, creative, thinking citizens of a democratic society, who can make intelligent choices and decisions, then we have to have programs that encourage such behavior. We cannot just sit them down and talk at them. If we want children to be thinkers, problem solvers and decision makers, we have to give them opportunities to think, to identify and solve problems, and to make decisions.

This is just another way of saying what the ancients knew long ago: If you give a man a fish, he eats for a day; if you *teach* a man to fish, he eats for a lifetime. If children learn *how to learn,* they will have the ability to acquire any knowledge or skill they seek to acquire—now and in the future.

THE ROLE OF MOVEMENT

Consider the following:

- Studies by Coghill (1929), Piaget (1952), Jersild (1954), and Strauss and Kephart (1955) suggest because the child's earliest learning is based on motor development, so too is subsequent knowledge.
- Jaques-Dalcroze (1931) asserted joy is the most powerful mental stimulus. And, for children, movement is most certainly joyous.
- After years of observing children, Montessori (1949) determined mental functioning is related to bodily expression.
- Einstein stated he *felt* an idea first, through visual and kinesthetic images, before he was able to put it into words (National Dance Association, 1990).
- Children think better when their daily routine includes physical activity (Taras, 1992).
- Body image influences a child's emotional health, learning ability, and intellectual performance.
- When children deal with the concepts of space and shape, they are learning to deal with abstract thought.

Several theories and research studies related to learning by doing have already been discussed. And movement, in a great many ways, is doing. This information, together with the data above, points toward a definite connection between body and mind—and, therefore, between moving and learning.

SAMPLE ACTIVITIES

Movement is less likely to stimulate learning if it is taught the way other subjects often are: through demonstration and imitation. Rather, teachers must offer children opportunities to solve problems, invent their own solutions to challenges, and make the abstract concrete. This is the key to learning for the young child.

Exploring Up and Down. Pose the following questions and movement challenges (Pica, 1990a):

- Do you know what *up* and *down* mean? Show me with your body.
- Can you make your body go all the way down?
- Make your body go all the way up. How high can you get?
- Show me you can go halfway down.
- Make yourself so tiny I can hardly see you.
- Now become as huge as a giant.
- Pretend your feet are glued to the floor.
- How can you move your body up and down without your feet moving?

Bridges and Tunnels. Talk with the children about the differences between bridges and tunnels. Then ask them to show you both with their bodies. To make the activity more challenging, ask them to show you how many body *parts* can create bridges and tunnels. Finally, if they are responsible enough to handle the challenge, have half the class act as tunnels and the other half act as trains or cars traveling through the tunnels.

Figure 1-9
"Make your body go all the way up."

Body Parts. In this activity, the children work with a variety of body parts in relation to other body parts or the floor, which requires them to think a bit more about the sum of their parts and about the space they occupy.

Ask the children to sit, and then present the following challenges:

- Place an elbow on the floor; move it as far from the floor as possible.
- Stretch a foot far away from you and then bring it back without touching the floor (until it is in its original position).
- Put a shoulder (the other shoulder; both shoulders) on the floor.
- Touch an elbow to a knee; take it as far away from that knee as possible.
- Touch an elbow to a foot.
- Can you touch your shoulder to your foot?
- Come up from the floor with your head leading and the rest of your body following.
- Go back down to the floor with your nose leading the way.
- Come back up with an elbow leading.

The American Flag. As discussed in Chapter 9, movement can be used to explore study units or classroom themes. The following is an example excerpted from Pica (1991b) that can be used for a history lesson or for several different holidays, including Independence Day and Flag Day.

Show the children an American flag and discuss it with them. What colors is it? What shapes are on it? What do the 50 stars represent? Have the children ever seen a flag being raised on a flagpole? Discuss some of the reasons a flag might be lowered to half-mast, the proper way to fold a flag, and the respect our flag deserves.

Now tell the children they are going to pretend to be a lot of different things associated with the flag, and ask them to show you the shape of a flag, a star, a stripe, a flagpole, a flag being raised on a flagpole, a flag at half-mast, a flag waving proudly in the breeze, a flag being lowered on a flagpole, and a flag being folded.

Exploring Upside Down. When a teacher uses guided discovery (also known as convergent problem solving; refer to Chapter 7), the challenges are intended to produce specific outcomes. Here is an example of an activity involving guided discovery that is suitable for children at the preschool or early elementary level.

The ultimate goal of the questions and challenges is a forward roll, but because this approach allows students to respond to challenges at their own developmental levels and rates, even if the children do not manage to perform the desired forward roll, their responses should be accepted. Ultimately, all children can be led to the "correct" answer through guided discovery.

Specific questions and challenges will vary according to the responses elicited from the students, but the following is an example of the process:

- Show me an upside-down position with your weight on your hands and feet.
- Show me an upside-down position with your weight on your hands and feet and your tummy facing the floor.
- Can you put your bottom in the air?
- Can you look behind yourself from that position?
- Can you look at the ceiling? Try to look at even more of the ceiling.
- Show me you can roll yourself over from that position. Can you do it more than once?

Creativity and the Young Child

What is creativity? Answers can differ, depending on whom you ask. Various definitions tell us creativity

- may be defined as the interpersonal and intrapersonal process through which original, high-quality, and genuinely significant products are developed (Tegano et al., 1991);
- is a way of thinking and acting or making something original for the individual and valued by that person or others (Mayesky, 1995);
- describes ideas, behaviors, and products (*not* a person) that are appropriately novel (Amabile, 1989); and
- is the sensing of problems or gaps in information, forming ideas or hypotheses, testing and modifying these hypotheses, and communicating the results. This process may lead to any one of many products—verbal and nonverbal, concrete and abstract (Torrance & Goff, 1989).

According to Torrance and Goff (1989, p. 142), the most extensive research in the field indicates a number of abilities are involved in creative thinking, including

1. sensitivity to problems;
2. fluency (the ability to produce large numbers of ideas);

3. flexibility (the ability to produce a variety of ideas or use a variety of approaches);
4. originality (ability to produce new, unusual, innovative ideas);
5. elaboration (ability to fill in details);
6. redefinition (ability to define or perceive in a way that differs from the usual, established, intended way).

Amabile (1989, p. 49) reports the key personality traits of highly creative people, if not naturally occurring, can be developed in childhood, and include

1. self-discipline about work,
2. perseverance even when frustrated,
3. independence,
4. tolerance for unclear situations,
5. nonconformity to society's stereotypes,
6. ability to wait for rewards,
7. self-motivation to do excellent work, and
8. a willingness to take risks.

When considering creativity in early childhood, it is important to note there is no one profile of the creative child; creative expression is a developmental process, as are other facets of the child's development. Also, educators and parents must focus on the *process* rather than end products, as young children do not always have the skills necessary to make creative products (Tegano et al., 1991).

One point the experts appear to agree on is that creative potential exists to varying degrees in all young children. Unfortunately, that potential is greatly diminished for the majority of individuals on their way to adulthood.

Why does this happen? Where does creativity go?

Dudek (1974) followed a group of children from first through sixth grade and found creativity begins to "dry out" at just 5 years of age. It then suffers drastic reductions at about age 9 (fourth grade) and again at age 12 (seventh grade). School—with its "restrictive classroom environments" (Gilliom, 1970), insistence on conformity, academic accountability, and emphasis on competition—is often blamed for squelching creative potential.

Because each child is born with creative potential and the ages between 3 and 5 are thought to be the critical years for the development of creativity (Schirrmacher, 1993; Fauth, 1990), early childhood professionals have a tremendous opportunity to encourage creativity and foster those personality traits that demonstrate creative potential. And they can take advantage of this opportunity simply by implementing developmentally appropriate practices and allowing children to play, explore, and solve problems. In addition, they must value process over product, allow children to express themselves in their own individual ways, and recognize and nurture creative potential. For more on the teacher's role, see Tegano et al. (1991).

FUTURE IMPLICATIONS

Unfortunately, a number of misconceptions related to creativity threaten its existence. One, children who show high academic achievement are the most creative. Given this belief, adults tend to value correct answers more highly than original thought, so children find it "less rewarding to express interest in things, to be curious, to be creative in investigating their world" (Mayesky, 1995, p. 3). In fact, a creative child may or may not be academically gifted; some children who struggle academically show tremendous creativity.

Two, creativity to many people is thought to be the domain of artists (painters, writers, composers, etc.). And, certainly, the world benefits from the creativity of its artists. But it also benefits from creativity in business and industry, science, education, and in life itself.

THE LOST ART OF SELF-EXPRESSION Self-expression is an integral part of the creative process. But many educators and parents knowingly and unknowingly discourage creative expression. An early childhood professional once told me he felt creative children were much more difficult to deal with, so he purposely tried to discourage creativity!

Though the following anecdotes are all related to self-expression in art, they are typical of some of the ways in which creativity is discouraged—too often, very early in life.

- Witkin (1977) relates the story of a young boy whose teacher assigned the class to draw horses and then received a grade of F for turning in a blue horse. The teacher explained that horses are either white, black, or brown; but the little boy, who went home in tears, was confused. In his house was a painting by Franz Marc in which three blue horses roamed a brightly colored field.

- Amabile (1989) writes of her excitement in getting to the easel and clay table every day in kindergarten, where she had access to bright colors and big paintbrushes and lots of other art materials. Her excitement was such that when she returned home in the afternoons she wanted only to play with crayons and paint. Although she did not completely understand, she was thrilled to one day overhear her kindergarten teacher tell her mother she had the potential for artistic creativity. The next year, however, art became "just another subject." Gone was the free access to art materials. Even worse, in second grade her class was given small reprints of painted masterworks and asked to reproduce them with their crayons! The children's reproductions were then graded by the art teacher.

- In Graham, et al. (1993), James Smith writes of the wonder he felt when his young daughter accompanied him to a lake with easels, paintbrushes, and watercolors and, in moments, perfectly captured the essence of the September scene before them. His wonder turned to dismay, however, when she came to him for help in drawing a sailboat soon after she began school. Her teacher, it seems, did not care for interpretive artwork. Rather, she insisted the class create sailboats from dittoed triangles.

- Not long ago, I heard a story about a first-grade girl who, when asked to draw a butterfly like the teacher had drawn on the chalkboard, happily put purple polka dots on her butterfly—and was promptly scolded. After all, the teacher's butterfly had no polka dots.

Are these isolated incidences, or typical of everyday occurrences in the lives of young children? Are adults who stifle children's self-expression merely guilty of not knowing any better, or are they trying to mold the children into conformity?

I do not know the answers to these questions, but I do know kindergarten was the pinnacle of Amabile's artistic career. Smith's daughter, when planning her semester schedule years later, was appalled by her father's suggestion she take creative writing or beginning painting. "Who me?" she asked. "Paint or write? Good grief, Dad, you ought to know better than that!" And I would guess the artistic—and creative—inclinations of the little girl with the polka-dotted butterfly and the little boy with the blue horse were similarly dampened.

Why is conformity valued more highly than creativity? Certainly people like Einstein, Florence Nightingale, and Albert Schweitzer were nonconformists whose problem-solving abilities played an invaluable role in their achievements. And if we wish to help create a generation of future Einsteins, Nightingales, and Schweitzers—not to mention Shakespeares, Michelangelos, and Bachs— we must encourage the children in our care to express themselves—through art, through movement, and through whatever medium they wish.

Goleman et al. (1992, p. 29) assert daily life is "a major arena for innovation and problem solving—the largest but least honored realm of the creative spirit."

Can you imagine a world without creativity and self-expression? Today, more than at any time in history, the ability to imagine may be in grave danger of disappearing. Current technology, including television, computers, and video, provide children so many ready-made images they have little need to create their own.

Creative people are those who can *imagine*. Thus, they can imagine the solutions to problems and challenges faced. They can imagine what it is like to be someone or something else (empathy). They can imagine answers to the question, "What if?" They can plan full and satisfying futures.

Goff and Torrance (1991, p. 302) contend creative activities give people a chance to communicate with each other and with themselves, while creative expression brings satisfaction, "arouses the adventurous spirit within and creates a zest for living." Schirrmacher (1993, 61) tells us, beyond personal development, "creativity advances civilization and society by addressing and attempting to solve the global problems of hunger, poverty, disease, war, and pollution."

THE ROLE OF MOVEMENT

Certainly, a movement program that requires the children merely imitate the instructor will do nothing to foster creativity. But a program using movement *exploration,* with its emphasis on problem solving, discovery, and self-expression, can make a substantial contribution.

When you present the children with a challenge like "Show me how crooked you can be," chances are no two responses will be alike. Divergent thinking, one of the cognitive skills required for creativity, will be enhanced through problem-solving challenges that allow for various responses.

Also, when you praise and validate the different responses, the children will realize it is okay to find their own individual solutions and they are not in competition with one another. Thus, their confidence will grow, and they will continue to take greater creative risks.

Creative movement activities also give children many opportunities to imagine. They must imagine the slowness of a turtle to replicate that movement. They must call to mind a time they were not happy to move as though sad. They must envision a partner balance or group shape to achieve it.

Goleman et al. (1992, p. 27) tell us creativity does not happen only in the mind. Rather, they say, the relationships "between thinking and feelings, between mind and body, are critical to unleashing

Figure 1-11
With divergent problem solving a challenge to "Find a way to move across the balance beam" can result in many possible responses— all of which are "correct."

creativity." What better medium for establishing relationships between thinking and feelings or between mind and body than creative movement!

SAMPLE ACTIVITIES

Self-expression is critical to creativity. The following activities, excerpted from Pica (1990a), encourage self-expression because they allow children to find their own way of responding to your challenges. Each activity, to a greater or lesser degree, also requires the children use their imaginations.

Make-Believe Walks.   Incorporating imagery into the locomotor skill of walking, ask the children to walk like they are big and strong, fat and jolly like Santa Claus, really mad, really sad, looking for the towel with soap in their eyes, in a parade, on hot sand that is burning their feet, and trying to get through sticky mud.

"At the Zoo."   Read the following poem in its entirety and discuss it with the children. Then read it again, as slowly as necessary, with the children acting out the movements of each of the animals mentioned.

Let's visit a while at the local zoo
And see what we might see
A tall giraffe or a kangaroo
Even a chimpanzee!

See the elephant swinging his trunk
And hear the lion roar
Could that black and white creature be a skunk?
Do you want to see some more?

Why, there's a gorilla in that cage
And, my, it seems to me
The tiger is in a terrible rage
But the bear is as calm as can be.

Well, it's getting late; but don't you fret
We'll come back another day
You haven't seen the hippos yet
Or the slippery seals at play!

Make-Believe Striking.   Before exploring the nonlocomotor skill of striking, explain to the children they are to hit only the air. Then ask them to strike as though playing a big bass drum, swinging a bat, hammering a nail, chopping wood, swatting at a mosquito, and hitting a ball.

Making Shapes.   Shape is a movement element that is fun to explore in one's personal space. Making sure the children have enough room to respond without touching one another, ask them the following:

- How round can you be?
- How flat can you be? Wide? Narrow? Long? Short? Crooked? Straight?
- Can you make your body look like a table? A chair?
- Can you look like a ball? A pencil with a point at the end?
- A flower? A teapot? A rug?

"A Face Has Many Roles in Life."   The lyrics to this song require the children to express themselves with only their faces. For the chorus, you can have them point to (or move) the parts named. On the next-to-last line they can cover their faces with their hands, uncovering them on the last line to display an expression or funny face of their choice.

The lyrics, which you can explore as a poem, are as follows:

A face has many roles in life
I guess you know that's true
It smiles and frowns and even cries
When you are feeling blue.

A face can show that you're angry
A face can show you're glad
A face can pout and sulk and whine
When you are feeling bad.

A face can show that you're tired
With yawns or drooping eyes
A face can even show delight
When someone yells, "Surprise!"

A face has many roles in life
But most unique by far
'Cause yours belongs to only you
I can tell who you are!

Chorus
A nose, a mouth, a couple of eyes
Two eyebrows that you raise
These belong to any face
But you use them in your own ways!

Key Points

- Maturation alone does not ensure proper development of motor skills. Continuous practice and instruction are required if movement skills are to be refined.
- There is considerable concern that children today may be leading more sedentary lives than their predecessors.
- Children who are physically active feel more accomplished and have a greater sense of self-esteem.
- Success and enjoyment are key elements in establishing a lifelong love of movement.
- Children exposed to music have a greater motivation to communicate with the world than those who are isolated from it.
- Music is vital to the development of language and listening skills.

- Children need to experience music *as a whole*—listening, singing, playing, creating, and moving.
- Social development is a long and continuous process that begins with self-discovery and results in the ability to interact well with others.
- To help ensure the movement curriculum has an impact on the children's social development, educators can choose to incorporate activities emphasizing cooperation, child-directed activities, and a creative problem-solving approach to instruction.
- The more senses involved in the learning process, the greater the impression made and the higher the retention percentage.
- Children acquire knowledge experientially, using different modalities (visual, auditory, tactile, kinesthetic). Many children who do poorly in school are predominantly tactile or kinesthetic learners.
- The potential for creativity exists in all people, but its greatest chance for development is between the ages of 3 and 5.
- Creativity is not necessarily related to academic intelligence.
- Creativity is not the domain of only artists.
- Self-expression and imagination are critical to creativity.

Assignments

1. Observe a group of children for a day, and note the ways you detect them learning *kinesthetically*.
2. Choose a preschool or early elementary child as a subject. Compare the time that child spends in sedentary activity versus that spent in physical activity during a week. (You can simply observe the time spent in child care or school, or you can enlist the aid of the child's parents. If they are willing to keep a log of the child's activities at home, you can gain a more accurate view.)
3. Experiment with music of varying moods and note its effect on a child or group of children.
4. Determine a benefit of movement not cited in this chapter and justify it in writing.

References

AAHPERD. (1989). *Physical best program*. Reston, Va.: American Alliance for Health, Physical Education, Recreation, and Dance.

Amabile, T. M. (1989). *Growing up creative: Nurturing a lifetime of creativity*. New York: Crown.

Bayless, K. M., & Ramsey, M. E. (1991). *Music: A way of life for the young child*. New York: Merrill.

Berenson, G. S., ed. (1980). *Cardiovascular risk factors in children: The early natural history of atherosclerosis and essential hypertension*. New York: Oxford University Press.

Blair, S. N. (1992). Are American children and youth fit? The need for better data. *Research Quarterly for Exercise and Sport*, 63(2), 120–23.

Blair, S. N., Clark, D. G., Cureton, K. J., & Powell, K. E. (1989). In G. V. Gisolfi & D. R. Lamb, eds., *Perspectives in Exercise Science and Sports Medicine, Vol. 2: Youth, Exercise, and Sport* (pp. 401–30). Indianapolis: Benchmark.

Bloom, B. (1964). *Stability and change in human characteristics*. New York: Wiley & Sons.

Bunker, L. (1991). The role of play and motor skills development in building children's self-confidence and self-esteem. *Elementary School Journal*, 91(5), 467–71.

Cleland, F. E., & Gallahue, D. L. (1993). Young children's divergent movement ability. *Perceptual and Motor Skills*, 77, 535–44.

Coghill, G. E. (1929). *Anatomy and the problem of behavior*. Cambridge: Cambridge University Press.

Corso, M. (1993). Is developmentally appropriate physical education the answer to children's school readiness? *Colorado Journal of Health, Physical Education, Recreation and Dance*, 19(2), 6–7.

Driver, A. (1936). *Music and movement*. London: Oxford University Press.

Dudek, S. (1974). Creativity in young children: Attitude or ability? *Journal of Creative Behavior*, 8, 282–92.

Fauth, B. (1990). Linking the visual arts with drama, movement, and dance for the young child. In W. J. Stinson, ed., *Moving and learning for the young child* (pp. 159–87). Reston, Va.: American Alliance for Health, Physical Education, Recreation, and Dance.

Flaherty, G. (1992). The learning curve: Why textbook teaching doesn't work for all kids. *Teaching Today*, 67(6), 32–33, 56.

Frostig, M. (1970). *Movement education: Theory and practice*. Chicago: Follet Education Corp.

Gallahue, D. (November 1987). *Developmental movement activities for young children*. Presented at Annual Conference of the National Association for the Education of Young Children, Chicago.

Garnet, E. D. (1982). *Movement is life*. Princeton, N.J.: Princeton Book Co.

Gilliom, B. C. (1970). *Basic movement education for children: Rationale and teaching units*. Reading, Mass.: Addison-Wesley.

Goff, K., & Torrance, E. P. (1991). Healing qualities of imagery and creativity. *Journal of Creative Behavior*, 25(4), 296–303.

Goleman, D., Kaufman, P., & Ray, M. (1992). *The creative spirit*. New York: Penguin Books.

Graham, G., Holt/Hale, S., & Parker, M. (1993). *Children moving*. Mountain View, Calif.: Mayfield.

Greenberg, P. (1992). How to institute some simple democratic practices pertaining to respect, rights, roots, and responsibilities in any classroom (without losing your leadership position). *Young Children*, 47(5), 10–17.

Groves, D. (1988). Is childhood obesity related to TV addiction? *The Physician and Sportsmedicine,* 16(11), 117–22.

Haines, B. J. E., & Gerber, L. L. (1992). *Leading young children to music.* New York: Merrill.

Institute for Aerobic Research. (1987). *Get fit.* Dallas: Author.

Isenberg, J. P., & Jalongo, M. R. (1993). *Creative expression and play in the early childhood curriculum.* New York: Merrill.

Jaques-Dalcroze, E. (1931). *Eurhythmics, art, and education,* F. Rothwell, trans.; C. Cox, ed. New York: A. S. Barnes.

Jersild, A. T. (1954). *Child psychology.* Englewood Cliffs, N.J.: Prentice-Hall.

Klein, J. (1990). Young children and learning. In W. J. Stinson, ed., *Moving and learning for the young child* (pp. 159–87). Reston, Va.: AAHPERD.

Lerch, H. A., Becker, J. E., Ward, B. M., & Nelson, J. A. (1974). *Perceptual-motor learning: Theory and practice.* Palo Alto, Calif.: Peek.

Mayesky, M. (1995). *Creative activities for young children.* Albany, N.Y.: Delmar.

McDonald, D. T., & Simons, G. M. (1989). *Musical growth and development: Birth through six.* New York: Schirmer Books.

Montessori, M. (1949). *The absorbent mind.* Madras, India: Kalakshetra Publications.

Morris, G. S. D. (1980). *Elementary physical education: Toward inclusion.* Salt Lake City: Brighton.

Mosston, M., & Ashworth, S. (1990). *The spectrum of teaching styles: From command to discovery.* New York: Longman.

NASPE Outcomes Committee. (1992). *The Physically Educated Person.* Reston, Va: National Association for Sport and Physical Education.

National Dance Association. (1990). *Guide to creative dance for the young child.* Reston, Va.: NDA.

Pangrazi, R. P., & Corbin, C. B. (1993). Physical fitness: Questions teachers ask. *Journal of Health, Physical Education, Recreation and Dance,* 64(7), 14–19.

Parker, F. C., Croft, J. B., Cresanta, J. L., Freedman, D. S., Burke, G. L., Webber, L. S., & Berenson, G. S. (1984). The association between cardiovascular response, tasks, and future blood pressures in children: Bogalusa heart study. *American Heart Journal,* 113, 1174–1179.

Piaget, J. (1952). *The origins of intelligence in children.* New York: International Universities Press.

Pica, R. (1990a). *Preschoolers moving & learning.* Champaign, Ill.: Human Kinetics.

Pica, R. (1990b). *Toddlers moving & learning.* Champaign, Ill.: Human Kinetics.

Pica, R. (1991a). *Early elementary children moving and learning.* Champaign, Ill.: Human Kinetics.

Pica, R. (1991b). *Special themes for moving and learning.* Champaign, Ill.: Human Kinetics.

Pica, R. (1993). *Upper elementary children moving and learning.* Champaign, Ill.: Human Kinetics.

Pica, R., & Gardzina, R. (1990). *More music for moving and learning.* Champaign, Ill.: Human Kinetics.

Poest, C. A., & Leszynski, L. (1988). *Kinderkicks: Preschool exercise and nutrition.* Unpublished manuscript.

Poest, C. A., Williams, J. R., Witt, D. D., & Atwood, M. E. (1990). Challenge me to move: Large muscle development in young children. *Young Children,* 45(5), 4–10.

Reiff, J. C. (1992). *Learning styles: What research says to the teacher series.* Washington, D.C.: National Education Association.

Ross, J. G., Pate, R. R., Lohman, T. G., & Christenson, G. M. (1987). Changes in body composition of children. *Journal of Physical Education, Recreation and Dance, 58*(9), 74–77.

Schirrmacher, R. (1993). *Art and creative development for young children.* Albany, N.Y.: Delmar.

Seefeldt, V. (1980). Physical fitness guidelines for preschool children. In *Proceedings of the National Conference on Physical Fitness and Sports for All* (pp. 5–19). Washington, D.C.: President's Council on Physical Fitness and Sports.

Seefeldt, V. (1984). Physical fitness in preschool and elementary school-aged children. *Journal of Physical Education, Recreation and Dance, 55*(9), 33–40.

Shapiro, L. R., Crawford, P. B., Clark, M. J., Pearson, D. L., Raz, J., & Hueneman, R. L. (1984). Obesity prognosis: A longitudinal study of children from the age of 6 months to 9 years. *American Journal of Public Health, 74,* 968.

Strauss, A. A., & Kephart, N. C. (1955). *Psychopathology and education of the brain-injured child.* Vol. II. *Progress in theory and clinic.* New York: Grune and Stratton.

Taras, H. L. (1992). Physical activity of young children in relation to physical and mental health. In C. M. Hendricks, ed., *Young children on the grow: Health, activity, and education in the preschool setting* (pp. 33–42). Washington, D.C.: Eric Clearinghouse.

Tegano, D. W., Moran, J. D., & Sawyers, J. K. (1991). *Creativity in early childhood classrooms.* Washington, D.C.: National Education Association.

Torrance, E. P., & Goff, K. (1989). A quiet revolution. *Journal of Creative Behavior, 23*(2), 136–45.

Williams, H. G. (1983). *Perceptual and motor development.* Englewood Cliffs, N.J.: Prentice-Hall.

Witkin, K. (1977). *To move, to learn.* Philadelphia: Temple University.

CHAPTER 2

Movement Education and the Young Child

*I*n Chapter 1, we looked at some of the many benefits children derive from participating in movement education. Although these benefits are generally reaped by all children, their impact can vary depending on the ages and developmental levels of the children participating. Reinforcing concepts such as *up* and *down,* for example, has much greater cognitive value for toddlers than for kindergarteners because toddlers are just beginning to understand spatial relationships. Kindergarteners, on the other hand, are at a higher level of cognitive development and require greater challenge. Movement activities, therefore, must be planned according to the developmental stages of the children participating. This, in essence, is what a *developmentally appropriate* program is all about.

According to the National Association for the Education of Young Children, the concept of developmental appropriateness has two dimensions: age appropriateness and individual appropriateness. The former reminds us "there are universal, predictable sequences of growth and change that occur in children during the first nine years of life" and "these predictable changes occur in all domains of development—physical, emotional, social, and cognitive" (Bredekamp, 1987, p. 2). The latter indicates all children are unique individuals who develop according to their own timetables.

Chapter 2 examines some developmental milestones in the cognitive, affective, and physical domains of toddlers, preschoolers, and early elementary children—specifically those that can have a significant impact on the movement programs of children in these age groups. For our purposes, cognitive development will include language development; affective development will encompass both the social and emotional realms; and motor development will refer only to gross motor, as opposed to fine motor, development.

The final section of this chapter deals with special populations and includes children with motor, visual, and auditory impairments, as well as those who are mentally and emotionally challenged. These children have special needs, and we will look at how the movement program can be planned and, when necessary, adapted to meet these needs.

Toddlers

In looking through books dealing with toddlers, one finds several definitions of these very young children. In some cases, toddlers are defined as those who have just acquired the ability to transport themselves in an upright position and are at the toddling stage between creeping and true walking. Often, the toddler years are described as falling between certain ages, but the ages vary considerably. For the purposes of this text, toddlers will be defined as children between the ages of 18 and 36 months.

Those who work with toddlers already know these children present a unique challenge—especially where movement is concerned. Although their motor abilities are rapidly emerging, toddlers do not yet possess enough gross motor skill to succeed at a wide variety of movement activities. Toddlers seem to be in almost constant motion, but due to an extremely short attention span, it can be difficult to channel that motion into organized movement activities. Also because of their short attention span, it is unrealistic to expect to keep these young children involved for longer than 20 to 30 minutes (at the most!); however, since it generally takes longer for toddlers to organize as a group, it is impractical to set aside fewer than 20 minutes each day for a movement session.

To make the most of a movement session for toddlers, you should, first and foremost, know what challenges they are capable of responding to. Plan more activities than you expect to use to allow yourself to move quickly from one activity to another and to switch gears should you find a particular activity is just not working. Whenever possible, plan movement sessions for morning, as this is the best time for toddlers to participate in movement exploration. If afternoon is your only option, wait until the children have been up from their naps for a while before expecting them to be creative. Toddlers thrive on individual attention, so the general rule for movement is to have no more than four toddlers per adult (again, whenever possible). Finally, Miller

(1985, p. 44) offers some attention-getting techniques that include enticing the children with a novelty factor and the "flop down and do" method. For the former, she suggests bringing out something the children have not yet seen that day, such as a music box, to grab their undivided attention. For the latter, she recommends, "Instead of calling toddlers over and trying to get them all to sit down and pay attention at the same time, simply flop down on the floor and start doing whatever it was you wanted to present to them." Once a couple children have joined you, others will want to "get in on the action" and they will "stay longer when it was their choice to come over in the first place."

Naturally, the better you understand toddlers, the easier it will be to plan and provide successful movement experiences for them. Excellent resources are cited in the References to contribute to your knowledge of children between the ages of 18 and 36 months.

COGNITIVE DEVELOPMENT

The emerging intellectual development of very young children is truly a wonder to behold. Between the ages of 18 and 24 months, toddlers are speaking in just two- or three-word sentences, with only about 66 percent of their speech intelligible. Within the next 12 months, their speech becomes about 90 percent intelligible; they are speaking in longer sentences and are able to associate word and object.

Words, in fact, are extremely important to toddlers, even though they are not yet proficient verbal communicators. Charlesworth (1992) tells us language and concept development go hand in hand, with verbal cues accompanied by demonstrations playing a vital role in the learning process. Toddlers learn much through imitation—and even more when imitating behaviors accompanied by a verbal explanation.

Among the quantitative concepts toddlers are busy discovering are *some, more,* and *big,* as well as spatial relationships like *up, down, inside, outside, behind, over,* and *under.* Understanding these "location words" is necessary so children can later "make sense of the order of letters and words on a page" (Miller, 1985, p. 73). Size, space, and shape are becoming increasingly meaningful concepts to toddlers; between 30 and 36 months, they are especially curious about how things work and what objects are made of. Number concepts are too abstract for toddlers—even those who can count by rote, because the numbers do not yet represent quantities or sequences for them (Miller, 1985).

An exciting development during toddlerhood is the beginning of the ability to use the imagination. From 18 to 24 months, children are

Figure 2-1
Size, space, and shape become increasingly meaningful concepts to toddlers.

in the stage of symbolic representation—they can internally visualize events and objects. This not only allows them a better understanding of cause and effect, but also enables them to fantasize. They can now pretend to be something else (a cat or a dog or something they saw on a field trip the day before), or imagine that one object is actually another (e.g., a block of wood becomes a fire engine) (Castle, 1991; Morrison, 1990; Miller, 1985).

By the time children are 2 years old, they can learn—and often sing—short, simple songs and like activities with short, simple directions. They enjoy the familiar, positively thrive on repetition, and are curious, information-seeking individuals. Toddlers can identify at least six body parts (Bredekamp, 1987).

But perhaps the most important bit of information comes from Morrison (1990, p. 298), who reminds us that "the way children see or represent things is not like adults. Therefore, care-givers should not emphasize 'right' answers as much as they should emphasize helping children have meaningful experiences, which will enable them to discover the right answers through the process of living and maturation."

Implications for the Movement Program.   Because movement exploration does not emphasize right answers, it allows young children the opportunity to experience and discover and to learn by doing. In particular, movement exploration can help toddlers identify body parts, understand quantitative concepts and spatial relationships, and make greater use of the imagination. Specific teaching methods, however, must be employed with toddlers if you and the children are to enjoy the utmost success.

One important word to keep in mind is *brief*. Due to toddlers' short attention span, activities must be kept brief, as must directions (one or two simple instructions). This is especially true if you have more 18- to 24-month-old children than 2-year-olds in your class. If this is the case, you may find it takes these young children longer to complete a single lesson—or you cannot keep their attention long enough to complete much of anything!

Whenever possible, accompany your directions with gestures and/or demonstrations. Labeling actions is a multimodal form of instruction that promotes concept and language development. Similarly, you should label the children's actions. For instance, if the children are crawling through a tunnel, you should say the word *through* as the children are experiencing it.

Although toddlers are learning to fantasize, their experiences are extremely limited. Using images they can easily relate to, therefore, is especially important. If you are going to ask them to move like certain animals or objects, they must be animals or objects the toddlers have personally experienced. Likewise, if you are going to ask toddlers to imitate, for example, straight and round shapes, *show* them straight and round objects.

Because distractibility is a real issue in working with toddlers, you will have to pay particular attention to helping them to focus. Using a single movement theme, rather than a variety of themes, for a single session (see Chapter 4) is a sensible practice. For example, if you plan three activities based on three different themes, your toddlers may enjoy the activities but will probably not readily grasp the three concepts. On the other hand, if you plan three activities centered around the movement theme of body-parts identification, the children will enjoy themselves *and* learn a lot about body part identification.

Also, although young children love music, you should use it sparingly as part of your movement program. Again, the fewer things we

Figure 2-2
Due to toddlers' short
attention span, directions
must be kept brief.

ask them to concentrate on, the easier it will be for them. In addition, moving without music allows children to find and use their own personal rhythms.

When you do use music, it should make a contribution to the learning experience involved in the activity. Use short, simple songs with basic melodies (nursery rhymes set to music and songs like "Row, Row, Row Your Boat" are among children's favorites). And be prepared to repeat them often!

Sample Activities. Body-part identification is the basis of any movement program, but is especially important for toddlers because their awareness and understanding of body parts is just developing. To help reinforce this growing awareness, perform activities like Heads, Bellies, Toes, in which you call out the names of these three body parts and the children must touch the part being called out. Start off slowly, saying the parts in the same order each time. Then, as the children gain experience, vary the tempo and the order. A bit more challenging is Heads, Shoulders, Knees, and Toes.

Simon Says is also an appropriate body-parts activity—*if* it is played without the elimination process. With toddlers, it should be performed at a very slow tempo, and you should also model the actions. You might consider saying, "Simon says" prior to every challenge. Also, if your toddlers are too young to grasp the concept of Simon, use the name of a favorite stuffed animal or character, or substitute with the phrase, "Show me."

Toddlers love fingerplays—even if they cannot perform them from start to finish. "Where Is Thumbkin?" is a fingerplay that incorporates body-part identification, singing, echoing responses, and the positional concepts of *in front* and *behind*.

Body Percussion is an activity that uses body parts to create sounds and offers a basic introduction to rhythm. In this activity, you first ask the children to clap their hands—something they have been doing since patty-cake. Then challenge them to use their hands to pat other parts of their body. Which parts make the most noise? What else can they pat with their hands to create sounds? How can they use their feet to make noise? Can they make a lot of noise? Just a little noise? Are there other body parts they can make noise with?

In addition to reinforcing body-part identification, Heads, Shoulders, Knees, and Toes and Heads, Bellies, Toes draw attention to the concepts of up and down—important spatial relationships for young children. You can specifically focus on up and down by doing gentle bending and stretching exercises with toddlers. Challenge them to show you they can make their bodies go all the way down and all the way up, using the words *low* and *high* in connection with their actions. Blast Off!, in which you count down from ten and the children "launch" themselves at the command to blast off, is another activity that reinforces the concepts of up, down, low, and high. (Until your toddlers become familiar with this activity, you will have to model.) Also ask the children to make themselves very *small* and very *big*.

"Ring Around the Rosie" is a traditional favorite that focuses on the spatial relationships of *around* and *down* and can serve as the children's first introduction to group participation. Simple obstacle courses or learning centers can also play a critical role in introducing and reinforcing spatial relationships. Tunnels (purchased, or created from desks or large boxes), balance beams (purchased or homemade),

Figure 2-3
"Ring Around the Rosie" can serve as toddlers' introduction to group participation and reinforces the spatial relationships of around and down.

ropes, hoops, and the like can all be used to develop greater understanding of important positional concepts.

AFFECTIVE DEVELOPMENT

During the first two years of life, a child's personality is forming, and she is rapidly developing a sense of herself as an individual. This sense is referred to as the self-concept.

According to Castle (1991, p. 5), the self-concept "includes what the child thinks about himself in terms of his capabilities, physical characteristics, and self-worth. . . . A child's self-concept affects everything he does. Children who have positive views of themselves are more successful in everyday life and later in school. Children who have negative views tend to do less well."

The self-concept is greatly influenced by feedback from the important people in a child's life. Toddlers, in particular, tend to seek approval and to act to please adults, so caregivers can play an enormous role in helping toddlers to develop positive self-concepts.

Of course, when toddlers are *not* acting to please adults, they are acting to assert their increasing independence and to gain some control over their world. They frequently display defiant, contrary behavior, with *no* being one of their favorite words. They occasionally throw tantrums and can be physically aggressive—perhaps because their limited verbal skills make it difficult for them to express themselves (Essa, 1992; Miller, 1985). Especially between 30 and 36 months, children feel a need to express their emotions strongly.

Though unable to adequately indicate what they want, toddlers are becoming increasingly aware of what they do and do not want and what they do and do not like. They *like* routine and derive much comfort and security from the familiar. They *do not like* having to wait for something they want.

From 18 to 24 months, toddlers are in the stage of solitary play (see Categories of Social Play). Two-year-olds, however, become increasingly aware of one another; and though there is still little interaction, they move on to the stage of parallel play and tend to imitate what others are doing. During this time, they also begin to understand others have feelings, too (the beginnings of empathy).

CATEGORIES OF SOCIAL PLAY Although play researchers continue to refine Parten's (1932) categories of social play, the six categories are still being used today. Their definitions follow, reprinted with permission from Frost (1992, pp. 85–86):

1. Unoccupied Behavior. The child is not playing but occupies him- or herself with watching anything that happens to be of momentary interest. When there is nothing exciting taking place, he plays with his own body, gets on and off chairs, just stands around, follows the teacher, or sits in one spot glancing around the room (playground).

2. Onlooker Behavior. The child spends most of his time watching the other children play. He often talks to the children being observed, asks questions or gives suggestions, but does not overtly enter into the play. This type differs from unoccupied in that the onlooker is definitely observing particular groups of children rather than anything that happens to be exciting. The child stands or sits within speaking distance from other children.

3. Solitary Play. The child plays alone and independently with toys that are different from those used by the children within speaking distance and makes no effort to get close to other children. He pursues his own activity without reference to what others are doing.

4. Parallel Play. The child plays independently, but the activity chosen naturally brings him among other children. He plays with toys that are like those the children around him are using but he plays with the toys as he sees fit, and does not try to influence or modify the activity of the children near him. He plays beside rather than with the other children.

5. Associative Play. The child plays with other children. The communication concerns the common activity; there is borrowing and loaning of play materials; following one another with trains or wagons; mild attempts to control which children may or may not play in the group. All the members engage in similar activity, there is no division of labor, and no organization of the activity around materials, goal, or product. The children do not subordinate their individual interests to that of the group.

6. Cooperative Play. The child plays in a group that is organized for the purpose of making some material product, striving to attain some competitive goal, dramatizing situations of adult and group life, or playing formal games.

Although Parten found the play categories demonstrate a hierarchy related to children's increasing age (i.e., from 2 to $2\frac{1}{2}$ years old, children engaged mostly in solitary play; from $2\frac{1}{2}$ to $3\frac{1}{2}$, parallel play; from $3\frac{1}{2}$ to $4\frac{1}{2}$, associative play; and from $4\frac{1}{2}$ on, cooperative play), later studies did not completely support these findings. (For example, preschoolers today are less skilled in associative and cooperative play than were preschoolers in the late 1920s.) Researchers generally agree, however, children do advance from playing alone to playing cooperatively with others, but they do not necessarily outgrow their need for solitary activity (Frost, 1992).

Implications for the Movement Program. As mentioned, a toddler's emerging self-concept is greatly influenced by feedback received from the important adults in her life. Therefore, not only is it essential for toddlers to have the successful experiences offered by movement education, but also caregivers must complement the success with praise and positive reinforcement to advance the development of healthy self-concepts.

Positive reinforcement can also help ensure a more manageable environment for the movement session, because it appeals to the toddlers' need for adult approval. By granting approval, you will be giving the children one of the things they most desire; thus, they will be less likely to act out. And because toddlers are prone to imitation, they will strive to replicate the behavior you have most recently praised.

Charlesworth (1992) tells us that adults who use "positive suggestions" are much more likely to receive compliance from toddlers. Therefore, "show me you can" introductions to challenges, as opposed to "can you . . ." questions (see Chapter 8), are especially useful when working with toddlers. Presenting challenges that assume the children can do what you ask addresses their desire to please you *and* helps offset that ever-present urge to say no.

Waiting for turns is never a good idea for children participating in movement activities. But it is especially critical that toddlers—with their short attention spans and inability to delay gratification—spend no time waiting. Your challenges should allow all the children to respond at the same time—each in his or her own way.

Finally, because toddlers derive comfort from routine, you may attract greater interest and participation from them by opening and closing your movement sessions the same way every time. By doing so, you will be addressing their need for repetition, while ensuring success and providing special satisfaction.

Sample Activities. As previously stated, the self-concept involves children's view of their capabilities, physical characteristics, and self-worth (Castle, 1991). Movement exploration contributes to self-concept precisely because it makes children aware of many of their capabilities and physical characteristics. And when the movement exploration offers numerous opportunities for success, it enhances self-worth as well. Therefore, any developmentally appropriate movement activities you perform with toddlers will promote the me-and-I-am-great part of affective development.

To take advantage of toddlers' increasing interest in one another and help promote their budding feelings of empathy, you can perform activities that specifically focus on the concept of feelings. "If You're Happy and You Know It" is a simple, repetitive song toddlers enjoy. Once you have experienced the "happy" verse, you can make up your own based on other emotions; for example, "If you're grumpy and you know it, stamp your feet."

See My Face (Pica, 1990, p. 29) challenges children to display angry, surprised, sad, and happy faces, among others. Once the children become familiar and comfortable with these challenges, you can ask them to show these same emotions, and more, with their hands and with whole bodies. For instance, how would they walk if they were very mad? These activities not only give toddlers a much needed outlet for their emotions, but also when they begin to see similar responses among their peers, they begin to realize they share similar feelings.

Asking the children to move like familiar animals can also help develop empathy. Although they are too young to really imagine what it is like to *be* the animals, they can become more *aware* of the animals through movement activities; and that is an important first step.

Of course, one of the wonderful things about moving with toddlers is they are probably the most uninhibited beings in the world. They, unlike their older counterparts, will gladly move in the way the music makes them feel—and you do not even have to ask them to. All you need to do is put on the music, and they will be dancing before you know it—especially if you start dancing yourself, or if you provide bright, colorful scarves for the children to dance with. Simply by participating in this group activity, young children experience not only the joy of movement but the joy of moving *together*.

Figure 2-4
Ask children to demonstrate various emotions with their faces only. *Note:* From *Preschoolers Moving & Learning, 2nd ed.* (p. 38) by R. Pica, Champaign, IL: Human Kinetics. Copyright 1990 by Rae Pica. Reprinted by permission.

MOTOR DEVELOPMENT

Control over the body occurs from top (head) to bottom (toes) and from the middle (trunk) to the outside (extremities) (see Figure 2.5). And it is one development area caregivers can actually see occurring during the toddler stage (Castle, 1991). Not only do children grow considerably during the first three years of life, but they also gain considerable mastery over their bodies. They become more coordinated, more stable, and more determined to explore every bit of space available to them. This determination, combined with their drive toward independence and their inexhaustible energy, make motor development one of the most important aspects of their young lives.

By the time children are 2 years old, they are walking more confidently, having lost most or all of the wobble. They are also running, but not with as much control; their ability to balance and to start and stop quickly needs improving. Still, these minor inconveniences do not keep them from *wanting* to run. Essa (1992, p. 47) says running is a "pleasure in itself rather than means of getting somewhere fast."

Figure 2-5
The pattern of development. From Mayesky, *Creative Activities for Young Children*, 4th edition, copyright 1990 by Delmar Publishers, Inc.

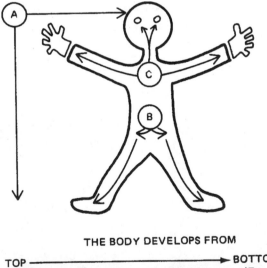

THE BODY DEVELOPS FROM

TOP ⟶ BOTTOM		
(Head)	*Cephalocaudal Development*	(Toes)

INSIDE ⟶ OUTSIDE		
(Trunk)	*Proximodental Development*	(Extremities)

LARGE ⟶ SMALL		
(Trunk, Neck, Arms, Legs)	*Gross to Fine Motor Development*	(Fingers, Hands, Toes, Wrists, Eyes)

Jumping is another newfound skill. It often begins with jumping off a low object, like a bottom step. Toddlers tend to land with their knees straight with one foot before the other. Later, when they begin to jump with both feet together, they will most likely jump from a flat-footed stance, with the body weight shifted backward. It is only after children become more proficient at the flat-footed jump that they can begin a jump from the balls of the feet, swinging the arms forward and upward and, finally, shifting body weight forward.

Climbing is one of the great adventures in the life of a toddler—and she or he will try to climb *everything*. Toddlers enjoy throwing and kicking, too, but will require another few years of practice and maturation before they approach a mature pattern in these skills. Two-year-olds can also roll a ball. Hand dominance is generally established by age 3.

Implications for the Movement Program.   Morrison (1990, p. 305) writes, "Activity is the normal pattern of toddler development, and to devise means for their inactivity is both pointless and harmful." If toddlers are going to be constantly on the move, however, we must also ensure they come to no harm through their activity. *Safety* is a key factor in working with toddlers.

Because they are going to walk and run and jump with a certain degree of instability, they are also going to fall. Thus, caregivers must take every precaution to ensure the falls are injury-free (see Chapter 5). If toddlers are going to practice throwing, lots of soft objects should be available for them to throw. If they are going to climb, Miller (1985) strongly advises providing a stable, toddler-sized climbing structure (with mats or padding beneath) toward which caregivers can "redirect" them from climbing on other, inappropriate, and perhaps unsafe objects, like tables and chairs.

Success is also especially important for toddlers, whose emerging self-concepts depend so much on early experiences. If they are going to practice kicking, their feet are more likely to actually strike something if very large balls are made available. Caregivers must also remember these young children are still only capable of performing a few movement skills, so they must avoid asking them to attempt skills for which they are not yet developmentally ready.

Sample Activities.   Follow the Leader and mirroring activities appeal to toddlers' knack for imitation. The Mirror Game, described in Chapter 1, is played in place and is therefore appropriate for experimenting with nonlocomotor movement. Although the only nonlocomotor skills with which toddlers are experiencing adequate amounts of success are bending and stretching, you can use this game to further explore the concepts of up, down, high, low, big, and small. Demonstrate simple shapes the children must replicate. Also, 2-year-olds are capable to imitating clapping, patting, raising their arms overhead, and other such simple actions.

Toddlers love Follow the Leader, which can be used to grant the children practice time with their newly acquired locomotor skills. Though this involves only walking, running, and jumping skills, you can use the elements of movement to vary how the children perform them (see Chapters 3 and 7). Children 30 to 36 months of age have usually acquired the ability to walk on tiptoe, so be sure to include this skill with your older toddlers.

Toddlers also love to throw things, and you can give them opportunity to practice the manipulative skill of throwing *safely* by providing lots of soft objects for them to toss—for example, stuffed socks, foam balls, and yarn balls. Striking at stationary objects with the hands or simple racquets can provide an introduction to yet another manipulative skill.

To help toddlers develop the skill of rolling a ball, provide playground balls, large foam balls, or beachballs and large, lightweight targets to give them a chance to practice "bowling." Targets can include objects large enough to hit and light enough to knock over, like empty plastic soft drink and dish or laundry detergent bottles. An additional benefit of practicing rolling and throwing is that it further familiarizes toddlers with the idea of cause and effect.

Hammett (1992) suggests children practice jumping and landing with an activity called Jack Be Nimble. For this game, each child needs a "candlestick" made from a bathroom tissue roll. You (and the children, if they know it) then recite the nursery rhyme "Jack Be Nimble." At "Jack jump over the candlestick," the children jump over their candles. You have to repeat this often so the children get a chance to do lots of jumping and landing—and because the children will insist on it!

Figure 2-6
Small beachballs and empty soda bottles can make "bowling" a successful experience for toddlers.

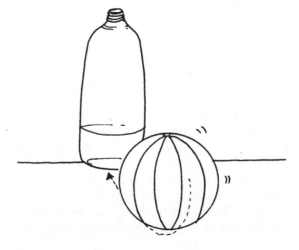

Preschoolers

Possibilities abound for exploring movement with preschoolers (within the scope of this book, children ages 3 to about $5\frac{1}{2}$). They are acquiring more and more motor skills, their cognitive abilities are increasing by leaps and bounds, and their social skills are rapidly improving. In general, this translates into fewer restrictions on the movement program. It does *not* translate into anything goes. Preschoolers still have special needs—including movement activities that are specifically designed with their capabilities and limitations in mind.

The following general points bear consideration when planning a movement program for preschoolers:

- The younger the preschoolers, the more time they will need to organize themselves as a group—an essential fact if you are planning movement sessions as short as 15 minutes.
- Forty-five minutes is generally the longest time you can expect to keep preschoolers interested and involved in movement activities.
- If you are working with mixed-age groups of children 3 to 5, you can expect the youngest children—at least initially—to respond by imitating the older children. This is a natural developmental stage and does not mean the younger preschoolers are not gaining anything from the experience; much is learned from imitation. As the movement program continues and individual responses are positively reinforced, the children's self-confidence will increase and all the participants will eventually respond in their own ways.
- Preschoolers run into objects and each other because depth perception is a learned ability. Therefore, their paths must be kept clear, and the children must be allowed enough time to change directions.
- When verbal instructions are given, the initial motor response of a preschooler will be toward the sound of your voice.

As mentioned earlier, children acquire gross motor skills according to their own individual timetables. They do not, however, instantly acquire the ability to perform these skills perfectly. Preschoolers will first execute each new skill in imperfect, individual ways; you should be concerned only if, after practicing the skill for a long time, a child shows no progress toward mastering it.

In planning and providing movement experiences for your preschoolers, keep in mind Sinclair's (1973, p. 64) words:

The preschooler up to the age of 5 is very busy learning new ways to move and practicing those he already knows. He can be helped best by being provided opportunity, motivation, encouragement, and a certain degree of protection, and by being allowed full rein for his creativity and discovery.

COGNITIVE DEVELOPMENT

As with motor development in toddlers, teachers and caregivers can almost literally *see* cognitive development taking place between the ages of 3 and 5. Speech goes from about 80 percent intelligible at age 3 to nearly 100 percent intelligible at age 5, with the children's interest in words and their ability to express themselves growing annually. Four-year-olds in particular have a fascination with words—especially silly ones.

Attention span increases significantly during the preschool years. Three-year-olds begin to be able to follow simple storylines, with 4-year-olds able to repeat stories, songs, and fingerplays. At 5, children are able to retell a story in the correct sequence (Feldman, 1991).

Curiosity increases, too. Four-year-olds ask many questions beginning with the words *why* and *how*. They enjoy stories about how things work and grow. And though they are not yet ready to sit still and learn, they do show interest in such academic subjects as letters and numbers—symbols that are becoming more and more recognizable for them. Between the ages of 3 and 5, children also learn to recognize shapes, sizes, and colors.

Three-year-olds understand more spatial concepts than do toddlers, including such positional words as *between, in back of,* and *on top of.* Four-year-olds understand many concepts related to space and time, and 5-year-olds comprehend *most* of them, including the days of the week, months, and seasons.

Implications for the Movement Program. Obviously, the increasing attention span of preschoolers will allow you to plan and provide longer movement sessions with them. Forty-five minute sessions *are* possible with 5-year-olds, and even 4-year-olds, if they are fast-paced. Not all activities should be fast-paced; rather, the activities should flow easily from one to the next. With 5-year-olds, you can even extend individual activities longer, providing extra experience with the movement skills and movement elements being explored. Five-year-olds are also able to handle combinations of movement elements (see Sample Activities).

The preschooler's lengthening attention span translates, too, into greater powers of concentration. Children from 3 to 5 become increasingly able to physically replicate what their eyes are seeing—for example, accurately imitating another's movement or shape. In addition, they become better able to respond to what they are hearing in a piece of music—for example, physically demonstrating changes in the music's tempo, volume, or pitch (see Chapter 6).

The preschool years are the perfect opportunity to take advantage of the children's fascination with words to encourage an appreciation for the language arts. Use nursery rhymes to inspire movement with 3-year-olds and, with preschoolers in general, lots of fingerplays, stories, poems, and songs (for 4-year-olds, the sillier the better!). Using descriptive words as the children move and pose will ensure their ability to provide their own descriptions of their actions, positions, and shapes by the time they are 5. Preschoolers, with their growing vocabulary and ability to express themselves, will also be glad to offer suggestions and ideas for movement activities.

Perhaps the most important opportunity is being able to validate and develop the children's creative ability. Preschoolers have a powerful curiosity and active imaginations. We can encourage and stretch these valuable tools by giving them chances, through movement, to imagine, explore, and discover.

Sample Activities. Bodily and spatial awareness continue to require emphasis during the preschool years. For the former, games like Simon Says can be played faster, with more body parts involved. (Elbows are particularly difficult for many preschoolers to find, so be sure to include them in your challenges.) "The Body Poem" (Pica, 1991a, p. 5) uses rhyme and simple numerical concepts to reinforce body awareness and also appeals to the 4-year-old's fondness for the silly.

> I have two feet,
> Two ears, two legs
> Ten fingers and ten toes;
>
> I have two knees,
> Two lips, two hands,
> And even two elbows
>
> I have two eyes
> And four eyelids.
> So why, do you suppose,
>
> With all these parts
> On my body
> I only have one nose?!

Read the poem slowly at first, asking children to touch or display the appropriate body parts as they are mentioned. For the third segment, they should shrug on "So why, do you suppose" and move their hands, from top to bottom, the length of their bodies on the next two lines. As the children become familiar with the poem, they will have fun if you do it faster each time.

As the children begin to master basic body-part activities, you can present them with greater challenges, such as the body-part activity described under cognitive development in Chapter 1. Eventually, you can introduce the concept of laterality, asking them to perform actions on only one side of their bodies. Later, you can ask them to perform opposite tasks with the separate halves of their bodies. For example, you might challenge them to stretch the top half of the body while bending the lower half, or to make a slow movement with one arm followed by a fast movement with the other.

Figure 2-7
Exploring the opposition of body halves can be as simple as stretching the top half of the body while bending the lower half.

As the children mature, you can provide greater challenges related to spatial concepts, too. Use imagery to explore up and down, asking the children to move like a yo-yo, popcorn popping, seeds growing, or ice cubes melting. Ask them to take on geometric shapes, beginning with vertical and horizontal lines, as described in Chapter 9. Obstacle courses and learning centers should become continually more complex.

Asking preschoolers to move with limitations enhances their critical thinking skills. You could, for example, challenge children to move while being very small, tall, round, or narrow. Can they move with the body very close to the ground? Is there another way? Can they move without using the feet at all?

Finally, as mentioned, older preschoolers can demonstrate success with *combinations* of movement elements. For instance, instead of merely asking them to move slowly, you can ask them to move slowly *and backward.* You might challenge them to walk backward while bending forward, or to walk quickly with a great deal of force.

AFFECTIVE DEVELOPMENT

Each year of growth during the preschool stage shows a corresponding growth in self-awareness, self-confidence, and self-control. Similarly, preschoolers show increasing interest and concern for one another, learning to take turns, share, and collaborate. Three-year-olds move from the parallel to the associative phase of play, with children 4 and 5 most often playing cooperatively.

Whether preschoolers are 3, 4, or 5, they show an eagerness to please adults and are susceptible to praise. Four-year-olds often seek adult approval, and 5-year-olds show a special fondness for their teachers.

Rules begin to take on greater meaning throughout the preschool years. Three-year-olds will learn some simple rules, but generally follow them according to their own interpretations (Harris, 1986). Four-year-olds are interested in rules and need to have limits set for them, but if the rules are within reason and consistently enforced, 4-year-olds generally have few problems with them (Miller, 1985). By the time children are 5, they have enough self-control so as not to require many rules; but they seem to enjoy having and following them (Mayesky, 1995; Allen & Marotz, 1994).

Preschoolers love to make believe. Although their experience is limited, 3-year-olds do engage in pretend play, alone and with others. At 4, children's pretend play ranges from the silly to the adventurous. By 5, children's imaginary play has become quite elaborate (Feldman, 1991; Allen & Marotz, 1994).

A few final points: Children of 3 often develop fears—of the dark, of animals, people, noises, and such. Four-year-olds display emotional extremes that change quite unpredictably, from one minute to the next. By the time children are 5, they generally "have their act together."

Implications for the Movement Program. Rules not only play a critical role in the lives of preschoolers but also in the movement program itself. To ensure that your rules are considered reasonable— and are therefore followed—ask the children to take part in the rule-making. They are less likely to break rules they themselves have established. Also, praise and positive reinforcement are still powerful tools during the preschool years; use them to further ensure a smooth-running movement program.

Because preschoolers are so fond of pretending, offer them frequent opportunities for role playing through movement, to help increase their creative potential while continuing to enhance their blossoming empathic feelings. As the children mature, they can express a greater range of emotions and take on more complex roles. In addition, allowing them to assume those roles that are important to them will add relevance to, and ensure greater interest in, the movement program.

When the children are 4 and 5, your program can include some activities that involve taking turns (on a limited basis, and only if they are not expected to wait very long). You can also incorporate some partner and simple group activities into the movement sessions.

And, of course, although children naturally develop greater self-confidence as they mature, this process could be seriously affected if the children's movement experiences are not positive and successful.

Sample Activities. As mentioned, preschoolers are able to display a greater range of emotions than their toddler counterparts. Clements and Schiemer (1993) suggest challenging the children to use their bodies to demonstrate many emotions, including mighty, friendly, proud, playful, gloomy, lazy, worried, and brave.

Although 3-year-olds might not be able to relate to all these feelings, they can identify with fearful things. Ask young preschoolers to act out their fears. If they are afraid of thunder, ask them to pretend to *be* thunder. If they are afraid of a certain animal, ask them to pretend to be that animal. Often, this role playing helps diminish the fear.

Because 4-year-olds love to be silly, you should give them occasional opportunities to move in silly ways or to make silly faces. An activity like Body Sounds (see Chapter 6), has special appeal to 4-year-olds.

Cooperation should be the key factor in partner and group activities. Touch and Move (see Chapter 1) and Footsie Rolls (see Chapter 3), are perfect examples of cooperative partner activities. Partners can also be asked to mirror and shadow one another's movements

Figure 2-8
Children ages 4 and 5 are ready to try simple partner activities.

and to create shapes and balances together. The Machine (see Chapter 9) and Musical Hoops (see Chapter 5) are examples of group cooperative activities.

MOTOR DEVELOPMENT

The preschool years are an exciting time for motor development. Three-year-olds begin simply by moving with greater ease and grace than their toddler counterparts; and by the time they are 5, preschoolers are executing most, if not all, of the basic locomotor and nonlocomotor skills as well as a number of manipulative and gymnastic skills.

Once 3-year-olds are walking and running comfortably, many begin to gallop. At about $3\frac{1}{2}$, children are even experimenting with brief hops on the preferred foot. Most preschoolers hop successfully on the dominant foot at age 4 and on the nondominant foot at about $4\frac{1}{2}$. Sliding and skipping are the two most challenging locomotor skills and are sometimes not acquired until children are more than $5\frac{1}{2}$. Many 4- and 5-year-olds first skip on one side only, and this should be considered a normal developmental stage. Older preschoolers are capable of combining some of the movement skills (see sample activities below).

Balance shows tremendous improvement during the preschool years. Three-year-olds can balance briefly on the preferred foot and walk a low balance beam with adult assistance. By the time children are 5, they can manage the balance beam by themselves, hop on either foot for 15 feet, and stand on one foot, hands on hips, for 10 seconds or longer (Skinner, 1979).

Manipulative skills also develop significantly during this time. Children begin to throw with greater accuracy, for longer distances; and their throwing pattern matures to the point where, at 5, they are stepping out with the foot opposite the throwing hand. Three-year-olds experience some success at catching a bounced ball, with 5-year-olds most often able to catch a medium-sized thrown ball. Four-year-olds begin bouncing a ball with control and can kick a ball with some accuracy toward a target. Five-year-olds are able to kick a rolling ball.

Though it is true children develop according to their own unique timetables, some general milestones normally take place by certain ages. Figure 2-9 highlights some of these milestones in the area of gross motor development.

Figure 2-9
Milestones in motor development.

18–24 Months
- Walks forward, backward, and sideways
- Runs with stops and starts, but unable to stop and start quickly
- Pushes and pulls objects while walking
- Climbs and ascends stairs
- Jumps up and down, but often falls

24–30 Months
- Ascends and descends stairs alone
- Imitates simple actions like clapping, patting, raising arms overhead
- Throws overhand
- Steps in place

Figure 2-9
(continued)

- Rolls a ball
- Bends easily at waist without toppling over

30–36 Months
- Walks on tiptoe
- Balances momentarily on one foot
- Jumps in place without falling, jumps forward, jumps off objects
- Kicks large ball

3-Year-Olds
- Change speed, direction, or style of movement at signal
- Walk a straight line and low balance beam
- Run on tiptoes
- Throw ball without losing balance and can throw underhand
- Gallop
- Hop briefly
- Use hands and feet simultaneously—for example, stamping feet while clapping
- Use alternate feet to ascend stairs
- Catch a large or bounced ball with both arms extended
- Jump to floor from approximately 12 inches

4-Year-Olds
- Start, stop, turn, and move easily around obstacles and others (well-oriented in space)
- Hop on nondominant foot
- Cross feet over midline of body
- Descend stairs with alternate feet
- Jump over objects 5 to 6 inches high
- Leap over objects 10 inches high
- Bounce and catch a ball
- May skip on one side only

5-Year-Olds
- Slide
- Skip using alternate feet
- Catch a thrown ball, though not always successful
- Balance on either foot
- Shift body weight to throw ("steps out" with foot opposite throwing hand)
- Execute simple dance steps
- Kick a rolling ball

6- to 8-Year-Olds
- Have well-developed gross motor skills
- Execute two or more skills concurrently—for example, running and catching
- Learn simple folk and partner dances

Implications for the Movement Program. Movement programs for preschoolers are tremendously exciting because there are continually more movement skills to explore—and more ways to explore them! As the children mature, they are gaining control over newly acquired skills and acquiring still others.

As this process unfolds, the focus gradually shifts from the elements of movement to the movements themselves (see Chapters 3 and 4). You will, of course, use the full array of movement elements to modify the ways movement skills are performed (providing the children greater practice, time, and experience with each skill). But during the preschool years, it is critical that you also begin evaluating how *well* the children are performing the movement skills.

If you are working with a mixed-age group of 3-to 5-year-olds, it is especially important that you be aware of their capabilities and limitations. Knowing the developmental stages of your students will allow you to phrase challenges so they can all experience success. For instance, if some children in your group can gallop and others cannot, rather than issuing a challenge to gallop, you might simply ask the children to move like horses. Those preschoolers who can gallop most likely will; the others will still be able to meet your challenge by pretending to be horses. They may even learn to gallop through imitation.

Similarly, if you are working on throwing, you could guarantee failure for some if you insist they all throw at a target from a specified distance. But if you permit the children to choose how far from the target they wish to stand, they will make choices that allow them to be successful. (Of course, these methods are part of the basic philosophy of movement education, but they are important enough to warrant reiterating here.)

Among preschoolers, 4-year-olds have the most energy and the greatest need to expend it. Plan your movement program for 4-year-olds accordingly, offering them the highest level of activity.

If you are working with 5-year-olds, possibilities truly abound. Not only can they manage many combinations of movement skills, but also they can learn some simple dances. They can even make up their own and should be encouraged to do so!

Sample Activities. Most or all of the locomotor and nonlocomotor activities suggested in Chapter 3 can be explored with preschoolers. As mentioned, with 5-year-olds, you can even begin working on combinations of skills. For example, you can challenge them to jump (or hop) and turn at the same time. Ask them to combine running and leaping. Can they execute several running steps followed by a leap? Can they run-run-leap? How about step-leap, step-leap, and so on?

Even simple locomotor skills become more challenging when performed with a partner. Ask pairs of preschoolers to move side by side, matching one another's movements. Challenge them to make one physical contact (e.g., holding hands, linking arms, placing inside hands on one another's shoulders) and to synchronize their movements. Can they smoothly change direction on signal? Can they find a way to execute the locomotor skill with one partner moving forward and the other backward?

Older preschoolers who have had adequate movement experience can also be asked to explore such nonlocomotor skills as pushing and pulling with partners. Sullivan (1982) even suggests having partners roll each other along the floor.

The Hokey Pokey is a simple group dance that is appropriate and fun for preschoolers. The song, "The Hokey Pokey," can be found on a number of recordings, including *The Hokey Pokey* (available from Melody House and Educational Record Center); *Kidding Around with Greg and Steve* (available from Kimbo); *Children's All-Time Rhythm Favorites* by Jack Capon and Rosemary Hallum and *Singing Action Games* (both available from Educational Activities); and *All-Time Favorite Dances* and *Around the World in Dance* (both available from Educational Record Center).

Early Elementary Children

Early elementary children, also referred to as primary-grade children, are generally about $5\frac{1}{2}$ to 8 years old and in kindergarten to grades two and three. In many ways, they are still developmentally similar to preschoolers. But their lives and learning experiences tend to change drastically upon entering public school—a situation the National Association for the Education of Young Children, the country's largest organization of early childhood educators, is greatly concerned about and has been attempting to change by educating teachers and parents as to what is developmentally appropriate for these young children.

Cognitively, for example, early elementary children are more like preschoolers than upper elementary children (Charlesworth, 1992). Yet, in many public schools, *all* elementary children are treated similarly. Gone are the days of active learning preschoolers engage in; early elementary children are frequently expected to learn through lectures, textbooks, worksheets, and other "seatwork." Subjects are studied in tightly scheduled time slots (Bredekamp, 1987) as opposed to being integrated. Student evaluations, rather than being determined by observation, often become grades based on the results of paperwork.

Opportunities for social development are also severely restricted as children are expected to work individually rather than as part of a group. And although primary-grade children are not yet physically mature and "are more fatigued by long periods of sitting than by running, jumping, or bicycling" (Bredekamp, 1987, p. 63), their need for activity is usually ignored and suppressed during the elementary years.

In a developmentally appropriate early elementary program, the emphasis will continue to be—as it was during the preschool years—on active, integrated learning experiences that address the whole child. This means movement will continue to play a critical role in the primary grades.

Some general information about the characteristics and development of 5- to 8-year-olds can help you better plan movement activities appropriate for early elementary children.

- Young children run into objects and each other because depth perception is a learned ability. By age 7, children should be able to travel freely throughout a room without collisions.
- Hand-eye and foot-eye coordination are not well established until 9 or 10. Both are difficult for the youngest primary-age children due to slow reaction time.
- Kindergarten and first-grade children may tire suddenly, but they recover quickly.
- Physiologically, girls are about a year ahead of boys in their development.
- Boys and girls share similar interests at the beginning of this age range, but interests begin to diverge toward the end.
- Self-consciousness tends to become more of a factor toward the end of this age span.

COGNITIVE DEVELOPMENT

As stated earlier, primary-grade children are cognitively more similar to preschoolers than to their upper elementary counterparts. Thus, they still learn best by doing and process should still receive more emphasis than product. These young children need most experiences that allow them to explore and discover, identify and solve problems, and to use and apply their burgeoning thinking skills. Traditional subjects will have greater meaning for them when they are integrated and relevant to their lives.

One major difference occurs, however, between the preschooler's and the primary-grade student's cognitive level; during the early elementary years, children begin to associate symbols with concrete experiences and, thus, to solve problems in their heads (Charlesworth, 1992; Bredekamp, 1987). They also begin to use logic in their attempts at understanding.

Another milestone is the realization differences of opinion exist. Early elementary children begin to accept this and to observe from other points of view—a significant development indeed.

Although still not able to think and solve problems as adults do, by the time they are 6 and 7 years old, primary-grade children have usually acquired the language skills of an adult. They talk almost nonstop, but rather than seeing this as an annoyance, adults should do everything possible to encourage the newfound ability to communicate. In fact, whenever possible, adults should make the comments necessary to prolong children's conversations and offer learning experiences that encourage verbal communication between the students themselves.

According to Charlesworth (1992, p. 542), primary-level children "still respond to adult approval and to task success . . . as criteria for their intellectual competence. Consequently, it is relatively easy to promote an atmosphere that enables them to feel good about themselves as learners."

Implications for the Movement Program.   Consider the following points:

- Primary-grade children continue to learn best by doing (Movement *is* doing.)
- Task success promotes feelings of intellectual competence. (Movement education is success-oriented.)
- Process is still more important throughout the primary grades than product. (Movement exploration is a process that leads to discovery.)
- For content areas to have greater relevance to young children, they should be integrated rather than studied in segments. (Movement, as discussed in Chapter 9, is a powerful tool to use in integrating traditional content areas.)

In short, movement is as important to primary-grade children as it is to toddlers and preschoolers. Of course, because the learning situation tends to change in elementary school, the ways in which movement is experienced must also change. In the best of situations, primary-grade children receive daily movement instruction from a physical education specialist as well as daily movement experiences related to the curriculum from their classroom teacher—*and* the specialist and classroom teacher work together to synthesize learnings.

Of the cognitive developments taking place during this period, increased problem-solving and communication skills will probably have the greatest impact on the movement program. First, teachers can present a much wider range of problem-solving challenges to early elementary children. And, by doing so, they will promote critical-thinking skills and help children learn how to learn. Teachers can test and stretch children's verbal skills by employing movement in the study of language arts and by soliciting their ideas and feedback. Also, by presenting children with challenges requiring interaction between partners or among group members, teachers can promote both problem-solving *and* communication skills.

Primary-grade teachers can expect their students' depictions of objects and animals to demonstrate much more realism at this stage. Because the children's understandings and powers of concentration are greater, teachers can also use a wider variety of music in the movement program and expect students to respond accurately to what they are hearing.

Sample Activities.   The early elementary child's level of cognitive development opens whole new possibilities for the movement program. For example, you can now explore laterality using the terms *left* and *right*. Rather than assigning specific body parts for weight placement and balance activities, you can simply challenge the children to place their weight or balance on a certain number of parts. You can also present more challenges beginning with the words, "Find (number) ways to _____ ." For instance, you might pose the following questions and challenges:

- Place your hands on the floor and show me how many ways you can move your feet (without moving your hands).
- Can you find different ways to move if you have just one hand on the floor?
- Try it with one foot and both hands. How many ways can you move the free foot?
- Put the top of your head on the floor and find at least four ways you can move the rest of your body.

Throughout this chapter, examples have been given of body-part activities appropriate for various development levels. During the early elementary years, less emphasis will be placed on body awareness. However, exploring the possible relationships among body parts will require primary-grade children to think a bit more about the sum of their parts and the space they occupy. Toward this end, you can present challenges similar to the following, adapted—as are all the activities in this section—from Pica (1991b).

- Touch a hand to an ankle; take it as far away from that ankle as possible.
- Bring your head to your knees; take it as far away from your knees as possible.
- Touch an elbow to the floor. What other body parts is it near?

Figure 2-10
Balancing on one body part only.

- Touch a shoulder to the floor. What other body parts are touching the floor?
- Touch an elbow to a knee; take it as far away from that knee as possible.
- Can you touch your elbow to your foot?
- Come up from the floor with your head leading and the rest of your body following.
- Go back down to the floor with your nose leading the way.
- Come back up with an elbow leading.

Primary-grade children are still attempting to grasp the concept of time, so an activity like 10 Seconds can be helpful because it limits the time they have to perform a movement or movements. Explain you are going to count 10 seconds in your head (so your counting does not influence their movement), telling them when to begin and end moving. During that 10 seconds, you want them to show you how many *different* movements it is possible to perform. After repeating this a few times, you can then ask them to prolong a *single* movement (like raising or lowering an arm, or making a single turn) for 10 seconds, this time while you count out loud.

In an activity called The Clock, you act as the timepiece. You raise your right arm overhead to the 12 o'clock position, with your left arm down, center front. You then sweep your right arm sideways in a smooth arc to center front, where it meets the left arm. When your palms touch, that is 6 o'clock. Both arms then separate and sweep out and up. When they meet overhead at 12, the activity is over. By watching the clock, the children should be able to determine the speed of their movements. They begin to move when the clock does; and when the clock strikes 6, they know the activity is half over. Either ask the children to move any way they like while the clock hands are moving, or assign them a specific movement they are familiar with. Vary the speed of the clock as you repeat this activity.

Kimbo has also produced *One Step at a Time,* an album to help children understand the concept of time. Songs on the album include "Minute Hand/Hour Hand," "Yesterday-Today-Tomorrow," and "60 Seconds/60 Minutes."

To enhance problem-solving skills and spatial awareness, choose a reference point, such as a table, a chair, or a column connecting floor to ceiling. Then ask your students to find and remember their personal space and to approach the reference point in the following ways, always returning to their own personal space:

- in a straight path;
- from one side and then the other;
- from the back;
- in a curving (zigzagging) path;
- walking forward to the reference point, but returning to personal space sideways;
- walking sideways to the point, but returning backward; and
- walking forward partway to the point, making a half-turn, and continuing toward the point backward.

AFFECTIVE DEVELOPMENT

Perhaps the most significant social development during the early elementary years is a growing interest in peers. Children easily establish—and abandon—friendships. Six- to 8-year-olds enjoy play-ing with one another in small groups. And, by first grade, children are beginning to compare themselves with others.

Although these young children still respond to adult approval, *peer* acceptance becomes a stronger force in the primary grades than adult acceptance. The adult's role, therefore, shifts primarily to one of facil-itator. And certainly teachers and caregivers should strive to facilitate positive relationships among the children.

Play, often seen as an activity for younger children, is still impor-tant in the cognitive and social development of primary-grade chil-dren. During the early elementary years, however, growing gender awareness and differences tend to change the way children play. Children between the ages of 6 and 8 generally play with others of the same sex. Yet, while they may not choose partners of the opposite sex, if assigned to each other for an activity, they still seem to enjoy it (Haines & Gerber, 1992). Boys are usually more concerned with sex-role stereotypes than are girls (Miller, 1985).

Although the emphasis in learning should remain on process through the primary grades, early elementary children do become increasingly interested in the final product. Task completion—and success—contribute to their feelings of self-esteem, with fears associ-ated with achievement—or lack thereof—common between the ages of 6 and 11 (Charlesworth, 1992). A desire to excel begins in the sec-ond and third grades; children in these grades like to be admired for doing things well.

Finally, although primary-age children show greater self-responsibility and are beginning to acquire a conscience, they still require adult assis-tance in achieving self-control and in monitoring their actions. Teachers and caregivers must allow them a certain amount of inde-pendence, encouraging them to take responsibility for themselves, but must also remember children of this age are sometimes *too* strict in their determination of what is right and wrong (Bredekamp, 1987).

Implications for the Movement Program.   Perhaps because chil-dren of this age begin to compare themselves with one another, the natural conclusion has traditionally been that this is the age when competition should play a prominent role in movement activities. However, there are a great many reasons why *cooperation,* rather than competition, should continue to be stressed.

For example, when students are given opportunities to work together toward a solution or common goal, they know they each contribute to the success of the venture. Every child plays a vital role in the outcome, and each accepts the responsibility involved in ful-filling that role. The children also learn to become tolerant of other's ideas, and to accept the similarities and differences of other children (Pica, 1993). And cooperative activities are far less likely to cause inferiority feelings that so often result from comparisons made during competitive situations. Furthermore, Grineski (1993) tells us self-esteem, motivation, and feelings of belonging are all enhanced through cooperative learning. Thus, physical educators and classroom teachers should make cooperative partner and group activities a major part of the curriculum. When competition is involved, it should be competition against oneself—that is, always striving to better an earlier "performance" (see More About Cooperation).

In addition, partner and group activities tend to alleviate the self-consciousness that begins to appear in older primary-grade children. When working with others, children are less focused on themselves than when they work individually.

To help break down sex-role barriers, teachers should avoid activities that involve any gender stereotyping. If, for instance, you ask the children to run as though carrying a football in a big game, both boys and girls should be expected to respond. Similarly, activities that

Figure 2-11
Cooperative group activities alleviate self-consciousness and help create feelings of belonging.

MORE ABOUT COOPERATION Sports psychologist Terry Orlick's two books of games are probably the most well-known collections of cooperative activities. Written in 1978, *The Cooperative Sports and Games Book: Challenge Without Competition* (Pantheon) contains more than 100 games. Orlick's *The Second Cooperative Sports and Games Book* (Nasco, 1982) consists of 200-plus additional games for players of all ages, including toddlers. The activities emphasize imagination as well as cooperative skills.

The games in Jeffrey Sobel's *Everybody Wins: 393 Non-competitive Games for Young Children* (Walker & Co., 1984) are designed for children 3 to 10 and are intended to promote feelings of self-worth and confidence—as opposed to rejection.

Supporting the argument for cooperation is Alfie Kohn's *No Contest: The Case Against Competition* (Houghton Mifflin, 1992), described as the first comprehensive book to show why competition is often damaging. It refutes the myths that competition builds character and is an instinctive part of human beings.

challenge children to take the roles of people in various occupations (from firefighters to flamenco dancers, homemakers to hairstylists) warrant a response from all children, regardless of gender. And to help get boys and girls together as partners, issue a challenge for the children to get back to back with someone else as fast as they can. They will be more concerned with how quickly they can do it than with whom they are back to back.

Sample Activities.   Many partner and group activities suggested for preschoolers are also appropriate for exploration with early elementary children, as long as they are made somewhat more challenging. For example, if the children are forming letters, numbers, and geometric shapes in pairs, they should be assigned more difficult letters, numbers, and geometric shapes—and sometimes encouraged to choose their own.

Palm to Palm is a partner activity that requires the children to consider the number of shapes they can assume with their arms and hands. Facing another child, who is standing close enough to touch, the first child assumes a shape with her or his arms. (Any shape is acceptable as long as palms face the partner.) The partner then forms the identical shape, bringing hands palm to palm with those of the first child. As soon as contact is made, the first child chooses a new arm position, and the activity proceeds accordingly. After a while, the partners reverse roles.

Children can gain experience with group cooperation with simple activities like Pass a Face, Pass a Movement, and Pass a Beat. With the first activity, the children sit in a circle and one child begins by making a face that is "passed" to the child to his right or left. That child makes the *same* face and passes it along in the same direction. When the face has been passed all around the circle, the process is repeated, with a different child beginning. With Pass a Movement, the children form a standing circle and pass around an *action*. The first child might, for instance, bend at the waist and straighten. Each child in succession must then do the same. In Pass a Beat, the first child claps out a rhythm (e.g., 1–2–3–4 at a moderate tempo, or quick-quick-slow). The object is for each child in the circle to repeat the rhythm *exactly,* keeping an even tempo all the way around. Even the interval between each child should be in keeping with the rhythm being passed.

More challenging group activities include Group Balance and Let's Slither. With the former, the children form a standing circle and place their hands on the shoulders of the children beside them. They must then maintain a steady balance through challenges to stand on only one foot, lean in various directions, rise on tiptoe, and such.

In Let's Slither, students begin by pairing off and stretching out on their stomachs, one in front of the other. The child in back takes hold of the ankles of the child in front, forming a two-person "snake" that starts to slither across the floor. This two-person snake then connects with another two-person snake, and the process continues until the entire group has formed one big snake.

MOTOR DEVELOPMENT

Fundamental movement abilities are usually present by 5 years of age. By the age of 6, children are able to perform most locomotor skills in a mature pattern, with sliding and skipping commonly the last two locomotor skills acquired. Generally, children are able to skip smoothly, alternating feet, by 5.6 years of age (Skinner, 1979).

By the time most children are 6 years old, they are capable climbers. Between the ages of 5 and 7, children nearly reach the mature stage of throwing, able to shift their weight to the foot on the same side as the throwing arm in preparation for the throw, and then to transfer the weight to the opposite foot during the throw (Morrison, 1990). By about 5.8 years of age, a child should be able to bounce a ball in place, catching each bounce (Skinner, 1979). Also, between 5 and 6, children are usually able to kick a rolling ball and to accurately roll a ball to hit a target.

Early elementary children are still physically active, with lots of energy and a desire to show off their newly acquired physical skills. During this time, development in all domains becomes integrated (Charlesworth, 1992). Gross motor skills are well developed; and this, together with newly acquired cognitive and social skills, makes it possible for primary-grade children to take part in games involving rules and combinations of skills. They are also able to learn the steps and sequences of partner and simple folk dances (Haines & Gerber, 1992).

Implications for the Movement Program.   Early elementary children should be given as much opportunity as possible to practice and perfect their movement skills, with particular attention being paid to those that are newly acquired. *Combinations* of skills, assigned by the teacher and created by the children, should receive special emphasis. Not only will they present greater challenge for the children, but also they will help prepare them for the games, dances, and movement activities that will likely be part of their later lives.

The primary grades present teachers with the perfect opportunity to incorporate dance (on a basic level) into the curriculum. Between the ages of 5 and 6, children are generally able to follow specific rhythm patterns (Mayesky, 1995), and the integration of the motor, cognitive, and affective domains enables them to work together, learning and performing dance steps and sequences. Also, it is significant that boys and girls at this level are usually still willing to cooperate.

Although primary-grade children are able to begin playing games involving rules and more complex skills, traditional games like kickball, basketball, and soccer are not developmentally appropriate at this level. Unless modified to meet the needs of young children, such competitive games are enjoyable only for those who have a chance for success. According to Grineski (1993), most participants fail due to the zero-sum (one winner and one loser) or negative-sum (one winner and many losers) results characteristic of competitive situations. Furthermore, learning and practice opportunities are extremely limited during such games. In studies conducted by Grineski, he discovered 75 percent of ball contacts were made by 40 percent of the players during a third-grade soccer game; three students neither touched the ball nor ran the length of the gym during a fifth-grade sideline soccer game; and only 60 percent of the players touched the ball during a fifth-grade sideline basketball game.

Obviously, teachers at the early (and even upper) elementary level must continue to plan movement activities that offer *all* children opportunities for participation, practice, and success.

Sample Activities.   A number of steps used in folk dance are simply combinations of locomotor skills. Furthermore, on their way to learning how to create and perform dances and master gymnastic and sports skills, children need to learn how to link the individual skills they have acquired to form movement "phrases," "sentences," and eventually "paragraphs."

Suggest combinations of skills to the children they must put together, in any order they choose, to form movement phrases. Possible combinations of locomotor skills include walk-leap-hop, run-jump-leap, or gallop-jump-hop, with possibilities for combinations of locomotor and nonlocomotor skills being walk-turn-jump, stretch-swing-jump, and hop-sit-roll. The children may perform as many repeats of each individual skill as they want, but must link them without lengthy pauses or extraneous movements between them.

A step-hop is a movement commonly performed in folk dances—and in a basketball lay-up shot. Like the skip, it is a combination of a step and a hop. With the step-hop, however, the two movements have the same time value, and the accent is on the step (the hop is accented in the skip). Provide an even 1–2 beat with your hands or a drum, and ask the children to practice combining steps and hops to match that rhythm. Can they perform repeatedly one step followed by one hop?

Once the children are able to slide, the "Mexican Hat Dance" is a perfect introduction to a group folk dance. It should, of course, be divided into manageable components, with the children learning the components individually before putting them together. Music for this dance can be found in *Early Elementary Children Moving & Learning* and *All-Time Favorite Dances* and *Folk Dance Fun* (both offered by Kimbo).

During the primary grades, children should also continue experimenting with locomotor movements performed with a partner. Once they are able to walk and run in synchronization, with one physical contact and in all possible directions, they should explore the possibilities for the remaining locomotor skills. Which are the easiest to perform together? Which are the hardest?

Children with Special Needs

Just as this textbook cannot do justice to the vast topic of child development, it cannot fully address the subject of children with special needs or cover all the different special needs teachers and caregivers may encounter. (For additional information, readers should refer to the References at the end of this chapter and to the ever-increasing number of resources becoming available on this topic)

Although movement entails an additional challenge for children with special needs, movement education is well suited to these children. Its philosophy and practice lend themselves to inclusion of—and success for—all children. And the benefits cited in Chapter 1 certainly apply to children with special needs. Coordination, listening skills, conceptual learning, and expressive ability are just a few of the areas enhanced through regular participation—at whatever level possible—in a movement program.

However, perhaps of greatest importance is the contribution movement programs can make toward the special child's self-concept. Often children with disabilities fail to form a complete body image due to exclusion from physical activity. Or because they do not necessarily perform like other children, they develop a distorted body image (Gallahue, 1993). Identifying and moving various body parts can "help the child discover how each body part fits into the whole schema of a human body. This enables the child to explore body boundaries and define his/her image" (Samuelson, 1981, p. 53). Achieving regular success in movement activities will contribute greatly to the child's confidence—perhaps offering for the first time an opportunity to feel good about oneself.

Another unique opportunity derived from the movement program is the chance to be part of a group. As the child's self-concept becomes more developed, she is better able to relate to others. As the child's movements and ideas are regularly accepted and valued, he receives greater acceptance from his peers. Becoming part of a group—making contributions, taking turns, following rules—has the additional benefit of enhancing social skills (Hibben & Scheer, 1982).

When incorporating children with special needs into the movement program, you must be sure your challenges can be met by all the children. In general, every child will be able to respond in some manner. For example, Samuelson (1981) reminds us the blink of an eye, the inhalation of a breath, and the twitching of fingers are all movements. Thus, they can be considered responses to challenges and can even be used for demonstration purposes, with the rest of the children being asked to replicate these movements. Not only does this include the child with special needs, but also places her in what is probably an unfamiliar role—that of leader.

Sometimes, of course, it will be necessary to adapt certain activities. For instance, some children with special needs have difficulty responding to an externally imposed rhythm (Krebs, 1990a). This does not mean rhythmic activities must be eliminated from the program; rather, the teacher can simply allow certain children to move to self-imposed rhythms.

Music can be an especially helpful addition to the movement program involving children with special needs. These children often show high levels of response, motivation, and enjoyment when participating in music experiences (Isenberg & Jalongo, 1993; Bayless & Ramsey, 1991; Zinar, 1987). Thus, you may want to make music a greater part of your movement activities than you normally would.

Naturally, you should always consult parents and therapists regarding movement activities and possible modifications. Public laws require children who qualify for special services and who are under the age of 5 be given individual family service plans (IFSPs), and school-aged children receive individual education plans (IEPs). Both plans are developed with input from parents, teachers, and service providers and outline short- and long-term goals in one or more developmental areas. Movement specialists who are in touch with parents, teachers, and therapists can help the children meet their goals by determining appropriate objectives.

In the following sections, we will address the special conditions teachers and caregivers of young children are most likely to find: physical impairments, hearing impairments, visual impairments, emotional disabilities, and limited understanding. Usually a small number of children with these special conditions are mainstreamed into the regular classroom, and their disabilities are not among the most severe. But the presence of any of these conditions can have an impact on the movement program; for that reason, they are addressed here. Implications for the movement program, as well as suggested activities, are incorporated into the discussion of each condition.

Two final points should be kept in mind when working with children with special needs. First, we must recognize that just as no two children are alike, neither are children with special needs—even if their disabilities fall into the same category. All conditions have a range of severity and a uniqueness directly correlated to the uniqueness of the child with the condition. Most importantly, as Bayless and Ramsey (1991, p. 193) point out, we must recognize that "there are more similarities than differences between handicapped and nonhandicapped children."

PHYSICALLY CHALLENGED CHILDREN

Physically challenged children are the fastest growing population of children receiving special education services (Knight & Wadsworth, 1993). Physical disabilities may be caused by birth defects, accidents, or illness and include such neurological or musculoskeletal impairments as cerebral palsy, arthritis, poliomyelitis, spina bifida, or multiple sclerosis. Severe chronic illnesses like asthma, diabetes, leukemia, and hemophilia are also included in this category (Knight & Wadsworth, 1993; Bayless & Ramsey, 1991; Zinar, 1987).

Perhaps the one thing children with these conditions share in common is their mobility is restricted in one way or another—and that, of course, will have an effect on their participation in the movement program. You, as teacher or caregiver, will have to understand the type and degree of the impairment and the physiological effects movement may have on these children.

Children with spina bifida, cerebral palsy, or arthritis, for example, will need periods of rest so they do not experience pain or discomfort. Children with epilepsy are just like their peers except for occasional seizures, which are usually controlled through medication; but climbing activities should probably be avoided (Gallahue, 1993). Children with multiple handicaps often require extra assistance where the concepts of laterality and directionality are concerned (Bayless & Ramsey, 1991).

Zinar (1987) suggests a number of activities to help accomplish specific goals with motor-impaired children. Among them are pretending to rock a baby to improve lateral movement of upper arms and shoulders; tossing a balloon into the air and watching it descend to strengthen the back of the neck; and waving streamers while peers are marching, to improve arm strength. According to Karnes (1992), fingerplays offer good fine-motor experience for children with muscle-control problems, but those children might have to start with larger movements and gradually work toward smaller ones.

In general, the child with physical disabilities should be encouraged to participate at whatever level is possible. A child may have to substitute swaying or nodding the head for more difficult rhythmic responses. If the child cannot hold rhythm instruments, he can wear bells attached to elastics placed around the wrists and simply *become* a musical instrument. Children in wheelchairs will have to experience locomotion on wheels rather than on foot—whether propelling themselves or being pushed by a peer. Krebs (1990a) suggests cane or crutch tapping as a substitute for hand clapping (or foot stamping), and replacing lower-body movements with upper-body movements.

The necessary modifications are often uncomplicated; it is simply a matter of focusing on what the children *can* do, as opposed to what they cannot.

CHILDREN WITH HEARING IMPAIRMENTS

Although of several types and degrees, all hearing impairments involve some malfunctioning of the auditory mechanism. The majority of people with hearing impairments are not totally deaf; rather, they have varying degrees of hearing loss (Craft, 1990).

Often, when hearing losses are not immediately diagnosed, children with hearing impairments are thought to be mentally retarded or slow learners, or to have behavior problems, because their impairments make communication difficult and they may not have received messages concerning what is expected of them (Gallahue, 1993; Craft, 1990; Zinar, 1987).

Movement, however, is generally not a problem for hearing-impaired children unless there is damage to the semicircular canals. If so, the child will have balance problems, which can result in delays in motor ability. Children with damage to the semicircular canals should refrain from taking part in potentially dangerous balance activities—for example, climbing or tumbling actions requiring rotation, unless assistance is provided. Craft (1990) does suggest balancing skills taught in safe situations should be included in the program to help hearing-impaired children make maximum use of visual and kinesthetic cues in balancing.

For all children with hearing impairments, the major challenges involved in participating in the movement program are related to the use of music and the presentation of instructions.

Teachers and caregivers can take a number of steps to help lessen the latter problem. Children with difficulty hearing should be placed in front of the room. Distractions like background music or others talking should be eliminated. Teachers, when speaking, should always face the child with a hearing impairment and avoid covering the mouth. Zinar (1987) also suggests teachers speak in low tones (not low as opposed to loud but as opposed to high-pitched) because the hearing-impaired are better able to hear low-frequency sounds. Flicking the lights off and on is a signal the teacher can use to instantly get the children's attention.

If the child uses sign language, the movement teacher should make every effort to learn simple signs that convey the day's objectives (e.g., walking, skipping, throwing, etc.). If sign language is not a possibility, teachers can communicate through facial expression, gestures, and pantomime. For other communication ideas, the speech and language therapist (assigned by the school district) is a valuable resource.

During music activities, teachers must remember that although a child may not be able to hear the music, he or she will be able to *feel* it. Children with hearing impairments can place their hands on the record or tape player, or the instrument being used to make music, to feel the vibrations and establish a rhythm. Lying on a wooden floor often enables the child to feel the vibrations with the whole body.

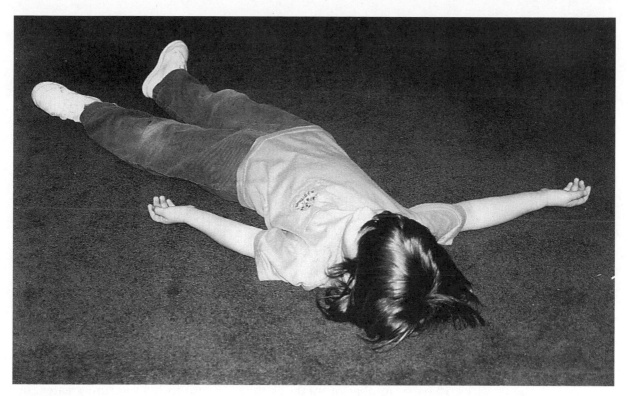

Figure 2-12
Lying on the floor often enables children with hearing impairments to feel the music's vibrations with the whole body.

Imitation is also an important tool in being able to experience rhythms—with and without music. Children with hearing impairments should be encouraged to imitate their peers as they clap hands, stamp feet, play rhythm instruments, march, gallop, and skip. Teachers may need to repeat more than usual to help children with hearing impairments gain a sense of rhythm.

Because movement education is one area that does not rely primarily on verbal communication, children with hearing losses can experience, as their peers do, all the benefits and joys of movement. For these special children, movement has the additional benefit of promoting social interaction that may be missing in other areas of their lives.

CHILDREN WITH VISUAL IMPAIRMENTS

The Education of All Handicapped Children Act (PL 94-142) defines visually challenged children as those whose visual impairments, even when corrected, adversely affect their learning. Included in the definition are blind and partially sighted children (Craft, 1990), more of whom are in public schools rather than in special schools for the blind (Zinar, 1987).

Usually, a movement education program that meets the needs of children at all levels of ability can similarly meet the needs of children with visual impairments, with minor modifications. Children with visual limitations tend to rely more heavily on adults than do sighted children and often display hesitation and caution when asked to move. However, they have to their advantage auditory and tactile skills that become increasingly stronger, and these senses can be used to enhance kinesthetic skills.

When working with children with visual impairments, teachers have a number of methods they can use to help ensure greater success. Children with poor vision should be placed near the teacher so they can see more easily. Holding hands with the teacher or with a responsible partner—or having a partner place her hands on the hips or shoulders of the visually impaired child—are ways of using the tactile and kinesthetic senses to encourage movement and alleviate fear. The teacher can also use touch to help a child achieve an appropriate shape or position.

To make use of the auditory sense, the teacher should use verbal cues and clear, succinct descriptions when presenting challenges and when offering feedback. Statements like "You are bending and straightening your knees to help you move up and down" have the additional benefit of increasing the visually impaired child's body awareness. Such statements as "Everyone swing their arms back and forth" help the visually impaired child realize his body is like the other children's (Karnes, 1992).

Craft (1990) suggests visual cues be enhanced through the use of such objects as brightly colored balls and mats that contrast with the background. Fluorescent tape placed on the edge of mats or on the floor can also help children with some vision. When working with blind children, she recommends choosing activities that are not heavily dependent on visual input and feedback and thus require little or no modification.

Finally, if the visually impaired child uses a cane, for safety, the class must learn how it is used.

CHILDREN WITH EMOTIONAL DISABILITIES

According to PL 94-142, a child with an emotional disability is "one who has an inability to learn that cannot be explained by sensory problems, health factors, or intellectual deficits; is unable to make and maintain satisfactory interpersonal relationships with peers and adults; demonstrates inappropriate behavior; is generally unhappy or depressed; or develops physical symptoms in response to school or personal problems" (Gallahue, 1993, p. 104). Gallahue further states that estimates of the number of children with emotional disabilities range from 2 to more than 20 percent of the total population, meaning, even at the most conservative estimate, more than 1 million school-aged children have serious emotional disabilities.

Loovis (1990) reports, although the term *emotionally handicapped* is regularly used to describe all the children fitting the above definition, these children exhibit quite varied behaviors, including hyperactivity, aggression "beyond what is considered normal or socially acceptable," withdrawal, impulsivity, and immaturity.

These behaviors commonly result in a lack of self-control and a refusal to participate, the two most common problems encountered during the movement program. In addition, some evidence indicates children with emotional disabilities also lag behind in physical and motor abilities, perhaps due to poor work habits, attention deficits, and other such common factors (Loovis, 1990).

To effectively remedy the latter problem, Loovis recommends an emphasis on basic movement skills, including balance, execution of fundamental locomotor and nonlocomotor skills, and perceptual-motor activities.

To help alleviate discipline problems, a number of teaching tips can be employed. In general, the methods that are an inherent part of movement education lend themselves to greater success for children with emotional disabilities. For example, presenting activities that are challenging yet not overwhelming will encourage children to participate and help guarantee success, which enhances self-esteem. Honest praise and positive reinforcement encourage desired behaviors. Dramatizing emotions and moving to action songs provide modes of self-expression and an outlet for feelings. Incorporating relaxation activities into the program promotes self-control.

Among the techniques specifically recommended for emotionally challenged children are the avoidance of physical contact during activities, shunning lyrics that could have disturbing associations for the children (e.g., "Rock-a-Bye Baby"), employing activities that require the children to concentrate (e.g., "Bingo"), and when appropriate, rewarding emotionally handicapped children by allowing them to assist in some way (Zinar, 1987).

CHILDREN WITH LIMITED UNDERSTANDING

For the purposes of this text, children with limited understanding include children with learning disabilities and those who are mildly to moderately retarded. (Children with severe and profound mental retardation are generally not mainstreamed into the regular classroom unless one-on-one with an aide is possible.)

Children with learning disabilities possess average or above-average intelligence but have difficulty in using written or spoken language (Gallahue, 1993; Essa, 1992). Because learning disabilities take many forms and are not as easily recognized as physical disabilities, children who have them are often mislabeled as hyperactive, immature, or emotionally disturbed. Many of them have problems with motor control, including difficulties with body and spatial awareness, coordination, directionality, and stopping once they are in motion (Essa, 1992; Zinar, 1987).

Although many different definitions of mental retardation exist, two criteria must occur between conception and 18 years of age (Krebs, 1990b) to be considered retardation: below-average intellectual functioning and an inability to mature personally and socially with age.

Mentally retarded children are usually also below average in motor development, possibly due to some extent to their cognitive difficulties and to a lack of opportunity for activity (Gallahue, 1993).

Generally speaking, children with limited understanding—no matter what the cause—will have shorter attention spans and may become easily discouraged. Using a multisensory approach (allowing the children chances to use body, voice, eyes, and ears—and often including music) and providing activities that incrementally become more challenging can help remedy these two problems. Mentally challenged children often require more repetition than their chronological counterparts and should not be asked to do two things at once (e.g., counting and clapping). Children with limited understanding may also rely more heavily on imitation. Teachers should accept this, but be sure to offer praise and encouragement once the child begins responding in her or his own ways (Hirst & Michaelis, 1983).

Movement, of course, can help improve problems with directionality, body and spatial awareness, coordination, and such. An activity

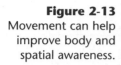

Figure 2-13
Movement can help
improve body and
spatial awareness.

like Statues can help children who have difficulty stopping gain greater motor control. Simple, familiar songs and rhythmic activities can help strengthen memory and powers of concentration. And, in all cases of children with limited understanding, movement should be used to reinforce academic concepts.

Key Points

- Developmental appropriateness has two dimensions: age appropriateness and individual appropriateness.
- The movement program for toddlers presents special challenges due to the children's short attention span, high energy level, and emerging motor skills.
- Teachers and caregivers should plan movement sessions for toddlers in the morning when possible, 20 to 30 minutes long.
- Language and concept development go hand in hand, with verbal cues accompanied by demonstrations playing a vital role in the learning process.
- Toddlers are busy discovering quantitative and positional concepts.
- The beginning of the ability to use the imagination occurs during toddlerhood; between 18 and 24 months, children can internally visualize events and objects.
- During the first two years of life, the child's personality is forming. This developing sense of oneself as an individual is referred to as the self-concept, which is greatly influenced by feedback from the important people in a child's life.
- Toddlers frequently display defiant, contrary behavior, occasionally throwing tantrums and becoming physically aggressive in their efforts to assert their growing independence and gain some control over their world.
- From 18 to 24 months, toddlers are in the stage of solitary play; 2-year-olds move on to the stage of parallel play.
- The ability to feel empathy begins to develop during toddlerhood.
- Toddlers are especially comforted by routine.
- Control over the body occurs from head to toe and from the middle to the extremities, with children gaining considerable mastery over their bodies during the first three years of life.
- Although preschoolers do begin to show an interest in "things academic," they are not ready to sit still and learn.
- Attention span increases significantly during the preschool years.
- Each year of growth during the preschool years shows a corresponding increase in self-awareness, self-confidence, and self-control.
- Three-year-olds move from the parallel to the associative state of play, with children 4 and 5 most often playing cooperatively.
- In developmentally appropriate early elementary programs, the emphasis should continue to be on active, integrated learning experiences that address the whole child.

- Cognitively, early elementary children are more like preschoolers than like their upper elementary counterparts. However, one difference between preschoolers and early elementary children is during the primary years children begin to associate symbols with concrete experiences and, thus, to solve problems in their heads.
- Children have a growing interest in peers during the early elementary years.
- Play is still important in the cognitive and social development of primary children.
- Fundamental movement abilities are usually present by 5 years of age, with children of 6 able to perform most locomotor skills in a mature pattern. Sliding and skipping are commonly the last two locomotor skills acquired.
- Movement education is well suited to children with special needs because it offers opportunity for inclusion and success.
- Teachers and caregivers should consult with parents and therapists when planning movement activities for children with special needs.
- Physically challenged children are the fastest growing population of children receiving special education services. Among these children are those with a wide array of physical disabilities caused by birth defects, accidents, or illness. In one way or another, the mobility of these children is restricted, but they should be encouraged to participate in the movement program at whatever level is possible.
- Hearing impairments involve malfunctioning of the auditory mechanism. Unless there is damage to the semicircular canals, which causes problems with balance, the major challenges for children with hearing impairments participating in movement programs are related to the use of music and the presentation of instructions. Teachers and caregivers can take a number of steps to help make these challenges more manageable.
- Visually challenged children are defined as those whose visual impairments, even when corrected, adversely affect their learning. The definition includes both blind and partially sighted children. With minor modifications, a movement education program that meets the needs of children at all levels of ability can similarly meet the needs of children with visual impairments.
- Children with emotional disabilities possess an inability to learn that cannot be attributed to sensory, health, or intellectual problems. Furthermore, they are generally depressed and have difficulties with social relationships. They exhibit quite varied behaviors, all of which have the potential to have an impact on their participation in the movement program. Avoiding physical

contact and lyrics that may have disturbing associations are two of the techniques that can be employed to help children with emotional disabilities participate more successfully.

- Children with limited understanding, whether mentally retarded or with learning disabilities, are especially in need of a multisensory approach to learning. They also require more repetition and may initially rely on imitation when taking part in movement activities. Because movement can do much to improve problems they commonly experience with body and spatial awareness, directionality, and the like, children with limited understanding should be given many opportunities to move.

Assignments

1. Choose a movement theme (e.g., body awareness or an element of movement) and develop and activity that explores that theme at the toddler level. Now make the necessary modifications to make the same activity appropriate for preschoolers. Change it once more to make it appropriate for early elementary children.
2. Observe the movement activities of a group that includes toddlers, preschoolers, and kindergarteners (or of three separate groups). Note differences and similarities among the children in the cognitive, affective, and motor domains.
3. Talk to several early childhood teachers or caregivers who conduct regular movement sessions, in an effort to discover the length of time they are able to keep children of varying ages actively engaged in movement activities.
4. Observe a large group of children at play (preferably of varying ages) and note the different stages of social play you witness.
5. Create a "silly" movement activity that would have special appeal to 4-year-olds.
6. Write a justification of the need for physical education specialists and classroom teachers to collaborate on the movement experiences of their students during the primary years.
7. Observe a movement session that includes at least one child with special needs. To what degree is that child involved in the movement activities? If participation is minimal, what do you feel could be done to ensure greater participation?
8. Create a movement activity and determine what adaptations could be made to accommodate children with physical, auditory, visual, learning, and emotional disabilities.

References

Allen, K. E., & Marotz, L. (1994.). *Developmental profiles: Pre-birth-to-eight.* Albany, N.Y.: Delmar.

Bayless, K. M., & Ramsey, M. E. (1991). *Music: A way of life for the young child.* New York: Merrill.

Bredekamp, S., ed. (1987). *Developmentally appropriate practice in early childhood programs serving children from birth through age 8.* Washington, D.C.: National Association for the Education of Young Children.

Castle, K. (1991). *The infant and toddler handbook.* Atlanta: Humanics.

Charlesworth, R. (1992). *Understanding child development.* Albany, N.Y.: Delmar.

Clements, R. L., & Schiemer, S. (1993). *Let's move, let's play: Developmentally appropriate movement and classroom activities for preschool children.* Montgomery, Ala.: KinderCare Learning Centers.

Craft, D. H. (1990). Sensory impairments. In J. P. Winnick, ed., *Adapted physical education and sport* (pp. 209–28). Champaign, Ill.: Human Kinetics.

Essa, E. (1992). *Introduction to early childhood education.* Albany, N.Y.: Delmar.

Feldman, J. R. (1991). *A survival guide for the preschool teacher.* West Nyack, N.Y.: Center for Applied Research in Education.

Frost, J. L. (1992). *Play and playscapes.* Albany, N.Y.: Delmar.

Gallahue, D. L. (1993). *Developmental physical education for today's children.* Dubuque, Ia.: Brown & Benchmark.

Grineski, S. (1993). Children, cooperative learning, and physical education. *Teaching Elementary Physical Education,* 4(6), 10–11, 14.

Haines, B. J. E., & Gerber, L. L. (1992). *Leading young children to music.* New York: Merrill.

Hammett, C. T. (1992). *Movement activities for early childhood.* Champaign, Ill.: Human Kinetics.

Harris, A. C. (1986). *Child Development.* St. Paul, Minn.: West.

Hibben, J., & Scheer, R. (1982). Music and movement for special needs children. *Teaching Exceptional Children,* 14(5), 171–76.

Hirst, C. C., & Michaelis, E. (1983). *Retarded kids need to play.* New York: Leisure Press.

Isenberg, J. P., & Jalongo, M. R. (1993). *Creative expression and play in the early childhood curriculum.* New York: Merrill.

Karnes, M. (1992). Music and movement with special needs children. In E. B. Church, *Learning through play: music and movement* (pp. 27–29). New York: Scholastic.

Knight, D., & Wadsworth, D. (1993). Physically challenged students. *Childhood Education,* 69(4), 211–15.

Krebs, P. L. (1990a). Rhythms and dance. In J. P. Winnick, ed., *Adapted physical education and sport* (pp. 379–89). Champaign, Ill.: Human Kinetics.

Krebs, P. L. (1990b). Mental retardation. In J. P. Winnick, ed., *Adapted physical education and sport* (pp. 153–76). Champaign, Ill.: Human Kinetics.

Loovis, E. M. (1990). Behavioral disabilities. In J. P. Winnick, ed., *Adapted physical education and sport* (pp. 195–207). Champaign, Ill.: Human Kinetics.

Mayesky, M. (1995). *Creative activities for young children.* Albany, N.Y.: Delmar.

Miller, K. (1985). *Ages and stages: Developmental descriptions and activities birth through 8 years.* Chelsea, Mass.: Telshare.

Morrison, G. S. (1990). *The world of child development.* Albany, N.Y.: Delmar.

Parten, M. (1932). Social participation among preschool children. *Journal of Abnormal Psychology,* 27:243–369.

Pica, R. (1990). *Toddlers moving & learning.* Champaign, Ill.: Human Kinetics.

Pica, R. (1991a). *Special themes for moving & learning.* Champaign, Ill.: Human Kinetics.

Pica, R. (1991b). *Early elementary children moving & learning.* Champaign, Ill.: Human Kinetics.

Pica, R. (1993). *Upper elementary children moving & learning.* Champaign, Ill.: Human Kinetics.

Samuelson, E. (1981). Group development and socialization through movement. In L. H. Kearns, ed., *Readings: Developing arts programs for handicapped students* (pp. 53–54). Harrisburg: Arts in Special Education Project of Pennsylvania.

Sinclair, C. B. (1973). *Movement of the young child: Ages 2 to 6.* Columbus, Ohio: Merrill.

Skinner, L. (1979). *Motor development in the preschool years.* Springfield, Ill.: Thomas.

Sullivan, M. (1982). *Feeling strong, feeling free: Movement exploration for young children.* Washington, D.C.: National Association for the Education of Young Children.

Zinar, R. (1987). *Music activities for special children.* West Nyack, N.Y.: Parker.

CHAPTER 3

Content of the Movement Program

*T*he decision as to what, specifically, will comprise your movement program must ultimately be yours. Time, space, availability or lack of equipment—and even regional weather—can be determining factors. Of course, the age of your children will also influence your program planning. Some of the skills described in this chapter (e.g., skipping and striking with implements) are too advanced for toddlers. Some skills, like the simplest locomotor and nonlocomotor movements, will not require much attention if you are working with primary-grade children. Some skills you may deem less important than others and thus unessential to your program.

Although they cannot be considered skills, this chapter begins with definitions of each of the six movement elements. An understanding of these is critical for anyone planning to teach movement to children—and for the children themselves. Exploring the movement elements, therefore, is an excellent starting point for any program.

Descriptions of the locomotor and nonlocomotor skills and the manipulative and educational gymnastic skills developmentally appropriate for preschool and early elementary children complete Chapter 3.

The Elements of Movement

Critical to any program of movement education is the concept of movement *variations,* or *extensions.* This concept, discussed further in Chapter 7, allows for the discovery of unlimited movement

89

possibilities for locomotor, nonlocomotor, and manipulative skills, as well as dance steps, gymnastic skills, and almost any other movement activity.

For instance, if the locomotor skill of walking were being explored, there would a number of choices with regard to *how* to perform the walking: forward, backward, to the side, or possibly in a circle (the element of *space* is being used here). The walk could be performed with arms or head held in various positions (*shape*), quickly or slowly (*time*), strongly or lightly (*force*), with interruptions (*flow*), or to altering rhythms (*rhythm*).

If we liken movement education to the study of grammar, the skills themselves can be considered *verbs,* while the elements of space, shape, time, force, flow, and rhythm are the *adverbs* modifying them. Each of these six movement elements, listed in a *general* progression from least to most challenging, is described in more detail below.

SPACE

The element of space is divided into two components. The first, *personal space,* is the area immediately surrounding the body and includes whatever can be reached while remaining in one spot; it can be likened to a large bubble surrounding the body. The rest is referred to as *general* (or *shared*) space and is limited only by floors, walls, and ceilings.

Both general and personal space consist of three levels. When standing upright, one is at the middle level. Anything lower to the ground is considered the low level. Positions or movements performed on tiptoe or in the air occur at the high level.

Space also considers the bodily and spatial directions of forward and backward and right and left. Finally, movement performed through general space also involves pathways, which will be straight, curving, or zigzag.

Sample Activities.   To explore *personal space,* provide carpet squares or hula-hoops for the children, or ask them to imagine they are each inside a giant bubble. Then present the following questions and challenges:

- Show me how low you can get in your personal space (in your "bubble;" on your "island" or "spot").
- Stay very low and move your arms in as many ways as possible all around your body.
- How high up can you get while staying in your own space?
  Find a way to get very high with your feet still on the floor.
  Now find a way with your feet coming off the floor.

Figure 3-1
Pathways traveled through
general space will be
straight, zigzag, or curving.

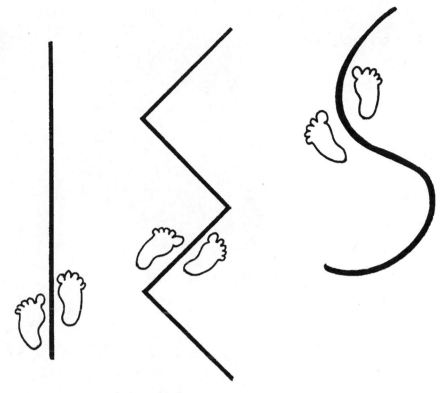

- Explore the area in between very high and very low. Move your arms in as many ways as possible all around your body.
- How far apart can you position your feet? With your feet like that, move you arms all around your body.
- Do the same thing at a lower (higher) level.

To explore *general space,* give each child a hula-hoop to pick up and hold around her or his waist, or ask the children to imagine they are each inside a giant bubble that stays all around them wherever they go. Now ask them to walk around the room without touching anyone else's hoop or bubble. Encourage them to make straight, curved, and zigzag paths. Once they have had ample time to experiment with a forward direction, ask them to try not touching one another while moving in a backward direction (with the back of the body going first). Can they do it with one (and then the other) side of the body leading?

If you have a large enough space, you can experiment with reducing the general space. First, allow the children to explore all the available space. Then pretend you are a wall and, a little bit at a time, move

toward the children until they are moving in as little space as possible while still not touching one another.

SHAPE

The study of shape relates to the various shapes the body is capable of assuming. This element is sometimes referred to as the relationship of body parts because whenever the relationship between or among body parts changes, so does the body's shape. For example, if an elbow is brought closer to a knee, the body bends and the spine curves. If that elbow is then taken as far from the knee as possible, the body must straighten.

Sample Activities. Making Shapes, described in Chapter 1, is a good introductory activity for exploring the element of shape. A more advanced activity, appropriate for early elementary children, would be a challenge to copy the shapes of numbers or the letters of the alphabet with their bodies.

Review the numbers or letters with the children, pointing them out on a chart or writing them on a chalkboard. Note some have straight and zigzag lines; some, curved lines; and some, both.

Choose numbers or letters easily formed by the body, and then ask the children to show them to you. You can also ask them to select partners and form the numbers and letters in pairs.

The children should be challenged to experiment with the different shapes they can make with their bodies while performing locomotor skills.

TIME

The element of time relates to how slowly or quickly a movement is performed. Movement, however, is not only slow or fast, but also includes the range of speed in between. With young children, it is best to introduce this element by contrasting the extremes of slow and fast before exploring the continuum from one to the other.

Sample Activities. Any movement can be performed at any speed. Spend lots of time exploring this with the children. What body parts can they move slowly? Quickly?

To explore time with music, see Contrasting Elements in Chapter 6. To explore this concept with imagery, ask the children to move like the following:

A rabbit	A bumblebee
A turtle	A snail or worm
A race car	A scurrying mouse
An old car	A stalking cat

FORCE

Force concerns how strongly or lightly a movement is performed and the amount of muscle tension involved. Tiptoeing, for instance, requires much less force and muscle tension than does stamping feet. Similarly, moving like a butterfly requires much less force than moving like a tin soldier. With this element, too, it is best to contrast the extremes before exploring the continuum from light to strong.

Sample Activity.   This activity is excerpted from Pica, 1990a, p. 40. Ask the children to do the following:

- Move very softly, like a feather floating (demonstrate with a feather if you have one!).
- Move very strongly, making lots of noise with their feet.
- Make strong movements with their arms, like propellers on a helicopter.
- Make light arm movements, like the wings of a bird sailing gently through the sky.
- Show you how hard they can push against the floor.
- Tighten all their muscles so they feel as stiff as robots (if possible, use a transformer for demonstration purposes).
- Be floppy rag dolls who have no muscles holding them up (again, show the children a rag doll!).

FLOW

The flow of movement is either *bound* (punctuated or halting) or *free* (uninterrupted). For example, bound flow would be motion resembling that of a robot, or a series requiring the children to hop-hop-stop, hop-hop-stop. Free flow is visible in the action of the skater gliding effortlessly across the ice or in the flight of an eagle. Free flow can also be likened to a sentence, which might have a breathing pause but not a complete pause until the period at the end.

Sample Activities.   Statues, described in Chapter 1, is an example of an activity involving flow. To explore this element without music, ask the children to move freely around the room until they hear your signal to freeze. As soon as they hear it, they must stop immediately and not move another muscle until they hear your signal to go again.

Vary the time between signals, sometimes letting the children experience free flow and sometimes interrupting frequently (bound flow).

Figure 3-4
Playing Statues offers children experience with bound flow.

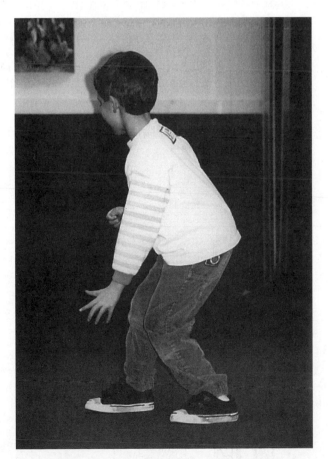

To explore flow with imagery, ask the children to move like an eagle soaring, a tin soldier, a happy person with no cares, and a robot.

RHYTHM

Rhythm, although often associated with the element of time, is mentioned separately because of its many facets and benefits to students. This element not only relates to music but also encompasses the many rhythms of life. Words, for instance, have rhythm, as do the various locomotor activities (e.g., the rhythm of a run differs from that of a hop). People, in fact, possess their own personal rhythms for both thinking and functioning (Gerhardt, 1973). The element of rhythm encompasses all of these aspects.

Sample Activities. Clapping activities can demonstrate the element of rhythm. Sit in a circle with the children. Then, saying your name aloud, clap one clap per syllable (Rae Pica, pronounced Ray Pee-ka, would involve three claps with a pause between the first and second). Now ask the children to do it with you.

Go around the circle, saying and clapping the rhythm of each child's name (first or first and last, depending on the developmental level of your group).

Clapping Rhythms and Exploring Common Meters, in Chapter 1, offer other possibilities for exploring rhythm.

Locomotor Skills

Locomotor skills transport the body as a whole from one point to another. Although it is commonly believed children acquire and develop locomotor skills automatically, they will be unable to reach a

THE QUALITIES OF MOVEMENT Not to be confused with the six elements of movement are the six *qualities* of movement, which you might also choose to explore with the children. The following qualities of movement describe the six *kinds* of movement that exist.

Sustained

Sustained movement continues through time and space without stopping and requires considerable control. Although movement at any speed can be sustained, this quality is usually associated with slow—even slow-motion—movement.

Suspended

In suspended movement, the body often acts as a base of support, above which one or more parts are temporarily interrupted in their flow of movement. In this case, the movement begins with an impulse, reaches its peak elevation, holds momentarily, and then continues once again. (An example would be a swinging arm that stops momentarily overhead before swinging once again.) Suspended movement involving the whole body requires control and balance.

Swinging

Swinging motion takes the form of an arc or a circle around a stationary base. It generally requires impulse and momentum, except perhaps when the swinging part is merely released to the force of gravity. Swinging movement can be executed by the body as a whole; by the upper or lower torso alone; and by the head, arms, and legs.

Percussive

Percussive movement is punctuated and accented. A head moves percussively when it drops sharply forward and then returns to center. Feet move percussively when they run. Hands and arms move percussively when they rapidly strike the air.

Vibratory

This quality relates to tremulous or quivering movement. Images that depict vibratory movement are bacon sizzling in the frying pan, a leaf quivering in the wind, a battery-powered toothbrush, and a baby's rattle being shaken. Body parts that can depict vibratory movement might be a rapidly shaking head, an open hand trembling in the air, or shoulders moving in a rapid shimmy.

Collapsing

Collapsing can be likened to movement that occurs when a puppet is released from its strings or when a building is demolished. A collapse of the human body, however, must always be executed with the necessary control to avoid injury. In addition to the body as a whole, other body parts can collapse, including the head (collapsing to chest, back, shoulder), an arm that has been suspended and then collapses through space, or the upper torso collapsing toward the lower torso.

mature stage of development without practice, encouragement, and instruction. Failure to reach the mature level will hinder their ability to perform specialized movements in the future (Gallahue, 1993).

Children acquire the ability to execute locomotor skills according to their own internal timetables. The following represents a general developmental progression of locomotor skills. Each skill—crawl, creep, walk, run, jump, leap, gallop, hop, slide, skip, step-hop—is defined, and sample activities are provided for each.

CRAWL

The crawl involves lying on the stomach, with head and shoulders raised off the floor and the weight of the upper torso supported by the elbows. Locomotion involves moving the elbows and hips.

Children should explore homolateral crawling (simultaneously moving the arm and leg on the same side of the body) as well as crawling with limbs in opposition (cross-pattern: left arm and right leg together, and the reverse).

Sample Activities. Talk to the children about crawling, differentiating between it and creeping. Then ask them to pretend to be worms, snakes, or seals. Or perform this group activity excerpted from Pica (1991, p. 101).

This group activity requires lots of cooperation. Make success a challenge and a goal for them.

Talk to the children about eels (show them a picture, if possible), explaining eels are actually fish that look like snakes. The electric eel is one type; it can grow up to 6 feet long and has the ability to shock in the way that electricity does.

Explain to the children that, together, they are going to form an eel—a very long eel—and they are going to pretend the eel is swimming in the ocean. The children begin by getting on the floor and moving individually, as they believe eels would. Then, at a signal from you, one by one, they start to join together by taking hold of another child's ankles—until all the children are joined and moving like a giant eel. Finally, when the children have successfully accomplished this, you tell them they have become an *electric* eel and you have just turned on their electricity! What would that look like?

If you find the indiscriminate joining is too confusing for the children, assign one child to take the ankles of another child nearby by calling out their names.

CREEP

This skill requires using the hands and knees or hands and feet to move the body through space and is the child's first efficient form of locomotion. Children who have not achieved a mature level of cross-pattern crawling should be given many opportunities to practice, even at ages 4 and 5 or older (Sinclair, 1973).

Sample Activities. Talk to the children about the differences among creatures, and then ask them to show you how each of them creeps. Possible creatures could include a dog, a cat, a spider, a baby, a turtle, and a crab.

Figure 3-5
Setting up tunnels as part of an obstacle course can give children opportunities to practice crawling.

WALK

The walk moves the body through space by transferring weight from the ball and toes of one foot to the heel of the other. Continual contact is made with the floor. Limbs are used in opposition.

Infants begin to walk about age 1; and by the time children are 6, they have usually acquired a mature level of development. However, posture and foot alignment should be monitored. The body must be kept straight and toes pointed straight ahead, with the weight evenly distributed over all five toes (rolling in, with the small toes lifting off the ground, is a common problem).

Sample Activities. As mentioned earlier, the elements of movement can be used to vary the way skills are performed. Following are examples of how you can use the elements of movement to modify walking; however, these same examples can apply to *all* of the locomotor skills.

Ask the children to walk in the following ways:

- in place (slower, faster);
- forward (slower; faster; in straight, curving, and zigzag pathways; as tall as possible; as small as possible; with tiny steps; with giant steps; in a funny shape; lightly; strongly; with pauses between steps);
- backward (same as above); and
- sideways (same as above).

Some examples for using imagery to explore walking are offered in Chapter 1. Other possibilities include walking as though sneaking up on someone, in deep snow, in a dense jungle, and in a haunted house.

RUN

Running transfers the body's weight from the ball and toes of one foot to the ball and toes of the other. The body should be inclined slightly forward, and the arms should be slightly bent, swinging in opposition to the legs.

According to Sinclair (1973, p. 23), running is one of the most demanding activities, requiring "much of the heart, lungs, and muscles. For the young child it also makes demands on the nervous system for all parts of the body must be used alternately, symmetrically, and yet with synchronous timing; contraction and relaxation must alternate smoothly; an even rhythm must be maintained;

balance makes new demands as strides lengthen and ground is covered rapidly."

Sample Activities.   To explore running with imagery, ask the children to run as though on hot sand, finishing a long race, playing basketball, trying to catch a bus, and trying to score a touchdown.

JUMP

A jump propels the body upward from a takeoff on one or both feet. The toes, which are the last part of the foot to leave the ground (heel-ball-toe) are the first to reach it on landing, with landings occurring on both feet (toe-ball-heel). Knees should bend to absorb the shock of landing.

Figure 3-6
A jump propels the body upward from a takeoff on one or both feet. Landing occurs on both feet.

Sample Activities. Jumping is explored in "Pop Goes the Weasel" and Rabbits and 'Roos, described in Chapter 1. You can also ask the children to jump in the following ways:

- with knees straight, but not locked (briefly!);
- with landing and takeoff on balls of feet only;
- with feet together, apart;
- with feet alternately apart and together;
- landing with one foot forward and the other back; and
- clicking heels together while in the air.

To add imagery to the exercise, ask the children to jump in these ways:

- as though they were bouncing balls (some high, some low),
- pretending to reach for something above them,
- as though startled by a loud noise,
- as though angry (having a tantrum), and
- with joy.

LEAP

This skill is similar to a run, except the knee and ankle action is greater. The knee leads forward following the takeoff and is then extended as the foot reaches forward to land. The back leg extends to the rear while in the air, but once the front foot has landed, the rear leg swings forward into the next lift. Leaps are often combined with running steps to achieve greater height and distance.

Sample Activities. Preschoolers may be able to relate best to this locomotor skill through imagery or with a prop. For the former, you can ask them to pretend to leap over a puddle, a hurdle, a tall building (like Superman), or like a deer over fallen trees in the forest. If you prefer a prop, hold a rope an inch or two off the floor and ask the children to leap over it. Either way, be sure they practice leading with both legs.

GALLOP

The gallop is performed with an uneven rhythm. It is a combination of a walk and a run in which one foot leads and the other plays catch-up. Children will lead with the preferred foot long before they feel comfortable with the other foot.

Some young children learn this skill most easily when they can hear the gallop's rhythm. Teachers can provide rhythmic accompaniment with hands or drum, or they can use the appropriate recorded music. "On Horseback" (Pica, 1990b) and "Giddy-Up" (Pica, 1990a) were written specifically for galloping, and Georgiana Stewart's album, *Rhythms for Basic Motor Skills* (available from Kimbo and from Educational Record Center), offers music for seven movement skills, including galloping.

Sample Activities.   Hammett (1992, p. 15) offers a game called Fox and Hound in which the children pretend the lead foot is the fox and the back foot is the hound trying to catch the fox. The fox always gets away. Eventually, the feet reverse roles. She suggests pipe cleaners shaped like fox ears and attached to the shoes can help some children remember which is the lead foot.

HOP

A hop propels the body upward from a takeoff on one foot (heel-ball-toe). The landing is made on the same foot (toe-ball-heel). The free leg does not touch the ground.

Children are usually able to hop at about age 4. To help them maintain the balance necessary for successful hopping, encourage them to lean slightly in the direction of the support (hopping) leg to shift the center of gravity. They should practice hopping on the preferred and the nonpreferred foot.

Sample Activities.   Provide a hoop or jump rope for each child, who places his or her prop on the floor in his or her personal space.

If using a hoop, the child should hop in and out, all the way around it. Having completed the circle, she should reverse direction and repeat the exercise on the other foot.

If using a rope, the child should make a straight line with it and then hop side to side over the rope, beginning at one end and hopping to the other. He should then reverse direction and repeat the exercise on the other foot.

SLIDE

This movement skill is a gallop performed sideward. One foot leads and the other plays catch-up, and the uneven rhythm remains the same as in the gallop. Because facing one direction and moving in another is difficult for young children, they will learn to slide much later than they learn to gallop. Once learned, the slide should be practiced in both directions.

Sample Activities. Sliding is best taught through demonstration and imitation. If you stand with your back to the children, you will lead with the same foot they do. If you stand facing them, you will have to lead with the opposite foot.

Once all the children can slide, a fun group activity is to practice sliding together. The children form a circle and hold hands, sliding first in one and then the other direction.

SKIP

A combination of a step and a hop, the skip, like the gallop and the slide, also has an uneven rhythm. With more emphasis placed on the step than the hop, the overall effect is of a light, skimming motion during which the feet only momentarily leave the ground. The lead foot alternates. For many children, skipping initially on one side only is a normal developmental stage.

Possibilities for teaching the skip include providing rhythmic accompaniment, holding the child's hand and skipping with him or her, breaking down the components of the movement, and demonstration and imitation.

Sample Activities. Cherry (1971, p. 45) offers a progression of skipping songs sung to the tune of "Ten Little Indians." For 2- to 3-year-olds, the lyrics prompt the children to lift one foot and then the other (e.g., "Lift one foot and then the other; repeat two times; all the little children. . ."). Three- to 4-year-olds are encouraged to hop on one foot and then the other. The lyrics for 4- to 5-year-olds are "Walk and hop and walk and hop now." And, at the teacher's discretion, they induce the "little children" to "skip and skip and skip and skip."

STEP-HOP

Like the skip, the step-hop combines a step and a hop. With the latter, however, the step and the hop have the same time value (it is performed with an even rhythm), and the accent is on the *step*.

This step is used often in folk dances; like many other folk dance steps, it is a combination of basic locomotor movements. The step-hop is included here because it has the same components as a skip, it is a common movement (it can even be part of a lay-up shot in basketball), and it is developmentally appropriate for primary-grade students.

Sample Activities.   For a step-hop activity, introduce the movement to your children by providing an even 1-2 beat with your hands or a drum and asking the children to practice combining a step and a hop. They can begin by performing as many of each as they want, eventually reducing the number until they are alternating one step with one hop. Can they match the steps and hops to your beats?

Later, you can use a piece of music in a 2/4 meter (at a moderate tempo) to continue exploring the step-hop. Use the elements of movement to vary the ways in which the children perform it.

Nonlocomotor Skills

Nonlocomotor skills are movements performed in place, usually while standing, kneeling, sitting, or lying. Sometimes called *axial* movements, they involve the axis of the body rotating around a fixed point. Some textbook authors label them *nonmanipulative* skills.

Murray (1975, p. 129) writes that nonlocomotor movements should not be considered only as exercises or warm-ups. Rather, she says they serve as "points of departure for exploration and as instruments for creative expression." However, many nonlocomotor skills can certainly serve in both capacities.

It is perhaps even more difficult to list nonlocomotor skills progressively than locomotor skills. Many nonlocomotor skills are acquired at approximately the same point in the child's development, but some *are* more challenging than others. The following list represents a general developmental order of nonlocomotor skills. It includes stretch, bend, sit, shake, turn, rock and sway, swing, twist, dodge, and fall. Again, each is defined and sample activities provided.

STRETCH

A stretch extends the body, its parts, and one or more joints vertically, horizontally, or any point between. This nonlocomotor skill, perhaps more than any other, is commonly regarded as an exercise. Although

STAGES OF SKILL DEVELOPMENT

Until recently, it was assumed children of the same age were at the same level of skill development. A physical education teacher planning lessons for second-grade classes, for example, asked all the children to perform identical tasks. Children who executed them well were given good grades; those who could not received lower or failing grades.

Today, it is understood each child goes through a developmental process in learning *every* skill. The stages of skill development are described by noted physical education textbook authors listed below.

Kirchner

Kirchner (1992) uses learning to ride a bicycle to explain the process everyone experiences in acquiring a new motor skill. If you think back, you will probably recall how unsteady your initial attempts were and how much concentration the effort required. Gradually, you became more proficient at keeping the bike upright; but stopping, turning, and other such tasks still required effort and concentration. Finally, with much practice, riding a two-wheeler became automatic.

Kirchner has labeled these stages the initial phase, the intermediate phase, and the automatic phase. The first, as he describes it, "involves *thinking* about a skill as much as it does trying to perform it" (p. 71). The intermediate phase represents a gradual shift from the acquisition of the fundamentals of the skill to a more focused effort to refine it. In the final phase, the skill feels and looks like it is automatic.

Gallahue

Gallahue (1993) describes essentially the same three phases of motor learning and labels them the initial stage, the elementary stage, and the mature stage.

The initial stage, he writes, is "characterized by relatively crude, uncoordinated movements" (p. 23) and can be seen among 2- and 3-year-olds attempting to perform fundamental movement skills. The elementary stage, which seems to depend primarily on maturation, means greater control and coordination, but awkwardness and a lack of fluidity are still evident. Although Gallahue notes this stage is typical of 3- to 5-year-olds performing fundamental movement skills, he points out many adults remain at the elementary stage in such skills as throwing, striking, and catching due to insufficient practice and instruction.

The mature stage can be attained in most fundamental movements by age 6 or 7, but children usually reach this stage at varying rates. This stage is characterized by "the integration of all the component parts of a pattern of movement into a well-coordinated, mechanically correct, and efficient act" (p. 25).

Graham, Holt/Hale, and Parker

Graham et al. (1993) have chosen four stages to describe what they call "generic levels of skill proficiency." The first, the precontrol level, represents the stage at which a child is unable to either "consciously control or intentionally replicate a movement" (p. 60). They use the example of a child's initial attempts to bounce a ball, during which the child spends more time chasing it than bouncing it. The ball, rather than the child, seems to be in control. Most preschool and kindergarten children are at the precontrol level.

At the control (advanced beginner) level, the movement is much closer to the child's actual intentions, although a good deal of concentration is still required. When children reach the utilization level in a particular skill, they do not have to think as much about how to execute the skill and are able to use it in different contexts. The proficiency level is the advanced stage and represents the stage at which a movement appears effortless and a child is able to use it in changing environments and repeat it with ever-increasing degrees of quality. Elementary school children rarely reach the proficiency level in a skill.

Summary

Although these authors have chosen to describe the various stages of skill development somewhat differently, they agree there is a developmental progression in learning and acquiring a movement skill. What we, as educators, have to accept is these levels cannot be unconditionally assigned to certain ages or grades. Rather, every child will move from the first to the last stage—however we choose to label them—as he or she learns *each new skill* and tries to master it.

Furthermore, it is not unusual to observe children in the same class who are at varying levels of skill proficiency. For example, primary-grade children who have been enrolled in gymnastics programs since they were preschoolers will often demonstrate utilization-level gymnastic skills, while those who have had no introduction to gymnastics will be at the precontrol level. And, of course, those children who have had *some* experience with gymnastics will show control-level abilities.

How do you manage to teach all these children? This is where the indirect styles described in Chapter 7 come in handy. For instance, if you challenge the children to balance on just two body parts, children at the precontrol level might respond by standing on two feet; control-level children might balance on two knees or on the buttocks only, in a V-sit; and someone at the utilization level just might perform a handstand. What is truly important is that *all* the children will have successfully answered your challenge!

frequently used as a warm-up, stretching better serves as a cool-down, preventing contraction of the exercised muscles. When using stretching for this purpose, children should be taught to hold a stretch for 8 to 10 seconds and not to bounce.

Sample Activities. Stretching as a cat does, or as though yawning, are good introductions to this nonlocomotor skill. You can also have the children experiment with stretching (gently) forward, backward, toward the ceiling, and toward the floor while standing, kneeling, and sitting. Then present the following challenges and questions:

- Lie on your back and show me how long you can be.
- Can you be just as long lying on your stomach?
- Can you stretch wide?

- Stretch one arm high and the other low (one toward the ceiling and the other toward the floor).
- Reach both arms to the right (one side). To the left (the other side).
- On your hands and knees, stretch one leg behind you and one arm forward.
- Show me you can lie on your back and stretch one leg long and the other toward the ceiling.

BEND

A bend brings two adjacent parts of the body together, generally toward the body's center, with ball-and-socket or hinge joints. In addition to the body as a whole, many body parts can bend, including arms, fingers, legs, and neck.

Bending and stretching are natural partners because, once a body part has been bent, it must eventually straighten again.

Sample Activities.   Have the children stand and experiment with bending forward, backward, and to both sides. Then issue these challenges:

- Touch your knees and straighten.
- Touch your toes (with knees bent, to avoid strain on the lower back) and straighten very slowly.
- Touch your toes and straighten halfway.

Then ask them to experiment with bending the waist, arms, and legs while kneeling, crouching, sitting, and lying on backs, stomachs, and sides. Are there any other parts of the body they can find that bend?

To explore and contrast bending and stretching, use imagery the children can relate to. Possibilities include asking them to do the following:

- Stretch as though picking fruit from a tall tree.
- Flop like a rag doll.
- Stretch as though waking up and yawning.
- Bend over as though to tie shoes.
- Stretch to put something on a high shelf.
- Bend to pat a dog, an even smaller dog, or a cat.
- Stretch to shoot a basketball through a hoop.
- Bend to pick up a coin from the floor.
- Stretch as though climbing a ladder.
- Bend to pick vegetables or flowers.
- Stretch as though reaching for a star.

SIT

A sit moves the body from any level to a position in which the body's weight is placed on the buttocks or thighs. Although young children certainly know how to sit, exploring the ways it is possible to get into a sitting position can enhance body and spatial awareness.

Sample Activities.   Ask the children to practice sitting from standing, kneeling, and lying positions, with and without the help of the hands, at varying tempos, onto both the buttocks and the thighs.

SHAKE

A shake is a vibratory movement involving tension and relaxation. It can be performed by the whole body as well as by individual parts.

Children love to shake, as they view it as a somewhat silly movement. With very young children, you can introduce shaking by asking them to wiggle.

Sample Activities.   To use imagery to explore shaking, ask the children to shake like

- jello when the bowl is moved,
- a baby's rattle,
- a piece of bacon sizzling in the frying pan,
- a leaf in the wind,
- a battery-powered toothbrush,
- a very cold person, and
- a very scared person.

Once the children have explored shaking the body as a whole, ask them to discover how many body *parts* they can shake. Does the number of body parts that can shake change when the body goes from standing to kneeling to sitting to lying positions?

Musical accompaniment for shaking can be provided by "Shake It High/Shake It Low" (Pica, 1990a, p. 112); "Wiggle, Wiggle, Shake and Giggle" (Pica, 1990b, p. 39); and Raffi's "Shake Your Sillies Out" from *Singable Songs for the Very Young.*

TURN

A turn is a partial or complete rotation of the body around an axis causing a shift in weight placement. Turns can be executed dozens of ways—on a variety of body parts, at a variety of levels, clockwise and counterclockwise.

Graham et al. (1993) advise using the terms *clockwise* and *counterclockwise* with children, rather than *right* and *left,* to describe the direction of a turn. Until young children are familiar with *any* of these four terms, however, it may be best to simply ask them to turn first in one and then the other direction, perhaps using room markings to indicate the desired direction. For example, you might ask the children to turn toward the chalkboard, the closet, or the windows. When the children are developmentally ready, you can use the terms *right* and *left* and *clockwise* and *counterclockwise* at the same time to describe the direction they are turning (also including hand signals, if necessary).

Sample Activities.   Use the elements of movement to explore the skill of turning on the feet; for example, slowly, quickly, in both directions, and at high and low levels. Then ask the children to discover other body parts they can turn on. Possibilities include the knees, bottom, tummy, and back.

ROCK AND SWAY

Although the rock and the sway share the common trait of transferring weight from one part of the body to another, they are essentially different. A rock is the more forceful of the two, using greater muscle tension and suspension. A sway is an easy, relaxed motion that sustains rather than suspends.

Sample Activities.   Demonstrate a gentle sway to the children and ask them to imitate it. Or challenge them to sway like flowers or grass in the breeze. What else can they think of that sways? Then ask them to gradually increase the force of the sway until it becomes rocking. Does the rocking bring any images to mind? Reverse the process until gentle swaying is once again being demonstrated.

SWING

A swing creates an arc or a circle around a stationary base. It generally requires impulse and momentum, except perhaps when the swinging part is merely released to the force of gravity. Swinging movement can be executed by the body as a whole; by the upper or lower torso alone; and by the head, arms, or legs (one at a time, unless the body is suspended off the ground).

Sample Activities.   Using a jump rope or another appropriate object, demonstrate swinging. Then challenge the children to discover how many parts of the body can swing, encouraging them to explore swinging back and forth and side to side. You can prompt specific responses by presenting the following challenges:

- Swing your head as though it were a windshield wiper.
- Swing your head as though it were the clapper in a bell.
- Swing your arms like an elephant's trunk (the pendulum in a clock).
- Swing your body as though you were on a flying trapeze.
- Find at least two more ways you can swing your body.

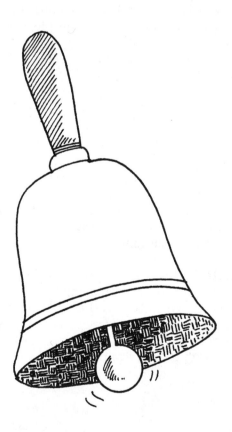

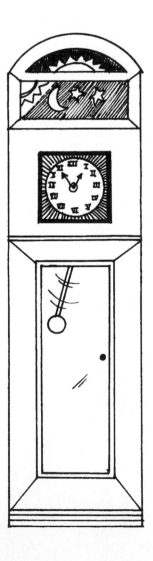

TWIST

Unlike a turn, which rotates the whole body, a twist rotates a *part* of the body around an axis. The neck, trunk, arms, and legs are the body parts most easily twisted. Wrists, ankles, shoulders, and hips can be twisted to a lesser extent.

Sample Activities.   Twisting is fun to do in conjunction with pretending. Ask the children to twist in these ways, excerpted from Pica (1990a, p. 70):

Like the inside of a washing machine

Like a screwdriver when someone is using it

Like a wet dishrag being wrung (if you have one, show the children how it looks)

As though wiping their bottoms with towels

As though digging a little hole in the sand with a foot

As though wiping with a towel and digging a little hole in the sand with a foot at the same time

You should also challenge the children to discover other ways they can twist their bodies and body parts.

DODGE

A dodge generally uses the whole body as it shifts quickly and forcefully to avoid an object (or person) moving toward it. When combined with the run, the dodge becomes a locomotor skill. However, it is often performed from a stationary position, where it may involve such other nonlocomotor movements as bending, stretching, twisting, or falling.

Sample Activities.   Use imagery to introduce the dodge to your preschoolers, asking them to pretend to dodge a flying Frisbee, a limb falling from a tree, a snowball, and a series of snowballs.

FALL

A fall moves the body from a higher position to a prone, supine, or on-the-side lying position. Falls are often sudden, forceful movements, but they may also be executed slowly and limply. Either way, the body should be relaxed to avoid injury.

Sample Activities.   You can introduce your children to the fall by concentrating first on collapsing. Sullivan (1982, p. 119) suggests an activity in which they each stand in their own personal space and make their bodies stiff and tight. At a signal from the teacher, the children "let go immediately of the stiffness and collapse to the floor like a wet noodle." Then they rise in slow motion, make their bodies stiff again, and repeat the process several times.

You can also use imagery to explore falling. Ask the children to fall like a limp rag doll, a puppet released from its strings, bowling pins, raindrops, snowflakes, Humpty Dumpty from a wall, and a melting candle.

Manipulative Skills

To most early childhood professionals, the word *manipulatives* conjures up images of puzzles, blocks, and other such materials that develop fine motor skills in young children. In the physical education field, manipulative skills involve *gross* motor skills and an entirely different object. In some physical education texts, manipulative skills are described as gross motor movements involving force imparted to or received from objects. Others characterize manipulative skills as activities using some implement, usually with the hands but sometimes with the feet or other body parts. For the purposes of this text, manipulative skills will be described as any gross motor skill in which an object is usually involved (manipulated).

For clarity, the skills are divided into two categories. The first group consists of pushing, pulling, lifting, and striking—skills that can initially be explored with imaginary objects, allowing the children to become familiar with the body movement itself. (Some very young children may experience greater success with a tangible object. You will have to use your judgment.)

PULL

A pull entails resistance and is used to move something from one place to another, toward the base of support. With this movement, the arms are first extended and then usually bent. Pulling may be prolonged by combining it with a locomotor movement, usually a walk.

CREATIVE DANCE Not to be overlooked is the possibility of making creative dance part of the content of your movement program. Although the terms *creative movement* and *creative dance* are often interchanged, they are not technically the same.

While it is true discovering the ways it is possible to move an arm or perform everyday movements falls under both categories, an element distinguishes creative dance from creative movement. Preschool children themselves have told Stinson (1988) the difference between dance and other movement is that dance is "magic."

In other words (that perhaps we adults can better understand), creative dance is an art form. Although it is based on natural movement and not the stylized movements used in ballet and other theatrical dancing, it is indeed art and it is the form of dance most appropriate for young children.

The National Dance Association (1990, p. 3) points out movement must first be expressive (i.e., the body is used as an instrument to express ideas and feelings) if it is to be considered dance and therefore art. Other factors are intent, form, and awareness. They write:

> *Intent* means that the movement is chosen by the dancer—not necessarily pre-planned, but under the dancer's own control. . . . The artistic *form* that a dancer or choreographer creates may be very complex. On the most basic level—that which is appropriate for young children—dance form involves a beginning, middle, and an end. Thus "dancing" is separate from "not-dancing" and each dance has a sense of wholeness. *Awareness* means sensing oneself moving. For example, walking may be used as dance movement, but the dancer senses the feet as they contact the floor, with lightness or strength, lingering or with quickness. This kind of awareness is the magic that transforms any particular movement into dance movement.

Creative dance, like other art forms, is important in early childhood education. Through creative dance, young children are given opportunities to express ideas and personal feelings, to learn more about themselves and others, and to make connections with different art forms and the rest of the world. To learn more about making creative dance part of your movement program, refer to these excellent resources, published by the American Alliance for Health, Physical Education, Recreation, and Dance and the National Dance Association: Fleming (1990); Gilbert (1992); Stinson (1988); and National Dance Association (1990).

Sample Activities.   Challenge the children to pull something imaginary

- with both hands;
- with one (the other) hand;
- alternating hands;
- forward, downward, upward, sideward;
- strong and hard;
- lightly (against less resistance);
- slowly, quickly; and
- with short (long) movements.

PUSH

A push moves something, also against resistance, from one place to another, *away* from the base of support. A push starts with the arms drawn in and continues into an extension of the arms. It may also be extended by combining it with a locomotor movement. Pushing seems to be more difficult for young children than pulling (Sinclair, 1973).

Sample Activities.   Repeat the pulling challenges, but substitute pushing. To contrast pulling and pushing, ask the children to move as though they are pushing a swing, pulling a rope, pushing heavy furniture, pulling a kite, pushing a balloon into the air, pulling a wagon or sled, pushing a car stuck in mud or snow, pulling a balloon from the sky, and pushing a shovel.

LIFT

A lift transports an object from one place to another, often from a lower to a higher level. This skill may require carrying the object and can, therefore, be a locomotor movement as well. When lifting from a low to a high level, the knees must be bent and then straightened as the lift is made.

In lifting, pulling, and pushing, the arms, legs, and trunk work together.

Sample Activities.   Ask the children to pretend to lift something very light, first with both hands, then with one and finally the other hand. Can they show you how it would look to lift this object from low to high and from high to low? Now challenge them to repeat the process, pretending the object is very heavy this time. How does that make lifting different? What would it look like to lift something very hot? What about something filled to the very brim with liquid that must not be spilled?

STRIKE

A strike is a strong movement of the arm (or arms) propelled in any direction for the purpose of hitting an object. The arm must bend to initiate the strike, extending with both force and speed. When performed without an implement (e.g., a bat or golf club), the movement abruptly stops, with no follow-through in the motion of the arm.

Sample Activities.   Suggestions for Make-Believe Striking can be found in Chapter 1. You can also challenge the children, while standing, kneeling, and sittÏing, to hit the air with both arms; with one (the other) arm; alternating arms; upward, downward, sideward, forward; and with long, short, medium, extension of the arms.

The second group—throwing, kicking, ball rolling, volleying, bouncing, catching, striking, and dribbling—are considered the more traditional manipulative skills. Because of the visual-motor coordination required by manipulative skills, they are generally more difficult for young children than the locomotor and nonlocomotor movements. Adapting the equipment to the child, rather than expecting the child to adapt to the equipment, can make a significant difference in success levels.

THROWING

Throwing consists of moving an object away from the body, through the air, using the hands. Following the infant/toddler phase of throwing small objects (food, bottles, etc.) in a downward direction (overhand), children generally progress from a two-hand underhand throw to a one-hand underhand throw to a one-hand overhand throw (Kirchner, 1992). Often, the size and weight of the ball dictate the type of throw.

Sample Activities.   Accuracy is not the first objective in teaching young children to throw. Rather, they must initially become familiar with the throwing action itself. You can begin simply by providing foam or yarn balls and asking them to practice throwing them against a wall. When the children are ready to move to a greater challenge, ask them to throw at a large target, such as a hula-hoop hung on the wall, the inside of a large box, or a rubber trash barrel. As they become more proficient, you can decrease the size of the targets.

KICKING

Kicking imparts force to an object (usually a ball) with the leg and foot (most often the side or top of the instep). This skill requires eye-foot coordination, body control and coordination, and accuracy of force and direction. Kicking for distance should be practiced frequently to develop a mature kicking pattern, while kicking for accuracy should not be a concern until after the mature pattern has been mastered (Gallahue, 1993).

Sample Activities.   Hammett (1992) advises beginning with beach-balls because they are difficult to miss, and simply asking the children to kick them any way they can, both with the preferred and the non-preferred foot. If space is limited, balloons can be substituted.

Later, she suggests the children can be asked to kick a beachball over and under a jump rope held by two classmates. With more skilled children, a large foam ball can replace the beachball.

BALL ROLLING

Like throwing, ball rolling involves moving a ball away from the body with the hands; but rather than through the air, the ball travels along the ground. Ball-rolling skills are most often associated with games like bowling and kickball, but are also used in such activities as boccie, shuffleboard, and curling. Gallahue (1993) writes that the basic pattern is also seen in underhand throwing (including softball pitching) and life-saving rope-tossing activities.

Sample Activities.   As with throwing, accuracy is not the initial objective in teaching the children to roll a ball. You can begin simply by asking them to roll balls of various sizes at the wall. When the children feel comfortable with this, you can substitute targets like plastic bowling pins and empty soda bottles, beginning with large balls and gradually decreasing their size.

If you have access to inclines, the children will enjoy rolling balls down them (this is a great way to ensure success for very young children) and discovering the balls do not go as easily uphill!

VOLLEYING

For the purposes of this text, *volleying* is defined as striking (imparting force to) an object in an upward direction with the hands or other body parts (excluding the feet). Typical body parts used for volleying include the head, arms, and knees, as witnessed during a game of soccer. Accurate visual tracking is necessary for this skill.

When working with young children on volleying, lightweight, colorful objects like balloons and beachballs should be used to help ensure success.

Sample Activities.   Provide a medium to large balloon for every child, and challenge the group to try hitting them upward and forward with both hands. The next step is to volley the balloon with just one (the preferred) hand, later trying it with the nonpreferred hand. Finally, challenge the children to volley the balloon with different body parts. How many can they volley with?

BOUNCING

Bouncing, sometimes referred to as dribbling, signifies striking an object (most often a ball) in a downward direction with one or both hands. Gallahue (1993, p. 315) tells us the developmental progression seems to be "(1) bouncing and catching, (2) bouncing and ineffective slapping at the ball, (3) basic dribbling with the ball in control of the child, (4) basic dribbling with the child in control of the ball, and (5) controlled dribbling with advanced abilities." Although bouncing a ball does not have much application later in life, it is an excellent tool for developing eye-hand coordination.

Sample Activities.   Beginning with large playground balls or small beachballs, the children initially bounce and catch with two hands, varying the number of bounces between catches. Once they have become proficient with this, they should be challenged to bounce continuously with two hands. The final challenge is to bounce with one (the preferred) hand, eventually bouncing with the nonpreferred hand as well.

CATCHING

The catching skill of receiving and controlling an object with the hands requires children to focus on the approaching object and make the adjustments necessary to receive it. Catching is often more difficult for some children, who experience fear as the object approaches. Using soft, colorful objects (scarves, beanbags, balloons, yarn balls) and large, soft balls (beach and foam balls) can help alleviate the fear *and* make visual tracking easier.

Sample Activities.   Children begin by catching their own bounced ball. Catching *from* someone (someone who is able to throw accurately) is the next challenge. Once they are achieving a certain measure of success, they can try catching an object (ball, beanbag, balloon, etc.) they themselves have tossed into the air.

Figure 3-9
Scarves are colorful, lightweight, and slow-moving—perfect for early experiences with catching.

STRIKING

Striking, as it is used here, refers to imparting force to an object using an implement (e.g., a racket, paddle, or bat). Graham et al. (1993) contend this is one of the last skills children develop because visual tracking is not refined until the upper elementary years and eye-hand coordination is more challenging at greater distances from the body. They also state the difficulty of striking increases with the length of the implement. However, with the proper modifications to the equipment (lightweight, short-handled implements and lightweight objects to be struck), young children can experience success with this skill.

Sample Activities.   A good rule for exploring this skill is, at first, the object and the child should be stationary, as when a child strikes a ball off a cone or tee with a bat. Next, the object moves but the child remains still (e.g., the child hits a pitched beachball with a paddle or large, lightweight bat). The final challenge occurs when the object and the child move (e.g., keeping a ball in the air with a paddle).

DRIBBLING

In the context of this book, dribbling refers to the manipulation of a ball with the *feet*. Force is imparted to the ball horizontally along the ground, but unlike kicking (in which the ball can also travel in a vertical direction), the goal is not to impart force for distance. Rather, the ball is controlled by keeping it close to the feet. Dribbling requires eye-foot coordination and a great deal of body control.

Sample Activities.   Using a small beachball or playground ball (8 to 12 inches in diameter), the children first begin controlling the ball with the inside and outside of their feet. Once they are able to do so, you can provide a pathway (and later an obstacle course) for them to dribble through. Encourage them to alternate their feet.

Educational Gymnastic Skills

Gymnastics teaches children body management skills—on the floor and with small and large apparatus—and develops strength, stamina, and flexibility. Although this is true of educational gymnastics and the more traditional, Olympic-style gymnastics, a vast difference exists between the two; that difference lies in their approach.

Olympic gymnastics is stunt-oriented, and the ability to execute the required stunts determines success or failure. Performances "are compared against a set standard, such as the Olympic '10,' and typically against others' performances" (Belka, 1993, p. 1).

Educational gymnastics, on the other hand, is *child*-oriented and is a natural progression of the exploration of fundamental movement skills. Its use of exploration and discovery allows children to progress at their own pace—and thus, to experience much success in body management.

Five skills—rolling, transferring weight, balancing, climbing, and hanging and swinging—are developmentally appropriate for preschool and primary-grade children and can introduce them to the experiences characteristic of gymnastics. Mats or carpeting should be used for rolling and transferring weight.

ROLLING

Rolling is a horizontal transfer of weight that can take many forms and move in forward, backward, or sideward directions. It is one of the most basic of movement activities and is excellent for developing balance (Skinner, 1979), as well as body and spatial awareness. Unlike Olympic gymnastics, which often begins with the forward roll, educational gymnastics considers the forward roll an advanced skill.

Sample Activities.   Several rolling activities are fun for children. Log rolls involve long, stretched bodies with arms overhead, rolling in both directions. Once the children are able to keep their bodies (and pathways) straight while performing log rolls, ask them to try initiating the rolls with first the upper and then the lower torso. A more advanced activity is "footsie rolls," in which pairs of children lie on their backs with the soles of their feet together and then attempt to roll without their feet breaking contact.

Egg rolls require getting into an egg shape—kneeling, with arms crossed and resting on the mat, knees pulled into chest, and head tucked. The children then roll sideways, in both directions.

An activity for initiating the forward roll through convergent problem solving is included in Chapter 1.

TRANSFERRING WEIGHT

Transferring weight, in its simplest definition, is the smooth shift of the body's weight from body part(s) to body part(s). Locomotion such

COMPARISON OF OLYMPIC AND EDUCATIONAL GYMNASTICS

Olympic

Stunt-oriented

Children's performances compared with others'

Children traditionally compete against one another

Mastery of specific skills required

Traditional demonstration/imitation method of instruction (command style) used

Children often scored on their performances

Often consists of skills too advanced for most preschoolers

Customarily requires use of large apparatus beyond capability of most preschoolers

Often developmentally inappropriate

Educational

Child-oriented

Children's performances compared only with their own previous performances

Children compete against selves to improve skills

Children progress at own developmental rates

Exploratory approach (problem solving) used

Children rewarded intrinsically through success achieved

A natural outgrowth of exploration of fundamental movement skills

Children explore possible uses of large apparatus according to their level of ability

Developmentally appropriate

as walking is considered weight transfer because it moves the body's weight from foot to foot. However, transferring weight can also take place without locomotion, as when an individual moves from a lying to a sitting position (simple weight transfer) or shifts the body's weight from the feet to the hands (advanced).

Sample Activities.   In one weight activity, the children experiment with the placement of weight on various body parts and the transfer of that weight to other parts.

You can explain the placement of weight by telling them only the body parts you assign will be touching the floor. They will then move their weight from those body parts to the next one(s) you mention. (Move somewhat quickly from one position to another so the children are not required to *balance* on these body parts.) Make it their goal to transfer the weight as smoothly as possible.

Body parts can include hands and knees, knees and elbows, knees alone, the tummy (nothing else should be touching the floor), the back, one (the other) side of the body, the bottom only, hands and feet, and just the feet.

BALANCING

When a person is balanced, his or her center of gravity is over the base of support, whether that base is a foot, two feet, two hands, or the head and hands. Balance over a wide base is, of course, easier than over a narrow one. Like transferring weight, balancing is possible both when moving and while remaining stationary; it is, in fact, *necessary* to both moving and remaining stationary.

Balances that occur in a stationary position, like standing on one foot, are known as *static* balances; maintaining balance while moving (for example, walking along a balance beam) is called *dynamic* balance.

Sample Activities.   A basic introduction to balance is walking a tightrope, whether imaginary or created with masking tape, string, or rope (younger children will benefit from having a visible tightrope). Begin by asking the children just to walk forward along the tightrope, placing one foot in front of the other. When they are ready, you can challenge them to try moving sideward and then backward. (These activities can later be transferred to a low balance beam, if available, giving children a chance to actually move above the ground.)

Young children should also practice balancing on various body parts, at low and high levels. Challenge your children to do the following balances at a low level: on two hands and one knee, on one

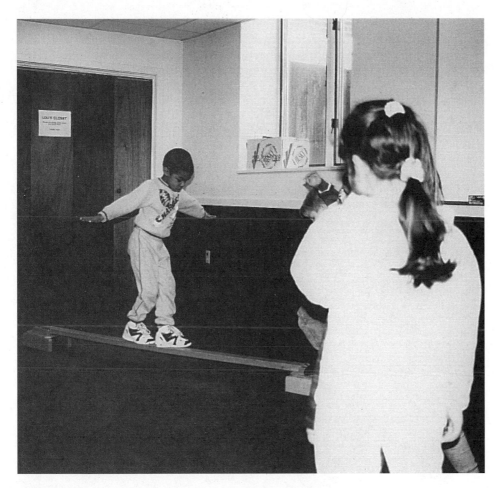

Figure 3-10
Maintaining balance while moving is known as dynamic balance.

hand and one knee, on bottom only, on knees only, on tummy only, and on one knee.

Challenges for a high level include on tiptoe, on one foot (flat), on the other foot, on tiptoe with knees bent, on tiptoe with eyes closed (briefly), and on tiptoe on one foot only (briefly).

CLIMBING

Children love to climb and are often fearless in their attempts to do so. This skill involves "pushing and pulling and supporting one's weight while moving the body up or down" (Belka, 1993, p. 6). It contributes to leg, arm, upper trunk, and shoulder strength.

Climbing requires apparatus, but if the necessary equipment is not available indoors, most playground structures will suffice.

Figure 3-11
An indoor slide offers children a chance to practice climbing.

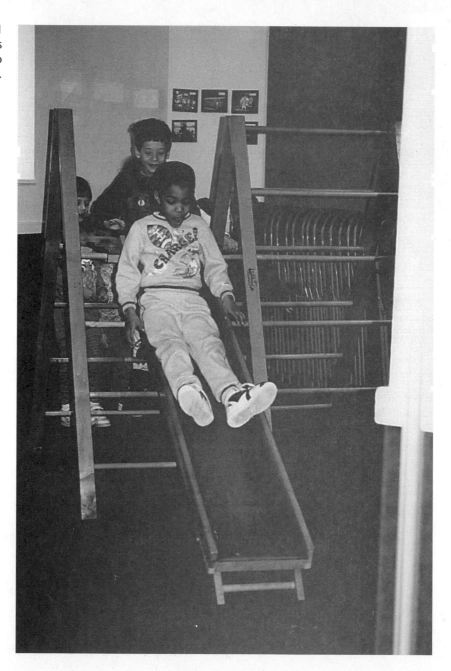

Sample Activities.   You can combine climbing with imagination by asking the children to pretend the climbing equipment is a mountain or the side of a building to be scaled. They should practice climbing up *and* down. Can they climb certain parts of the equipment facing *away* from it? Can they climb up part of the equipment in a forward direction and climb down that same part in a backward direction?

CATEGORIES OF MOVEMENT SKILLS

Locomotor Skills	**Nonlocomotor Skills**
Crawl	Stretch
Creep	Bend
Walk	Sit
Run	Shake
Jump	Turn
Leap	Rock and sway
Gallop	Swing
Hop	Twist
Slide	Dodge
Skip	Fall
Step-Hop	

Manipulative Skills	**Gymnastic Skills**
Pull	Rolling
Push	Transferring weight
Lift	Balancing
Strike	Climbing
Throwing	Hanging and swinging
Kicking	
Ball rolling	
Volleying	
Bouncing	
Catching	
Striking	
Dribbling	

HANGING AND SWINGING

Hanging and swinging, like climbing, require apparatus, and help develop arm, upper trunk, and shoulder strength. Most children will use an overgrasp and can hang four or more seconds (Sinclair, 1973). Arms should remain fairly straight (the elbow should be slightly bent) while hanging and swinging.

Without supervision, children should hang from apparatus no higher than their heads. Even with supervision, the apparatus should not be more than twice the child's height.

Also, children should be taught to dismount (i.e., let go) on a backward rather than forward swing.

Sample Activities.   No one hangs and swings better than a monkey, and children love to pretend to be monkeys! Challenge them to hang and swing with two arms, one arm (trying it on both sides), and eventually in an inverted position (with supervision only).

Key Points

- An understanding of the six elements of movement—space, shape, time, force, flow, and rhythm—is essential for teachers and children in a movement program. Exploring these concepts is a good place to start the program.
- If we liken movement education to the study of grammar, the movement skills can be considered verbs, with the elements of movement acting as the adverbs modifying them.
- Locomotor skills transport the body as a whole from one point to another. Children acquire the ability to perform locomotor skills at their own rates, but will be unable to reach mature performance patterns without instruction and practice.
- Nonlocomotor skills, sometimes called axial or nonmanipulative movements, are performed in place and involve the axis of the body rotating around a fixed point. Although often considered in terms of muscle warm-ups, nonlocomotor skills are vital to movement education and physical self-expression.
- Manipulative skills, as described in this text, involve the body's large muscles and manipulation of objects. Because of the visual-motor coordination required by traditional manipulative skills, they are more difficult for children than the locomotor and nonlocomotor movements.
- When exploring manipulative skills, teachers must adapt the equipment to the children rather than expecting the children to adapt to the equipment.

- Both educational and traditional gymnastics teach body management and develop strength, stamina, and flexibility. Traditional, Olympic-style gymnastics is stunt-oriented, and educational gymnastics is child-oriented, using an exploratory approach that allows children to progress at their own pace.

Assignments

1. Not all the skills described in this chapter are explored in every movement program. Choose those skills you consider most critical for preschool children and provide justification for your choices.
2. Create one activity for each movement element and skill in the chapter.
3. Write an explanation, in your own words, of how the movement elements and skills are used in conjunction with one another.
4. Using early childhood catalogs, compile a wish list of equipment you consider necessary for exploring manipulative and educational gymnastic skills.
5. Observe a preschool class at a gymnastics center. Is the class content educational or Olympic gymnastics? Explain the reasons for your determination.

References

Belka, D. (1993). Educational gymnastics: Recommendations for elementary physical education. *Teaching Elementary Physical Education, 4*(2), 1–6.

Cherry, C. (1971). *Creative movement for the developing child.* Carthage, Ill.: Fearon.

Fleming, G. A., ed. (1990). *Children's dance.* Reston, Va: American Alliance for Health, Physical Education, Recreation, and Dance.

Gallahue, D. L. (1993). *Developmental physical education for today's children.* Dubuque, Iowa: Brown & Benchmark.

Gerhardt, L. (1973). *Moving and knowing: The young child orients himself in space.* Englewood Cliffs, N.J.: Prentice-Hall.

Gilbert, A. G. (1992). *Creative dance for all ages.* Reston, Va: American Alliance for Health, Physical Education, Recreation, and Dance.

Godfrey, B. B., & Kephart, N. C. (1969). *Movement patterns and motor education.* New York: Appleton-Century Crofts.

Graham, G., Holt/Hale, S., & Parker, M. (1993). *Children moving: A reflective approach to teaching physical education.* Mountain View, Calif.: Mayfield.

Hammett, C. T. (1992). *Movement activities for early childhood.* Champaign, Ill.: Human Kinetics.

Kirchner, G. (1992). *Physical education for elementary school children*. Dubuque, Iowa: Brown.

Murray, R. L. (1975). *Dance in elementary education*. New York: Harper & Row.

National Dance Association. (1990). *Guide to creative dance for the young child*. Reston, Va: National Dance Association.

Pica, R. (1990a). *Preschoolers moving & learning*. Champaign, Ill.: Human Kinetics.

Pica, R. (1990b). *Toddlers moving & learning*. Champaign, Ill.: Human Kinetics.

Pica, R. (1991). *Special themes for moving & learning*. Champaign, Ill.: Human Kinetics.

Pica, R. (1993). *Upper elementary children moving & learning*. Champaign, Ill.: Human Kinetics.

Schurr, E. (1980). *Movement experiences for children*. Dubuque, Iowa: Brown.

Sinclair, C. B. (1973). *Movement of the young child: Ages two to six*. Columbus, Ohio: Merrill.

Skinner, L. (1979). *Motor development in the preschool years*. Springfield, Ill.: Thomas.

Stinson, S. (1988). *Dance for young children: Finding the magic in movement*. Reston, Va.: American Alliance for Health, Physical Education, Recreation, and Dance.

Sullivan, M. (1982). *Feeling strong, feeling free: Movement exploration for young children*. Washington, D.C.: National Association for the Education of Young Children.

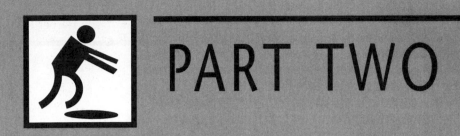

PART TWO

Planning for Movement and Music

Lesson Planning

Much of lesson planning is a matter of personal choice. You can choose a lesson plan format from the numerous possibilities found in physical education texts—or you can create one of your own. You may choose to build your lesson plans around movement themes, in which case you will have to decide whether a lesson will consist of a single theme or a variety of themes. Or you may choose to build your lesson plans around content areas or classroom themes.

There are, however, some suggestions for lesson planning in general; these are covered in the following section. The next segment examines general progresssions, helping you know where to begin your lesson plans and where to go from there. We then look at the possibilities for planning lessons based on a variety of movement themes, on just one movement theme throughout, and on unit themes related to content areas. This information will help you decide how you want to design your movement program.

Gallahue (1993, p. 192) writes: "Experience has shown that teachers who fail to plan are really in essence planning to fail." As often mentioned, movement education is success-oriented. Thus far, we have considered the term only as it applies to the children participating in the movement program. Success, however, should also be the end result for those who are *conducting* the movement program; well-prepared lesson plans can help ensure it will be.

Creating Lesson Plans

A lesson plan, as defined by Weiler et al. (1988, p. 43), "specifies procedures for teaching one class period of a planned learning unit."

However, there may be as many ways to create lesson plans as there are teachers. Here are some suggestions to get you started devising your own.

1. The lesson plan itself should be considered a flexible guideline (Kirchner, 1992), because no two classes are ever alike. Even children of the same age will be at different levels of motor ability, experience, and emotional maturity. Thus, you will have to adapt your lessons accordingly. You should also be aware—and open to the idea—that changes can occur as you go along, over time or during an individual lesson. For example, you may decide, based on your observations during one lesson, you would like to further develop a particular activity or skill, thus causing you to change your next lesson plan. Or the children may make a suggestion you had not considered, or ask to repeat something they especially enjoyed. (For more on flexibility, see Chapter 8.)

2. Although you do not want to be rigid in your preparation and use of lesson plans, you want to have clear—and realistic—objectives. Although it may seem overwhelming, the best plan of attack is to know what objectives you would like the children to meet during the entire school year. You can then begin to break these into goals for weekly or daily lesson plans.

If, for instance, your prime objective is for your kindergarten children to experience some success with all the basic locomotor and nonlocomotor skills, you must first define what you mean by success. You can then begin to prepare your schedule accordingly. What activities will you include in each lesson to help the children reach this goal by the end of the year? What exactly do you want the children to accomplish in each meeting?

Graham (1993, p. 24) advises being realistic and specific. He writes that expecting children to learn to volley a ball in a 30-minute class is an example of an unrealistic and overly general goal. Rather, he suggests a narrower focus that provides a guideline for observation and evaluation: "The children will learn to bend their knees as they receive and volley a ball." In other words, the yearly objectives are rather like a sumptuous banquet, and the daily or weekly objectives are the many, many ingredients that go into making the banquet possible.

3. The more experienced you become at teaching, the less actual planning you will have to do. (This is certainly good news in light of the above point!) It only makes sense; the more familiar and comfortable we become with anything, the less concentration it requires.

Take the lesson plans themselves. When you first begin teaching movement, it is likely the more detailed the lesson plans, the easier the actual teaching will be. Figure 4-2 is an example of a lesson plan outline that allows you to record most of the specifics in teaching a movement class.

Figure 4-1
One of your primary—and constant—objectives should be the children's enjoyment.

The first four items—class, skill level, length of lesson, and number of meetings per week—are helpful for teachers with several classes each week, especially if the classes are not identical. The space allotted for equipment allows the teacher to list the materials required for a specific lesson and make a quick and easy inventory prior to class.

Primary theme refers to the main focus of the lesson—for example, a movement element or skill, or a classroom theme—with the secondary theme(s) as subfocus. If the primary theme were jumping, the secondary theme might be the movement element of force; the lesson

Figure 4-2

Sample lesson plan outline

Class _____   Skill Level _____

Length of Lesson _____   Lessons per Week _____

Equipment Needed _____

_____

Primary Theme _____

Secondary Theme(s)   1. _____

                                2. _____

Objectives _____

_____

Activity	Organization/ Equipment	Observation Cues

Notes

_____

_____

_____

_____

_____

would then involve jumping lightly and heavily. The objectives (also written on the lesson plan) might then be that the children learn to land toe-ball-heel, with knees bent, and demonstrate an understanding of the difference between light and heavy jumps.

The next part of the lesson plan format has space to list the activities, organization/equipment needs, and observation cues for each activity. (An actual lesson plan would require more space for the activities than shown.) Organization simply means the formation in which an activity will be performed—for example, circle, single-file lines, scattered, and so on. Small x's representing students' bodies can be used to demonstrate the formation of choice. Any equipment required for the activity can also be noted here. (You can later scan this section to prepare your overall list of equipment needed, for notation at the top of the lesson plan.)

Until you become adept at observation and evaluation, you will certainly want to write observation cues on your lesson plan: questions you will ask yourself as you analyze the children's movement (based on your lesson's themes and objectives) and will use to help the children refine their movements. (There is more on this topic in Chapter 7.) For instance, using the jumping themes and objectives as an example, the observation cues appearing on the lesson plan might be: Are the children landing with knees bent? Are their heels coming

Figure 4-3
You will get your movement session off to the best possible start by making the first activity fun!

all the way to the floor, or are they landing on balls of feet only? Are they demonstrating a clear difference between light and heavy jumps? Is there a discernible difference in the amount of muscle tension being used for each?

The last section should be used immediately following a class (or as soon after as possible) to make notes regarding your evaluation of the activities, the children's performance, and your own teaching. These notes can help you make the necessary adjustments in future lessons.

4. The number of activities you plan for a single lesson will vary according to the ages of the children and the time allotted for

Figure 4-4
Activities involving the whole body and that move the child through general space should alternate with less lively activities.

movement. Regardless of the number of activities, a lesson plan should have a beginning, middle, and end.

The beginning should be an activity that focuses the children on you and on the reason why you have come together: to move! If you want to add an element of predictability to your movement sessions, you can begin each one with the same activity (e.g., touching heads, shoulders, knees, and toes). On the other hand, you might choose an opening activity that specifically focuses the children on the theme of that day's lesson. Whichever you decide, you will get the session off to the best possible start by making the first activity fun.

The middle of the plan comprises the body of the lesson—the activities you have designed to meet the objective(s) you have outlined. The activities should build on each other and flow easily from one to the other. Writing them will keep you focused on the tasks at hand and avoid lulls in the lesson (Graham, 1993; Sullivan, 1982).

The end of the lesson, which could also be the same activity each time, should bring closure to the session and wind the children down. (For more on this, refer to The Role of Relaxation in Chapter 8.)

5. To maintain interest and order, the activities you plan should alternate between lively and not-so-lively. This may mean following a locomotor activity with a nonlocomotor activity, or an activity that moves through general space with one peformed in personal space— perhaps sitting or even lying down. Another possibility is to follow an activity involving the whole body with one requiring the use of just the hands. (For more on pacing sessions, see Chapter 8.)

Developmental Progressions

Although much choice is available with regard to the design of lesson plans and the movement program itself, one factor must be present in all instances if a program is to be truly successful: developmental progression. In other words, you must begin at the beginning and proceed in a logical, developmental order.

What should be "the beginning?" There is no one right answer to this question. You must determine this for yourself, depending on the developmental level of the children you are working with. There are, however, some guidelines you can follow in making this determination.

With young children, the initial focus of the lessons should be on the elements of movement, rather than the movements themselves. This can be somewhat confusing because, naturally, you cannot have one without the other. For example, if the focus of a lesson is pathways and you ask the children to gallop in zigzag paths, they will be concentrating on the zigzags (the movement element), but they will also be practicing the gallop (a movement skill). Thus, the two are interrelated. Initially, however, your objectives would be concerned with their understanding of the movement elements and not necessarily with the quality of their execution of the movement skills.

Chapter 3 outlined a general developmental progression for the movement skills (locomotor, nonlocomotor, manipulative, and educational gymnastic). Based on these progressions, you would not explore skipping before working on the locomotor skills leading up to the skip. You would not focus on dodging before other, simpler nonlocomotor skills. The same applies for the exploration of the movement elements. Generally speaking, the developmental progression for the movement elements—from least to most challenging—is space shape, time, force, flow, and rhythm.

Space—in particular, personal space—is the logical starting point for a movement program with young children. To further narrow the focus, however, we should consider two underlying principles: (1) The young child is concerned primarily with self; and (2) before children can focus on moving the body and its various parts, they should be able to identify body parts. Thus, identifying body parts—while in personal space—is the most logical answer to the question regarding where to begin.

In working with children 2 to 8, you could well choose to begin at the same point with all of them, regardless of age. However, in keeping with the premise that you should begin where the child is, you would adapt the particular activities according to the children's developmental stages. For example, you might begin all of your lessons—for toddlers, preschoolers, and early elementary children—with a focus on body-part identification. You might challenge toddlers simply to point to the various body parts whose names you call out. With preschoolers, you might play a game of Simon Says (without the elimination process, of course). You could also play Simon Says with the early elementary children but substantially increase the pace.

Three general progressions should be remembered when planning your lessons:

1. Children should work individually before exploring movement with a partner and then, in cooperation with a group.
2. For the most part, children will first use the body as a whole. They can be asked later to move both arms and/or both legs together, separate from the rest of the body. Laterality is then introduced, followed by the opposition of body halves; here students discover, for example, the lower half of the body can bend while the top half stretches. Finally, body parts are isolated and used individually. Use of parts, such as hands and face, can be introduced early, but much experience is required before a child can isolate and move *only* the head, hips, or shoulders.

3. Generally, children between 3 and 5 would rather pretend to *be* something than pretend to *do* something. In other words, they would rather pretend to be an airplane than pretend to fly that plane. And only much later can they demonstrate how such experiences might *feel*. So the natural progression is being, doing, and then feeling (Pica, 1990a).

You, of course, are the only one who can judge when it is time to move from one step to another, and you may have to rely on some experimentation to make your judgment. For instance, if the children have been working individually for quite a while, you can try a partner activity with them. If it is successful, you know they are ready to add more partner activities to their repertoire. If, on the other hand, the initial attempt results in chaos or lack of understanding, the children should continue to work individually a little longer.

Figure 4-5
Children ages 3 to 5 would generally prefer pretending to be an airplane than pretending to fly the plane.

As mentioned, there are no fixed formulas for the developmental design of lesson plans. However, if you keep the preceding points in mind and plan your activities and lessons so they build on one another—and give yourself permission to make changes based on trial and error—you will create a successful movement program.

Using a Variety of Movement Themes

Some teachers, perhaps abiding by the adage "variety is the spice of life," prefer to create lesson plans consisting of multiple themes, rather than a single theme throughout. As there are no hard and fast rules concerning the "best" way to plan lessons, this is a perfectly acceptable option. It does not, however, lend itself to classroom or unit themes, as classes usually explore only one unit theme per week or month. But it is possible to create lesson plans using a variety of *movement* themes.

A movement theme, as opposed to a classroom or unit theme, is based on a movement element or skill. Thus, a lesson plan consisting of multiple movement themes might focus on body-part identification, one element of movement, one locomotor skill, and one nonlocomotor skill. Figure 4-6 presents an example of a lesson plan, adapted from Pica, (1990a), using multiple movement themes. The lesson is appropriate for toddlers and preschoolers; but depending on the children involved, it might be too many activities for a group of toddlers to complete in one session. Also, although a suitable first lesson for preschoolers, it is somewhat too advanced for most toddlers.

In Figure 4-6, the first activity—Simon Says—focuses on body-part identification and is a great opening activity because it is fun and immediately attracts the children's attention. Obviously, the focus of Let's Walk is the locomotor skill of walking, which The Tightrope takes a bit further by introducing the concept of balance (this can also be considered an introductory educational gymnastics activity). Exploring Up and Down, while emphasizing the three levels in space, also uses the nonlocomotor skills of bending and stretching. Finally, "Where Is Thumbkin?" is a basic body-part activity stressing the use of the hands. Because this exercise brings the children to the floor and is relatively low-key, it is a suitable closing activity.

Of course, developmental progression is a must even when using multiple themes. It may also be a bit more complicated than when planning single-theme lessons. With multiple themes, each one must develop from lesson to lesson, building naturally and logically. Being aware of the developmental progression of the movement elements and skills can make this happen.

Figure 4-6
Sample lesson plan using
multiple movement themes

Simon Says

This game is an excellent body parts activity and a good way to begin because it is familiar to most children. In the traditional game, those who need to participate the most are usually the first to be eliminated! You can enhance *all* the children's enjoyment if you play Simon Says without the elimination process. You can still remind the children they are not supposed to move without Simon's saying they may; then, if they do move when they're not supposed to, simply repeat the challenge.

"Simon" might make the following requests:

Raise your arms.

Touch your head.

Stand up tall.

Touch your toes.

Touch your shoulders.

Pucker up your mouth.

Stand on one foot.

Place hands on hips.

Bend and touch your knees.

Close (open) your eyes.

Reach for the sky.

Give yourself a hug!

Let's Walk

This activity provides an excellent opportunity for you to observe the children's strengths and weaknesses regarding posture and alignment, weight distribution, and use of body parts—while the children simply have fun walking. Observing closely, have the children walk freely (with good posture and alignment), in place, forward and backward, on tiptoe, on heels, and with tiny (giant) steps.

Any of these challenges can be modified using the elements of movement. For example, you might challenge the children to walk in place *as lightly as possible* (the movement element of force), or to walk *as slowly as possible* (the movement element of time).

The Tightrope

For this very basic introduction to balance, you need tightropes, whether imaginary or created with masking tape, yarn, or string on the floor. Most young children find a visible tightrope much easier to walk on. Be sure to make enough available so children do not have to wait long for a turn.

After presenting the tightropes, ask the children to pretend they are tightrope walkers in the circus, balancing high above the crowd. You

continued on next page

Figure 4-6
Continued

might want to remind them there is a net below and real tightrope walkers extend their arms to the sides for better balance.

If you use visible tightropes as opposed to imaginary ones and the children have to wait for their turns, you might have those waiting pretend to be other circus characters (clowns, lion tamers, trapeze artists, etc.).

Exploring Up and Down
Pose the following questions and movement challenges:

- Do you know what up and down mean? Show me with your body.
- Can you make your body go all the way down? All the way up?
- How high up can you get?
- Can you go down halfway?
- Make yourself so tiny I can hardly see you.
- Show me you can become as huge as a giant.
- Pretend your feet are glued to the floor. Can you move your body up and down without those feet moving?

"Where is Thumbkin?"
Perform this old standard in the usual manner, asking the whereabouts of thumbkin, pointer, middle finger, ring finger, and baby finger. The children, displaying the appropriate finger, respond, "Here I am, here I am." And to the question, "How are you this fine day?" they sing, "Very well, I thank you."

Initially, you should model as you sing along with the children.

Using a Single Movement Theme

Teachers who plan lessons consisting of activities with a single theme generally do so because they feel it helps the children focus more effectively on the subject at hand. For certain groups of children—toddlers, in particular—this is sound reasoning.

As mentioned, designing lessons around movement themes involves the movement elements and skills. Therefore, in a lesson plan with a single movement theme, the activities focus on one element of movement or movement skill. Figure 4-7 demonstrates an example of such a lesson plan. Adapted from Pica (1990b), this lesson uses the theme of body-part identification. Though not technically a movement element *or* skill, body-part identification is an important starting point and can be considered part of the exploration of personal space. The lesson in Figure 4-7 could easily be the first movement session conducted with children aged 18 to 36 months.

In considering a developmental progression of lessons using a single movement theme, it is important to realize each movement element and skill has its own progression. If you choose to design your

Figure 4-7

Sample lesson plan using single movement theme

Heads, Bellies, Toes
Ask the children to touch heads, bellies, and toes (and then the reverse) as you call out the body parts. Begin with a slow, rhythmic chant that gently moves the children down and up. Then, if your toddlers are ready for it, you can make the activity more challenging by increasing the tempo or by frequently changing it.

Simon Says
This activity can be performed as described in Figure 4-6. However, you will need to keep the pace slower with toddlers.

Counting Fingers
Ask the children to make a fist. Then, as you slowly count 1-2-3-4-5, have them display their fingers, one at a time. Reverse, counting backward, with the children "closing" one finger at a time. Repeat a few more times, gradually increasing the tempo.
   This may be hard for some to coordinate, but assure them it will come with practice.

"Where is Thumbkin?"
Sing this song as slowly as necessary to ensure success for your toddlers.

program this way, you will not want to plan your first lesson around one element of movement, your second around the next element of movement, and so forth. And it would not be practical to plan to cover every aspect of one movement element before exploring the next.

Rather, you could plan to initially acquaint your students with the least challenging aspects of the least challenging movement element (i.e., space). Once the children have mastered the introductory concepts, you can move to the least challenging aspects of the next movement element. Remember, though, repetition is important to young children; it will benefit them to periodically review concepts they have previously experienced.

Using a Single Unit Theme

Many schools and child-care centers design their yearly curriculums around weekly or monthly themes. A quick flip through any thematically organized curriculum resource will display the most popular of these themes: self-concept, the senses, hygiene, nutrition, families and friends, seasons, weather, animals, occupations, transportation, and holidays and celebrations. All these relate in some way to the children's lives—which, of course, is why they have become the most popular units. And all, with a little imagination, not only lend themselves to field trips, art activities, story time, and such, but also to movement activities.

Teachers who organize the rest of their curriculum around a single unit theme usually choose a similar plan for their movement programs. Figure 4-8 shows a lesson plan adapted from Pica (1991). The theme is the sky, which falls under the broader heading of nature and the overall content area of science. This lesson plan is appropriate for early elementary children.

Developmental progression is a bit more abstract in lessons organized around unit themes. In studying Figure 4-8, for instance, you might wonder how you will know if your students are ready to be "clouds" or the "solar system." More appropriate questions might be: At what stage of cognitive development are the children? Will they grasp the concepts involved? Are they ready to work cooperatively as a group? Does the lesson require them to understand movement elements, or perform movement skills, they are not yet ready for?

Whether the classroom teacher is planning movement activities to accompany a weekly or monthly theme, or a movement specialist is working in conjunction with the classroom teacher to enrich the academic experience, exploring content areas through physical activity is valuable for young children in numerous ways, as detailed in Chapters 2 and 10.

Key Points

- A limitless number of ways exist to plan a movement program and design lesson plans. However, lessons typically are built around a single movement theme, multiple movement themes, or a single classroom theme.
- Because no two classes are ever alike, the lesson plan itself should be a flexible guideline.
- Every lesson plan should begin with clear and realistic goals. It is best to determine the objectives you want the children to meet during a school year, later breaking these into goals for weekly or daily lessons.
- For beginning teachers especially, the more detailed the lesson plans, the easier the actual teaching will be.
- Every lesson plan should have a beginning, middle, and end.
- Alternating activities between lively and not-so-lively will help maintain interest and order.

Theme: The Sky
Content Area: Science

Clouds

Ask the children for their impressions of clouds. How many different kinds of clouds have they seen? What do they think clouds are made of? Have they ever sat looking up at the sky, watching the clouds form the shapes of objects or animals? (If possible, bring the children outside or to the window to do just that before this activity.)

Now ask the children to move like big fluffy clouds, wispy clouds, dark storm clouds, and clouds drifting and slowly changing shape.

Time permitting, ask the children to cooperate as a group, each beginning as a single cloud but gradually drifting together and apart, forming larger and then smaller clouds. Sometimes two "clouds" will drift together to form a floating shape; sometimes larger groups of clouds will join and separate.

The Solar System

Talk to the children about the solar system, which includes nine planets that revolve around the sun. They are, in the order of their distance from the sun (from nearest to farthest), Mercury, Venus, Earth, Mars, Jupiter, Saturn, Uranus, Neptune, and Pluto. The solar system also consists of moons (Earth has only one) and stars.

If you want, you can show the children pictures of the planets, discussing the characteristics of each. Also, you should discuss solar and lunar eclipses, which are described in the activity.

For the activity itself, you will need as many scraps of paper as there are children in your group. On each piece of paper, write the name of a planet or *sun, moon,* or *star.* The children draw one scrap apiece from a container. They then form a "solar system."

The sun, of course, will be in the center, "radiating light." The planets should each revolve around the sun at an appropriate distance (Mercury, for instance, will be the closest and Pluto the farthest away). The stars should "twinkle," and the moon revolves around the earth (from west to east, if you can work that into the exercise). When the moon blocks the sun, a solar eclipse occurs; when the moon is in the earth's shadow, that's a lunar eclipse. How do the children want to depict solar and lunar eclipses?

(This is a difficult activity and it may take many repetitions before it is performed smoothly.)

Sunrise/Sunset

Talk to your group about the rising and setting of the sun. Have they ever watched a sunrise or sunset? Explain the sun rises in the east and sets in the west, and it takes from early morning to early evening (and sometimes longer) for the sun to move from east to west. (Remind them, of course, the sun does not actually move; the earth revolves around *it.*)

Now ask the children to each get into a very small shape on one side of the room (the eastern side, if possible). Then they pretend to be the sun *slowly* rising over the horizon. Once fully risen, the sun moves *in very slow motion*—shining all the while— across the "sky" (to the other side of the room) and begins setting, until it is no longer in sight.

If you like, you can accompany this activity with a piece of slow, soft music, helping to set the mood and tempo.

Figure 4-8
Sample lesson plan using single unit theme

- A developmental progression of the movement elements and skills is a must in a successful movement program.
- Identifying body parts is a logical starting point in a movement program for young children.

Assignments

1. Determine how you want to design your lesson plans—built around a variety of movement themes, a single movement theme, or a single classroom theme. Justify your choice in writing.
2. Choose an age group and make a list of movement objectives you would want them to meet in a school year. (You can use the information in Chapter 2 to determine what objectives are realistic for children of a particular age.)
3. Using the sample lesson plan in Figure 4-2, create three lessons that are appropriate for the age group you selected in assignment 2. These lessons should include objectives that will help the children meet the yearly goals you have outlined, and they should demonstrate a developmental progression (both within the lessons themselves and from one to the next).

References

Gallahue, D. L. (1993). *Developmental physical education for today's children.* Dubuque, Iowa: Brown & Benchmark.

Graham, G. (1993). *Teaching children physical education.* Champaign, Ill.: Human Kinetics.

Kirchner, G. (1992). *Physical education for elementary school children.* Dubuque, Iowa: Brown.

Pica, R. (1990a). *Preschoolers moving & learning.* Champaign, Ill.: Human Kinetics.

Pica, R. (1990b). *Toddlers moving & learning.* Champaign, Ill.: Human Kinetics.

Pica, R. (1991). *Special themes for moving & learning.* Champaign, Ill.: Human Kinetics.

Sullivan, M. (1982). *Feeling strong, feeling free: Movement exploration for young children.* Washington, D.C.: National Association for the Education of Young Children.

Weiler, V. B., Maas, J. M., & Nirschl, E. (1988). *A guide to curriculum planning in dance.* Madison: Wisconsin Department of Public Instruction.

The When, Where, and What of Movement Sessions

*P*art Four explores some possibilities for weaving movement and music throughout the daily fabric of early childhood and primary-grade programs. In Chapter 5, however, we will look specifically at planning movement *sessions* (blocks of time devoted exclusively to movement activities) as regular components of the curriculum.

How do you fit movement into an already busy schedule? How much—and what kind of—space is required? What size groups should you work with? What should the children wear? Will you need equipment and props?

Of course, many factors will influence the answers to these questions. Among them are the ages of the children, the number of children and assistants you have, the space you have to work in, the equipment available to you, the funds that may or may not be available to purchase new equipment, and the human resources for constructing equipment you may or may not have at your disposal.

Experience and personal preference can also play roles in the decisions you make. For instance, if you are a fledgling instructor, you may make some initial choices for scheduling and group size that continue to change as you gain experience. Or you might feel strongly the children explore movement with minimal—or no—props or equipment.

Although every situation is different and you will ultimately make—and continue to make—decisions based on the logistics of each situation, the following information can help establish a framework from which to begin.

Scheduling

With the many physical, social, emotional, cognitive, and creative benefits to be garnered from movement education, young children deserve the opportunity to experience planned movement activities daily. Yet daily movement sessions are seldom offered in early childhood programs or the primary grades. The reasons are many and varied and range from lack of time to lack of space to lack of money for hiring specialists.

In elementary schools, movement is typically planned only if the school employs a physical education specialist. Due to budget cuts, however, physical education teachers are seeing the children less often and for shorter periods, or are being removed completely from the staff rosters. The responsibility for movement education then falls to the classroom teacher, who commonly feels she is inadequately trained for such a task, and/or is already pushed to the limit in trying to meet all the curriculum objectives demanded by the recent clamor for accountability.

Similar reasons exist in early childhood programs, as evidenced by the comment of the director of a privately owned kindergarten, who stated, "We don't have time for movement; we're too busy preparing the children for first-grade academics."

But an increased understanding of how children learn, the need to address the whole child, and the importance of physical fitness has led classroom teachers and early childhood professionals to make greater efforts to overcome the problems of incorporating movement education into their programs.

What, then, is the best way to go about it? Because children are comforted by predictability, the best plan is to schedule movement sessions for the same time each day or each week. Most early childhood programs, whether half- or full-day, already schedule one or more periods for large group activity. And since these periods typically alternate with quieter activities, like time to explore learning centers or nap time, they can easily be used for movement. One note of caution: They should also alternate with periods when the children have had a chance to work or be alone. Otherwise, they may have had enough, temporarily, of being together as a group, and your movement sessions may end up more frustrating than fulfilling.

If lack of time is a concern but you feel strongly about offering the children movement every day (or as many days as possible), particularly in light of young children's need for repetition, one option is to set aside a 30- to 45-minute period at the beginning of the week, during which you complete one whole lesson plan. Then, during the remainder of your movement sessions, which could be as brief as 15

Figure 5-1
Group activities are scheduled three times in this example of a full-day program excerpted from Essa (1992). From Essa, *Introduction to Early Childhood Education,* copyright 1992 by Delmar Publishers Inc.

7:30–9:00	**Staggered Arrival:** Teachers greet children and talk to parents; self-selected activities such as books, manipulatives, play dough, and blocks.
7:30–8:30	Breakfast available.
9:00–9:20	**Group Time:** Introduction of day's activities; story or discussion related to day's topic.
9:20–10:30	**Activity Time:** Self-selected activities from learning centers, or teacher-planned projects.
10:30–10:40	**Cleanup Time.**
10:40–11:00	**Snack.**
11:00–11:15	**Small Group Activity:** Teacher-initiated, small group actvity to reinforce specific concepts.
11:15–12:00	**Outdoor Time:** Self-selected activities.
12:00–12:20	**Group Time:** Recap of morning; story; music.
12:20–12:30	**Wash for Lunch.**
12:30–1:00	**Lunch.**
1:00–3:00	**Nap:** Transition to nap and sleep for those requiring a nap.
1:00–1:30	**Rest:** Quiet individual activity for nonsleepers.
1:30–3:00	**Activity Time:** Self-selected activities, both inside and outside; as sleeping children wake, they gradually join others.
3:00–3:20	**Snack.**
3:20–4:00	**Activity Time:** Continued self-selected activities both inside and outside.
4:00–4:10	**Cleanup.**
4:10–4:30	**Group Time:** Closing of day; story; movement activity.
4:30–5:30	**Staggered Departure:** Self-selected activities until all children leave.

Figure 5-2
Essa's sample half-day program includes two group times. From Essa, *Introduction to Early Childhood Education,* copyright 1992 by Delmar Publishers Inc.

8:50–9:00	**Arrival.**
9:00–9:20	**Group Time:** Introduce day's activities; story, music.
9:20–9:40	**Snack.**
9:40–10:30	**Activity Time:** Self-selected activities.
10:30–10:40	**Cleanup Time.**
10:40–11:00	**Small Group Activity.**
11:00–11:40	**Outdoor Time.**
11:40–11:55	**Group Time:** Closing and recap of day.
11:55–12:00	**Departure:** Gather belongings; teachers talk to parents briefly.

to 20 minutes each, you would use the same lesson plan, repeating those activities that required extra work or ones your children especially enjoyed (Pica, 1990).

The children's ages are the most significant factor in determining the length of your sessions. Even so, great disparity is found among the suggestions offered by some experts. Sinclair (1973, pp. 85–86) states:

> For two-year-olds and younger three-year-olds one or two simple motor tasks might be sufficient; for children in the older four- and five-age bracket, group activity might be successful for a period of 20 minutes—seldom longer unless there is a sharp change of pace or focus. For full-day programs indoors, vigorous activity should be offered at least four times during the day; for shorter programs indoors, two or three times may be sufficient.

Fowler (1981, p. 108, 109), on the other hand, contends children "can be involved happily in movement activities for as long as 45 minutes or more, providing that the teacher is prepared to offer a wide variety of activities that range from vigorous and challenging tasks to those which are quieter and less demanding." He recommends "at least two opportunities during the day for movement if children are in school all day."

Sullivan (1982) suggests that 7- and 8-year-olds can easily manage a one-hour session while classes for 3-year-olds are best kept at 15 minutes per day. And Stinson (1988, p. 42) simply says the children themselves determine the length of each session. Once they are "finished," she asserts, the most you can expect from them is "going through the motions."

As mentioned, every situation is different. A small group will require less time to complete a lesson than a large group. A mixed-age group may or may not take more time to complete a lesson. A very young group will certainly need more time to get through fewer activities; it generally also takes longer to transition into and out of group activities. Due to the natures of children and movement exploration, lessons with the same number of activities can last 45 minutes one day, the next day only 30 minutes, and the following day just 20. Probably as the year progresses and the children (and you) gain more experience, the sessions can be extended.

One thing is certain: You must remain flexible. Children's moods vary from day to day. The weather can force you to explore indoors what you had planned for outdoors. Carefully planned lessons can take much less—or more—time than you expected. Simply put, where movement and young children are concerned, you should be prepared to occasionally (and perhaps frequently) "play it by ear."

Remember, it is better to *over*plan than underplan so you do not find yourself finished with a lesson long before the session is scheduled to end. Keep a list of activities from previous lessons that could use some additional work or were particular favorites of the children. Or compile a list of extra activities to choose from—locomotor and nonlocomotor, vigorous and quiet—just for those occasions when the class runs short. You can also ask the children for ideas.

Space

Is there such a thing as the perfect space in which to conduct movement sessions? To some teachers it must seem a rare commodity indeed. But, as the saying goes, "Where there's a will, there's a way." In a field test conducted by Gilliom (1970), teachers held movement sessions in a gym, half of a gym (with another class in the other half), a multipurpose room, a blacktopped schoolyard, a grass lawn schoolyard, a wide hall, a classroom with desks pushed to the edges, a stage, a cafeteria, and a lobby.

Of these, a gym is certainly the ideal. It usually offers a large, open space (although if too large, boundaries should be established, as described in Chapter 8), and a smooth, resilient, wooden floor. It typically does not contain objects like pieces of furniture with pointed corners that would be hazardous to moving children. The gym also has the advantage of being a place children associate with movement and can therefore help set the proper mood.

If a gym is not available, you will have to choose an appropriate area. Here are some points to bear in mind.

- Find—or create—the most open space you can. (Space set aside for circle time is often large enough for movement.) Each child should have a personal space to call his or her own, and participants should be able to move freely through general space without colliding. If you must use a classroom, push the furniture to the walls. Or, if possible, set up a permanent movement center in the room.
- Sometimes what seems like too little space can actually be adequate for movement. Asking the children, for instance, to gallop in a circle, rather than back and forth across the area, can ensure they have a chance to gallop "full out." You can also divide a large group in two, asking half the group to act as the audience while the other half performs an activity. (Keep activities brief in this case to avoid too much time spent waiting.

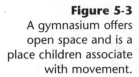

Figure 5-3
A gymnasium offers open space and is a place children associate with movement.

Also, ask the audience to watch for something in particular so they are participating visually.) If you cannot perform locomotor skills indoors, consider planning nonlocomotor activities for the classroom and locomotor activities for outdoors.

• Whenever possible, avoid cement or concrete flooring; it does not yield. Wooden surfaces are the best for movement, and a carpeted floor is second best (unless the carpet is laid over cement). If using a cement floor is unavoidable, decrease or eliminate high jumps, leaps, falls, and other such movements from your program.

• Find an area with as few distractions as possible. Distractions can be caused by people coming and going, excessive noise, and equipment and objects that provide either a safety hazard or overwhelming temptation (like tables "begging" to be climbed on, or wheel toys just "asking" to be ridden). If the material distractions cannot be removed, consider covering them before your movement sessions to help eliminate the temptation.

• Take all possible safety precautions. Place obstacles along a concrete wall to prevent children running into them, or put foam rubber on the sharp corners of pieces of furniture that must remain in the area.

WORKING CONDITIONS When I first started my company, Moving & Learning, I was hiring and training instructors and sending them to local child-care centers and preschools to teach my movement program. Once a month, we would get together to share stories about what was or was not working. And what *was not* often turned out to be the space the instructors and I were trying to teach in.

Floor-to-ceiling columns throughout the movement area were a problem for one instructor. They posed a definite hazard to the children, who did not always look where they were going! The only solution was to wrap the columns in padded material, similar to how pipes are wrapped for insulation in a cold basement.

Figure 5-4
Floor-to-ceiling columns are common obstructions.

Another instructor informed us, in one center, the only room in which to conduct movement sessions had a *wood stove* in the center! During warm weather, the heavy cast iron object could be extremely dangerous if a child were to trip and fall against it. In cold weather, when lit, it posed two dangers. Although detracting from the space available for movement, the only alternative in this situation was to surround the object with a barricade—a series of gates, like those used to keep children from falling down stairs, or something like large cardboard boxes.

The most problematic situation I ever encountered had several factors working against it. The center's director had determined the larger, basement area would be more appropriate for movement than the classrooms. The floor, of course, was cement; and although covered with indoor/outdoor carpeting, it limited the movements we could explore. A large fan was going at all times, which circulated the air nicely, but was impossibly noisy. I was unable to use a range of vocal expressions to elicit what I wanted from the children. The space was also long and narrow, which sometimes kept the children and me from being able to see one another, and also allowed children to remove themselves quite a distance from the group.

But the many distractions were the biggest problem. Play equipment lined one side of the area, offering irresistible temptation to some children. The kitchen was on the other side. Since this was a large child-care center, there were three or four kitchen employees constantly bustling about, and lots of clanking pots and pans. The program director's office was at one end of the basement and the restrooms at the other, resulting in an endless stream of people coming and going. If I had previously imagined the worst possible scenario for teaching movement, this situation would have made an almost perfect match.

I taught in that space twice before asking the director if we could use the classrooms instead. She agreed, and everyone was happier as a result. Although the furniture had to be moved prior to my arrival and the space was limited, the cozier, more familiar area was less stimulating and thus more appropriate for these particular children. With fewer distractions, less noise, and greater visibility, we were able to get down to the business of having fun with movement!

Unfortunately, the situations described here are far more common than "ideal" working conditions. I was unprepared for them; after reading Chapter 5, you will not have to be.

Although problems are bound to exist with any location, most can be overcome. With a little creativity and a lot of desire, just about any space can become a movement space.

Group Size

Again, many factors come into play. The first consideration in determining group size must be the space available to you. If the space is only large enough to accommodate half of your class at a time, you may have to make arrangements for the other half. If aides or other teachers are available, they can attend to the nonparticipating children as they circulate through the learning centers; or they could take the children to the playground or library. Could half of your class go to another classroom during movement sessions? If so, you could reciprocate by allowing your colleague's groups into your room while he or she is conducting movement sessions.

If your space does accommodate all the children, you must ascertain how many students you feel comfortable working with. Will you be working alone or will you have assistance? Probably, if you are a beginning teacher, you would do best with small groups of children. If circumstances allow, you can increase the size of the group as you gain experience.

Sullivan (1982) suggests one adult for every five 3- and 4-year olds and one adult for every ten to 15 older children. She recommends groups number from eight to 15 so there are enough children to "generate energy from members" but few enough children for individual attention.

Naturally, the situation itself will be the ultimate determinant. Seasoned teachers realize a vast discrepancy frequently exists between the ideal group size and the group size they must actually work with. (Many teachers find themseles working alone with as many as 25 preschoolers!)

One bit of advice you *should* make every effort to follow is Stinson's (1988) recommendation to keep the children in groups to which they are accustomed, because they are already used to being together and to interacting as a group.

Attire

Most young children dress casually enough, so clothing is not usually a problem. The two most important considerations are that the clothing be unrestrictive, allowing for freedom of movement, and that it not increase the possibility of injury. Overly long pant legs, for example, could cause a child to trip, and tights are slippery on most surfaces.

If you find you often have children dressed inappropriately for your movement sessions, consider asking for the parents' assistance. Tell them why you make movement part of your curriculum, explaining

Figure 5-5
Clothing worn for movement should be unrestrictive and comfortable.

its many benefits and how essential it is for the children to experience movement in unrestrictive attire. Ask them to send an extra T-shirt and pair of shorts so their child will have the appropriate clothing for movement sessions.

If health regulations do not forbid it and the floor's surface is clean and smooth, you should absolutely encourage the children to move in bare feet. Children have been moving in sneakers for physical activity for so long we seem to have forgotten the feet *do* have sentient qualities. They can be used to grip the floor for strength and balance, and their different parts (toes, ball, sole, heel) can be more easily felt and used when bare. Young children also feel a natural affinity for the ground that can be enhanced by removing all the barriers between it and the feet. In addition, toes accidentally stepped on and body parts accidentally kicked are much less likely to be hurt by bare feet than by those wearing sneakers or shoes.

Children who are reluctant to remove shoes and socks can be encouraged by concepts like "barefoot time" or, for the toddlers, "tippy-toe time." They will also become more enthusiastic about bare feet if you remove your shoes and socks, too. (To save time and eliminate potential chaos, establish—and practice—routines for removing and retrieving footwear. Socks should be put inside shoes and shoes lined up against a wall or placed in each child's cubby prior to the movement session.)

Of course, sometimes the children cannot perform barefooted (for instance, when a child is wearing tights). If so, and the choice comes down to sneakers or stocking feet, then choose the sneakers. Even on a carpet, it is much too dangerous to move in socks or tights; and if children sense it would be easy to slip, their freedom of movement will be greatly restricted.

Equipment and Props

The most important, and only absolutely necessary, prop in a movement program is the human body. Some consider music the second most important. Using additional props and equipment, however, can enhance the movement program and certainly merits consideration.

Equipment like mats, inclines, balance beams, crawl-through shapes, and climbing structures offer many movement possibilities the children might not otherwise encounter. Manipulating objects provides opportunities to move in new ways that require different levels of coordination and lets them become comfortable with objects (Weikart, 1987). And focusing on the movement of a prop can help alleviate

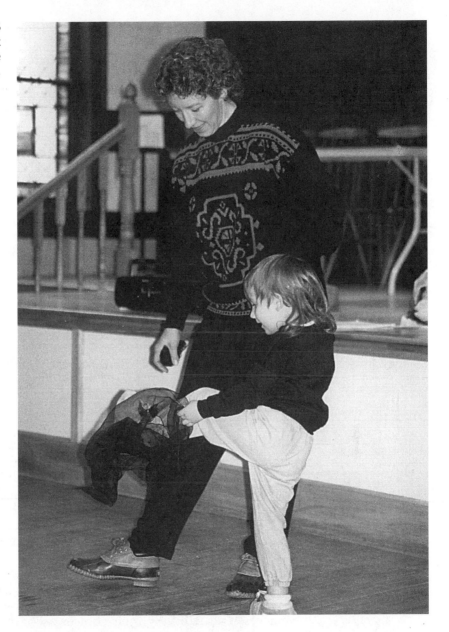

self-consciousness and encourage children who might not otherwise want to participate.

Often, the decision to incorporate props and/or equipment into the movement program is more a practical rather than a personal choice. Are the materials available? If not, is there funding to purchase some or all of what is desired? Are parents willing to donate their time and expertise to help make some equipment? Is there space for storing equipment?

Sanders (1992) suggests schools with limited budgets purchase small items first—and only those not easily homemade—then gradually acquire other items. He outlines activities requiring equipment and offers instructions for making such items as ribbon sticks, rhythm sticks, target boards, beanbags, balance beams, and balance boards. Stillwell (1987) is another excellent resource for simple, inexpensive instructions for making the aforementioned materials, as well as hoops, parachutes, yarn and rag balls, and geometric cutouts for target boards and crawl-through shapes. He also suggests activities that use these materials.

When purchasing equipment, you will find many possibilities listed in early childhood catalogs such as Childcraft, J. L. Hammett, Kaplan, and Lakeshore (see Appendix 2). Because equipment is their business, physical education suppliers like Flaghouse and Bell (Appendix 2) offer a greater selection of materials and, sometimes, better quality (see Selecting Equipment: Practical Considerations at end of chapter).

In the following pages, some of the relatively small, inexpensive props—balls, hoops, beanbags, streamers, scarves, rhythm sticks, and parachutes—commonly found in early childhood and early elementary programs are discussed and activities are suggested for each.

BALLS

Since ball-handling skills comprise the majority of manipulative skills described in Chapter 3, balls are necessary for any program in which these skills are taught.

A wide variety of balls should be available to the children. Beachballs and balls made of foam or yarn are easier for young children to catch and eliminate the fear of being hit that often occurs with harder balls. Since small balls are easier to throw and large ones easier to catch and bounce, many sizes should be offered. Children will generally select equipment with which they can have the greatest success and will vary their choices according to need and developmental progression.

Sample Activities. An introductory-level activity requiring one ball per child is to simply ask the children to move the ball all around the body, using both hands, the preferred hand alone, and then the nonpreferred hand. How many ways can they accomplish this task? Challenge them to try it with balls of different sizes and textures.

Curtis (1982) suggests a partner activity in which pairs of children attempt to move while holding a ball between them without using

Figure 5-7
Children should have access
to balls of different sizes
and textures.

hands. The ball can be balanced between the children's backs, tummies, hips, foreheads, or shoulders. Can they sit down and stand up without losing the ball?

Passing a ball overhead is appropriate for small groups of children. In this activity, the children stand in a single-file line. The first child passes a ball overhead to the next child without looking back, and so on down the line. The last child then comes to the front, until all the children have had a chance to be first. Later, to make this activity more challenging, the children can pass the ball, alternately, over and under (overhead and through their legs) (Pica, 1990).

For activity suggestions exploring specific ball-handling skills, refer to Manupulative Skills in Chapter 3.

HOOPS

Formerly, there was little choice in hoops that could be purchased; a hoop was a hoop. Today, they are available in a wide variety of colors and in different sizes and styles. According to Hammett (1992), the 24-inch, flat hoop is the most versatile, offering the best possibilities for manipulation and other activities. Flat hoops, she says, also tend to be sturdy and outlast the less expensive tubular ones.

Sample Activities.   Possibilities abound for using hoops. They can be spun, rolled, swung, jumped (like a rope), twirled around the body or various body parts, tossed and caught, and crawled through (when held upright by a person or styrofoam hoop holder). They can be used as targets and, when lying flat or held around the waist, are an example of personal space.

To explore the concept of *around,* provide each child with a hoop, and challenge the children to discover how many body parts the hoop can be twirled around (clockwise and counterclockwise). Or specifically direct them to try twirling it around the waist, the neck,

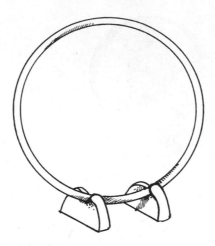

Figure 5-8
Hoops held upright by styrofoam
holders can be crawled through or
used as targets.

an arm, a wrist, a leg, or an ankle. Can they do it both quickly and slowly? While remaining in place and while moving through general space? With the body at different levels?

To explore *in* and *out,* ask the children to lay their hoops flat on the floor and find how many ways they can move into and out of them. (Possibilities include stepping, jumping, leaping, and hopping.) Ask them to walk around the hoop with one foot in and one foot out, trying it in both directions. What other locomotor skills can they perform this way? Then challenge them to discover how many other ways they can be inside and outside the hoop at the same time. Possibilities include having feet on the outside and hands on the inside; sitting or kneeling inside with hands and feet on the outside; lying on back or tummy inside the hoop with arms and/or legs extending over and outside the hoop; balancing on different body parts inside the hoop, with arms and/or one leg extended over and outside.

Hammett (1992) suggests a game of Musical Hoops as a fun alternative to Musical Chairs. In this game, hoops are scattered throughout the room, with one child inside each hoop. When the music starts, the children walk around the room. When the music stops, they step inside the closest hoop. Each time the music starts, a different locomotor skill is substituted. To make this a cooperative game, one or two hoops are removed as the music plays. When the music stops, the children have to share the remaining hoops. When there is only a single hoop left, the children must decide how to share it. (One possibility is for each child to place one foot inside the hoop.)

Figure 5-9
To explore the concept of around, challenge children to discover how many body parts the hoop can be twirled around.

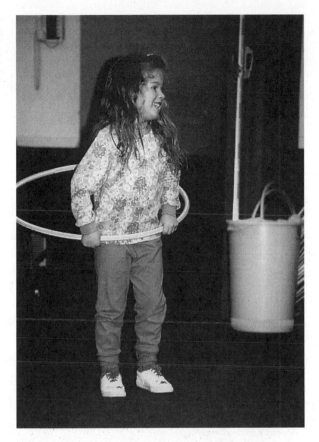

BEANBAGS

Beanbags are more fun today than ever before and offer a great variety of learning experiences. They come in different geometric shapes, in numerous colors (with the name of the color sometimes printed on the bag), and with letters (upper- and lowercase) and numbers (number and written word) printed on them—in English, Spanish, and French! Bell (see Appendix 2) offers beanbags with sign language.

Sample Activities.   Children enjoy (and have much success) throwing and catching beanbags, which are lightweight, flexible, and colorful. When used with target boards, boxes, hoops, or tires, beanbags provide practice with throwing for accuracy. Beanbags can also be manipulated with the feet, offering some introductory experience with dribbling. These activities are invaluable for developing eye-hand and eye-foot coordination.

To explore concepts like up and down, near and far, high and low, and front and back, ask the children to move a beanbag around the

Figure 5-10
Beanbags are more fun and educational today than ever before!

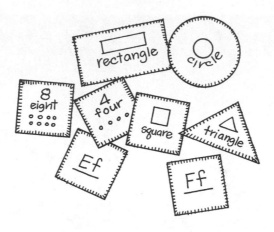

body at all possible levels. How far away from the body can they get the beanbag? How near to the body without touching it? Ask them to explore all the possibilities while standing, kneeling, sitting, and lying.

Perhaps the most popular beanbag activity is balancing a beanbag on various body parts. From the simplest challenge (balancing the bag

Figure 5-11
Balancing beanbags on body parts is probably the most popular beanbag activity.

on the palm of the hand) to the more difficult (balancing it on an elbow, a knee, or the nose), children love to test their skills this way. At first, you should challenge them to see on how many parts they can balance the beanbag while remaining in personal space. How many ways can they find to move the body part balancing the bean-bag? Later, you can suggest the children try balancing the beanbag on different body parts while executing various locomotor skills.

To combine beanbag activities with music, choose *Me and My Bean Bag, Bean Bag Activities,* or *Bean Bag Fun* (available from Kimbo Educational Records).

STREAMERS

Streamers, sometimes called ribbons (or ribbon sticks, if they are attached to sticks) can be made from lightweight cloth, satin ribbon, plastic surveyor's tape, plastic ribbon, crepe paper, or even strips of newspaper. Commercial ribbon sticks can be purchased from early childhood and physical education supply catalogs.

The children will need a lot of room to move with ribbons since they extend beyond the body and can cause injury if they should

Figure 5-12
Streamers and ribbon sticks can be homemade or purchased from catalogs.

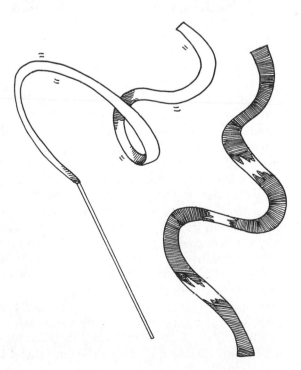

Figure 5-13
Children need to space themselves when working with streamers.

catch someone across the face or in the eye. (This can occur even with shorter ribbons made especially for young children.)

Sample Activities.   Streamers are ideal for exploring the concepts of over, under, around, in front of, and behind—the pathways around the body. With very young children, you may have to make specific suggestions for moving the streamer (e.g., in small and large circles, swinging, etc.). When the children are developmentally ready, simply ask them to discover how many ways they can find to move the streamer over, under, around, in front of, and behind various body parts.

Pathways through the air (like the arcing pathway made by a home-run ball on its way out of the park) are more abstract than those made by the feet on the ground, but streamers can help make these above-ground pathways "visible." Children enjoy pretending the air is a giant chalkboard and their streamers pieces of chalk. Ask them to "write" various letters in the air, or draw favorite shapes. Then introduce them to typical streamer patterns—circles, spirals (small circles), swings, figure eights, and zigzags (snakelike movements).

Kimbo produces a recording called *Ball, Hoop and Ribbon Activities for Young Children,* by Carol Hammett and Elaine Bueffel, if you wish to explore moving to music with any of these objects. Or you could simply play pieces of music in different styles, asking the children to see how each style makes them feel like moving their props.

SCARVES

You can purchase scarves, 8 to 16 inches square, in department stores (the inexpensive, lightweight type) or through early childhood or physical education supply catalogs (they are sometimes listed as juggling scarves). Or if you need a truly inexpensive alternative, paper towels will suffice.

Although scarves can serve many of the same purposes as streamers, some children find scarves easier to manipulate because they are smaller and do not extend as far from the body.

Figure 5-14
Scarves are easier to manipulate and therefore more appropriate than streamers for toddlers.

Sample Activities.　If the scarves are large enough, the children can explore the same aerial pathways and designs suggested earlier for streamers. Scarves are also excellent for developing tossing and catching skills. They float slowly enough to give children ample time to adjust and, if brightly colored, are easy to focus on. In addition, they are fun and practical for juggling for those children developmentally ready to try it.

Tying large scarves around wrists and ankles can motivate the children to see what effect various arm and leg movements have on the scarves. Play music of different tempos and moods to alter the children's movements each time you repeat this activity.

RHYTHM STICKS

Rhythm sticks, also known as lummi sticks, are common and popular items in early childhood and elementary settings. They can be purchased from catalogs or homemade. Either way, they should be lightweight, no longer than 18 inches (although a maximum of 12 inches

Figure 5-15
Whether purchased from catalogs or homemade, rhythm sticks should be lightweight and no longer than 12″ to 18″.

is best for young children), and one-half to one inch in diameter. If homemade, an alternative to wooden doweling is PVC pipe, available at hardware and plumbing supply stores.

Because they are short and manageable, rhythm sticks are excellent for familiarizing young children with the feel of a held object, which prepares them to later manipulate short- and long-handled implements like racquets, paddles, and hockey sticks.

Sample Activities. For a beginning stick activity, ask the children to determine what sounds are created by the two sticks striking against one another. Give them time to experiment, suggesting they try both loud and soft sounds, using different parts of the sticks. You can later suggest they try some of these movements commonly associated with rhythm sticks:

Figure 5-16
Drumming, rapping, hammering, and scraping.

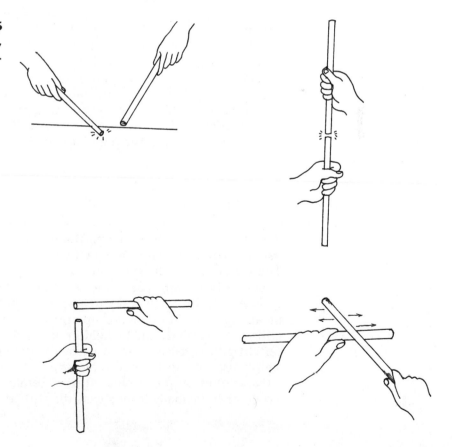

- drumming (using the floor as a drum and the rhythm sticks as drumsticks);
- hammering (one stick is held vertically, like a nail, and the other stick is used as a hammer);
- scraping (this is also known as Peel the Carrot, because one stick is held horizontally, like a carrot to be peeled, and the other moves along it like a vegetable scraper); and
- rapping (both sticks are held vertically and the two ends strike each other; this is more challenging because the ends are so small).

All the above movements involve making sounds with the sticks. Movements that make little or no sound include rolling the sticks around one another, shaking them, flipping and catching one or both, and tapping various body parts with them (e.g., heads, shoulders, knees, and toes).

The most common use for rhythm sticks, of course, is tapping them together in time with a musical beat. Musical selections for this activity should have a strong, even beat. Marches, with their even 1-2 rhythm, are most appropriate. You will want to begin with the children using the rhythm sticks while *sitting,* gradually advancing toward the more developed skill of simultaneously marching and playing the sticks. Weikart (1987) refers to this complex combination of locomotor action—what the feet are doing—and nonlocomotor action—what the hands are doing—as "integrated movement."

Kimbo Educational offers several albums for rhythm stick activities: *Multicultural Rhythm Stick Fun, Rhythm Sticks for Kids, Lively Music for Rhythm Stick Fun,* and the popular *Simplified Rhythm Stick Activities.*

PARACHUTES

While the above mentioned props are primarily intended for individual use, parachutes are designed to be used by groups of children. Thus, they are excellent for promoting cooperation.

Before beginning parachute activities, you should introduce the children to the three ways to grip the chute: (1) palms down, (2) palms up, and (3) one palm up and the other down. With all three grips, the thumb should be held in opposition to the fingers. Unless a certain grip is required for a particular activity, the children should simply use the most comfortable grip.

Parachutes can be purchased from catalogs or government supply stores, or homemade from sheets (brightly dyed if possible).

Sample Activities.   The two main possibilities for exploration with a parachute are moving it up and down and rotating the parachute. To rotate the chute while remaining in place, the children simply pass it to the right or left. This excellent introductory activity familiarizes the children with gripping the chute.

Next, you can challenge the group to create waves, using large arm movements to raise and lower the chute. They can experiment with this while sitting, kneeling, and standing. (Does a change in level have any effect on the waves?) Experiment with unison movement (all the children raising and lowering their arms at the same time) and with alternating movement (one child raises her arms as the next lowers his, and so on around the circle). Then, challenge the group to make small ripples by moving the arms up and down in opposition (one hand going up and the other coming down). Once the children are adept at making waves and ripples, you can place a lightweight ball or other object in the center of the chute, challenging the children to keep it bouncing.

Another in-place movement children enjoy is the creation of an "igloo." They start by holding the parachute close to the floor. They then raise it, eventually reaching as high into the air as possible, and pull it quickly back down, trapping air under the chute. Once the children have the knack of this, they can lie down as the parachute is

Figure 5-17
Making waves with
the parachute.

Figure 5-18
Children enjoy the challenge of bouncing balls off the parachute and trying to keep them inside the circle.

lowered, hands on the inside and bodies on the outside. Older children can hold the parachute with crossed hands, turning to face the outside as the parachute is lowered. This places them inside the igloo when the chute is brought to the floor.

Challenge the children to hold the parachute at waist height and discover how many locomotor movements they can use to move the parachute around in a circle. Can they find a way to rotate the parachute while facing it (i.e., sliding)? Be sure the children practice moving in both directions.

Kimbo offers six recordings to stimulate parachute play, including *Playtime Parachute Fun* by Jill Gallina; *Pop Rock Parachute,* set to con-

SELECTING EQUIPMENT: PRACTICAL CONSIDERATIONS
by Keith Gold, Product Manager, Flaghouse, Inc.

Being an early childhood professional carries the great responsibility of caring for the "future of our society." Part of that responsibility involves keeping the children safe.

When selecting equipment for the children's use, all items must first pass the "difficult to swallow" test. Additionally, any item a child could mouth or lick should be tested for toxicity and proven safe if accidentally ingested. All materials, including the inks and dyes, should be nontoxic. A typical problem area is the ink used on products like foam dice and beanbags.

Another area of concern with beanbags is what is inside of them. Some manufacturers use peas or other bean products. This filler is not recommended as it can attract vermin into your classroom. You should look instead for beanbags filled with plastic pellets. Reinforced stitching will inhibit ripping. Also available are beanbags covered with gym-mat material, which is washable and generally antifungal and antibacterial. These may cost a bit more than fabric-covered bags, but are well worth the investment when considering their longer life and greater hygienic value.

This gym-mat material is also important when purchasing shapes, wedges, and tumbling or safety mats. Many of the early childhood suppliers sell lightweight vinyl shapes in cute designs, using yellow foam as filler. These are generally inexpensive pieces that have a one- to two-year life. At the opposite end are professional-quality mats constructed of nylon-backed vinyl, weighing at least 13 to 15 ounces and with nylon stitching. They are antifungal, antibacterial, flameproof, and tearproof. These items, while not necessarily cute and certainly more expensive than low-end shapes, are functional and have an 8- to 10-year life, thus costing your program much less in the long term.

Safety and practicality also come into play when purchasing other common items, like hoops, parachutes, and balance beams. Traditionally, hoops were bendable, hollow plastic, with the pieces stapled together. Today hoops come staple-free, with plastic inserts, or in one-piece molded forms that are virtually unbreakable. Parachutes can now be bought with handles all around the outside edges so small hands can grip them more easily. And regardless of the balance beam you choose—and the variety includes padded beams very close to the ground, variable-height beams, foam beams, wooden beams, and beams made of plastic links that bend and curve—a safety mat should be placed underneath it because a falling child can be injured from any height.

As a rule of thumb, common sense and some experience should tell you whether a product seems safe and of good value. Your biggest problem may be lack of knowledge as to what is available. With this in mind, when you are ready to purchase new items, do not hesitate to ask questions, including questions about the materials used to construct the products. And, remember, no matter what equipment you use, no product is completely safe without proper supervision.

temporary music; and *Parachute Activities with Folk Dance Music,* which incorporates folk dance steps into the activities.

Key Points

- Among the factors that will determine the when, where, and what of your movement sessions are the number and ages of the children in your program, the number of assistants who will work with you, the space where the movement will take place, the available equipment, the funds (or lack thereof) for purchasing equipment, and personal preferences.
- Because children are comforted by and respond well to rituals and familiarity, it is best to schedule movement sessions for the same time each day or each week.
- In early childhood programs, one or more blocks scheduled for large-group activity each day can be used for movement. These blocks of time work especially well if they alternate with blocks used for quieter activities when the children have time to be alone.
- The length of individual movement sessions cannot always be planned or predicted. Chances are, the length of your sessions will be determined by the children themselves. Once you know a group of children well, you will have an educated idea of what to expect from them.
- Teachers should be prepared for those occasions when the class runs short by keeping a list of extra activities, or activities from previous lessons that bear repeating. The children themselves can also be asked for ideas.
- The ideal space for movement is a rare commodity. Teachers must often create a space in less-than-perfect conditions.
- Beginning teachers often find they are most comfortable working with small groups, gradually increasing the group's number as they gain experience. Working with children who are accustomed to being together as a group can make both teacher and children more comfortable.
- The clothing the children wear for movement should be unrestrictive and safe. Whenever possible, children should explore movement in bare feet.
- Moving with props can help alleviate self-consciousness, provide opportunities for children to become comfortable with objects, and offer movement possibilities the children might not otherwise encounter. Because they are fairly small and relatively inexpensive—and offer a variety of movement experiences— balls, hoops, beanbags, streamers, scarves, rhythm sticks, and parachutes are often included in movement programs.

Assignments

1. Design a weekly schedule for a full-day and a half-day program, incorporating movement into it daily.
2. Observe movement sessions held with toddlers, preschoolers, and early elementary children. Note the length of the sessions and your observations regarding the children's staying power. How long did the sessions last? Did the children lose or maintain interest?
3. While observing the previously mentioned sessions, also note the spaces in which they are held. Are any ideal? If any have drawbacks, how does the teacher compensate? Could you do anything differently to minimize the drawbacks?
4. Write a sample letter addressed to parents, justifying the necessity of children moving in bare feet.
5. Write a statement regarding your philosophy concerning the use of (or the decision not to use) props.
6. Using early childhood and/or physical education supply catalogs, prepare three five-year plans for purchasing equipment, based on annual allotments of $50, $100, and $200.

References

Curtis, S. R. (1982). *The joy of movement in early childhood.* New York: Teachers College.

Essa, E. (1992). *Introduction to early childhood education.* Albany: Delmar.

Fowler, J. S. (1981). *Movement education.* Philadelphia: Saunders College.

Gilliom, B. C. (1970). *Basic movement education for children: Rationale and teaching units.* Reading, Mass.: Addison-Wesley.

Hammett, C. T. (1992). *Movement activities for early childhood.* Champaign, Ill.: Human Kinetics.

Pica, R. (1990). *Preschoolers moving & learning.* Champaign, Ill.: Human Kinetics.

Sanders, S. W. (1992). *Designing preschool movement programs.* Champaign, Ill.: Human Kinetics.

Sinclair, C. B. (1973). *Movement of the young child.* Columbus, Ohio: Merrill.

Stillwell, J. L. (1987). *Making and using creative play equipment.* Champaign, Ill.: Human Kinetics.

Stinson, S. (1988). *Dance for young children: Finding the magic in movement.* Reston, Va.: American Alliance for Health, Physical Education, Recreation, and Dance.

Sullivan, M. (1982). *Feeling strong, feeling free: Movement exploration for young children.* Washington, D.C.: National Association for the Education of Young Children.

Weikart, P. S. (1987). *Round the circle.* Ypsilanti, Mich.: High/Scope.

Choosing and Using Music

As mentioned in Chapter 1, it is impossible to consider movement and music as separate entities. And although it is important for children to experience movement without music (so they can get a sense of their own personal rhythms), it is not surprising accompanying movement activities with music is often the more popular way of exploring movement. Music, after all, is enjoyable and provides an additional source of inspiration. It can be energizing or relaxing. It can make abstract concepts like slow and fast, light and strong, or free and bound more concrete. It can help a child to hear and feel the difference between the rhythm of a skip and that of a step-hop, or between sustained and suspended movement. Music is also a source of new ideas for activities. Finally, movement is an important instructional tool in the music education of children (Andress, 1991).

Chapter 6 looks at further ways the early childhood professional can make significant, simultaneous contributions to the movement and the music education of young children.

Choosing Music

Teachers and caregivers often say they have a difficult time finding music "for movement"—they do not know where to look or what to look for. But "movement music" is all around us, if only we are open to the possibilities.

Two critical factors should be recognized when making musical selections. The first is the *quality* of the music you provide, as quality listening experiences have been linked to the ability of children to concentrate and to their later language development (Jarnow, 1991).

Therefore, the recordings you choose to accompany movement activities must be clear and uncluttered. If you expect students to move to the music's rhythm, that rhythm must be easily heard. If instrumentation is the focus of the listening/movement activity, the instrumentation must be distinctive. If you are asking children to respond to the lyrics of a song, the words must be audible.

Throughout their life, children will have far too many opportunities for less-than-perfect exposure to music. They will hear it played in the background in doctors' offices, elevators, and supermarkets. They will hear it played indiscriminately at home, at school, and in the car. And they will learn to *tune it out*.

Haines and Gerber (1992, p. 13) contend the child "must be exposed to good musical sound, for anything less will inhibit or damage her awakening sensitivity." When selecting music for movement activities (or for any other purpose in your classroom), you should remember there is a major difference between hearing and listening. Listening involves perception; hearing does not. If you want your students to really listen to the music as they move, it must be music that *invites* them to listen.

Second, *variety* is also critical, from the student's and the teacher's point of view. Variety not only helps maintain interest, but also familiarizes students with musical elements—and movements—they might not otherwise experience. Following are several aspects of musical variety—styles, periods, nationalities, and textures—to consider when selecting music.

STYLES

Style is difficult to define. In music, styles technically differ from one another in how they treat form, melody, harmony, sound, and rhythm. For the most part, however, people can simply judge one style from another. We know, for instance, rock and roll certainly differs from opera, but most of us would have trouble saying why. Other examples of musical styles include jazz, folk, country and western, bluegrass, blues, rhythm and blues, disco, gospel, New Age, swing, and Dixieland.

Chances are, your students are exposed primarily to the music they hear on radio and television, which can offer only limited movement possibilities and does little to broaden music education.

THE MUSIC AND MOVEMENT CENTER

Learning centers offer children—individually and in small groups—opportunities to further explore their interests. When you provide a music and movement center in your classroom, children can listen to music, play instruments, and experiment with sound or movement at their own developmental levels and without adult supervision.

To achieve maximum success with your center, keep the following points in mind.

Location is critical. Choose an area where children making noise will not disturb those involved in quieter activities. Church (1992) suggests a spot near the dramatic-play space, or next to the circle-time area, and reminds teachers they can designate certain times of the day when the music/movement center is open or closed. Also, the area should be large enough so children actually *can* move.

Make your center inviting. If you have space, a table and chairs and additional comfortable seating (beanbag or beach chairs, throw pillows, scatter rugs) let your children know they are welcome to take their time in the center. Movement and music pictures hung on the walls will inspire the children and identify this as a special place.

Make your center accessible to young children. Tape players should be easy for children to operate. Materials should be stored in easy-to-open containers, on easily reached shelves. Instruments should be readily available.

Figure 6-1
An example of the "ideal" music-and-movement center.

Change the materials (tapes, props, instruments, and other sound-making devices) periodically for maximum interest and experimentation.

Though space and funding often keep us from achieving the ultimate, imagining it can help. The following wish list consists of items found in the ultimate music and movement center:

- A tape player designed for children, with a wide variety of cassettes (some with recordings of the children's own voices)

- A listening center for the tape player, with several headphones and a jack box so several children can listen at once (listed under Music or Audiovisual Equipment in the catalogs of early childhood suppliers like Kaplan, Lakeshore, and J. L. Hammett (see Appendix 2)

- Percussion instruments—maracas, tambourines, castinets, finger cymbals, and rhythm sticks

- Melodic instruments—bells, small keyboards, tone bars, xylophones, and a piano (to really achieve the ultimate)

- Miscellaneous, constantly changing sound sources: coffee cans, paper bags, or oatmeal containers filled with beans, beads, rice, or sand; coffee-can or oatmeal-box drums (i.e., with lids); different-sized stainless steel mixing bowls; blocks of wood; kitchen tools; and a variety of rocks

- A prop box, possibly including scarves, streamers, elastic bracelets or anklets with bells sewn on them, and rag dolls or stuffed animals (to serve as dance partners)

- An ever-changing selection of books to read or look at while listening

- A small selection of art materials to encourage children to combine drawing with music and offer a rich creative experience (Church, 1992)

Of course, if your music/movement center is going to be welcoming, accessible, efficient, and successful, it has to be maintained. Everything in the center should have a special place, and the children should learn to return each item to its appropriate spot. Andress (1973) suggests plastic bleach bottles with cut-out sections, ice cream cartons, shoe boxes, silverware trays, and coffee cans with plastic lids for storage containers. Cup hooks under a shelf are appropriate for hanging small items like castinets and triangles; many other instruments can be hung on a pegboard. Most importantly, the children must be taught to handle every item in the music and movement center with care and respect.

PERIODS

It would take an extensive course in music history to cover all that past ages have produced. The periods comprising the history of classical music alone offer an almost unlimited number of possibilities for use with the children.

From the Renaissance era, for example, came pieces such as *Greensleeves,* played during Christmastime under the title *What Child is This.* Bach's many works were products of the Baroque era, as was Pachelbel's lovely *Canon in D-Major.* From the Classical period are Haydn's *Surprise Symphony (Symphony No. 94 in G-Major)* and Mozart's *Eine Kleine Nacht Musik (A Little Night Music).* The Romantic period gave us Prokofiev's *Peter and the Wolf;* the Strauss waltzes; and Tchaikovsky's *Swan Lake, Nutcracker Suite,* and the forceful and expressive *1812 Overture.*

All these selections easily lend themselves to movement, as do those belonging to the decades of American music. The 1920s, for example, were the years for the Black Bottom, the Charleston, and other flappers' delights. The 1930s ushered in an era of Latin rhythms. The 1940s produced the big bands and their particular brand of swing. Elvis Presley was a product of the 1950s, which introduced rock and roll. During the 1960s, young people were performing such solo dances as the swim, the pony, and the mashed potato to the accompaniment of Top 40 hits. And with disco in the 1970s, partner dancing returned and opened the way for a revival of ballroom dancing in the next decade. The 1980s also saw an eclectic variety of musical styles, including everything from punk rock to New Age, as well as a fusion of styles from various parts of the world. In the early 1990s, country music and line dancing seem to be leading in popularity.

NATIONALITIES

The world is peopled with hundreds of nationalities, each of which has its own musical heritage: Polish and Mexican polkas, German and Austrian waltzes, Italian tarantellas, Irish jigs, Scottish Highland flings, and English folk songs. African chant and drum music, calypso, reggae, the hora, Latin rhythms, Greek dances, Native American songs, Spanish flamencos, and many, many others are further examples.

All these inspire different movements and contribute to the children's multicultural education.

TEXTURES

Although it may surprise many teenagers, songs do not always consist of vocals backed by guitar, bass, and drum. And every instrumental number does not have to be orchestral. Exposure to varying textures means students will become accustomed to hearing and moving to sounds produced by different instruments.

For example, a piece consisting only of percussion instruments (an African song, perhaps) may produce percussive and staccato movement (punctuated, like bound flow). In contrast, a Brahms violin sonata would generally tend to result in balletic or legato (smooth, like free flow) motion. Other musical textures are created by solo piano, full orchestra, brass, woodwinds, voice alone (a cappella), electronic instruments, acoustic guitar, or harp, to name a few.

Although the children may not enjoy everything you play for them, your enthusiasm, coupled with continued exposure, can make a difference in how they perceive music (see The Magic of Exposure). Even if they never learn to fully appreciate all the music they hear, they will at least make future choices based on knowledge rather than ignorance.

Of course, most of us do not have record collections encompassing all the music suggested here. And we do not have the funds to buy everything we need. But most of us do have local libraries—and librarians whose expertise we can rely on. Take advantage of these resources, keeping variety and quality in mind!

Using Music

There are certainly more ways to incorporate music into the curriculum than can be covered within the scope of this book. For our purposes, we will consider how music, together with movement, can provide the well-rounded introduction to music discussed in Chapter 1. We will look specifically at the musical experiences children should have and the musical elements children should encounter. All these elements can be explored through movement.

Two points must be made in regard to music and the teacher of young children. First, you need not be an expert in the field of music—or have an experienced singing voice—to offer your children valuable musical experiences. Children are not critics, and they will not be judging you on the quality of your singing, instrument playing, or musical creations. Second, you must possess only two qualifications to make music part of your program: a desire to do so and a

THE MAGIC OF EXPOSURE Your children are not going to enjoy all the music you play for them. Like adults, they have musical preferences. In fact, some evidence indicates the musical preferences of 4- to 6-year-olds are fairly set and not easily changed (Schukert & McDonald, 1968). But exposure is a powerful factor in bringing about change, especially if the exposure is coupled with enjoyment.

Several years ago, a teacher at one of my workshops shared a story about her husband with the group. Her husband's profession was installing siding on homes, and for a while, he was working on a home owned by people who loved polkas. Day in and day out, the sound of polkas floated through the windows, exposing him to a style of music he had never paid much attention to. At the end of one day, he went home to his wife and announced, "You know, I *like* polkas!"

More recently, I experienced the magic of exposure firsthand. My own husband, a musician/composer with fairly eclectic musical tastes, suddenly began listening to country music. I was amazed, as this was one style neither of us cared for, but assumed it was just a phase he was going through. Well, this phase did not pass; moreover, he was determined to get me to share his enthusiasm. I dug in my heels and refused to be swayed—until one day in the car an especially beautiful lyric brought a tear trickling out of the corner of my eye. Still, I remained steadfast in my determination—for at least three more days. And then, almost against my will, I found myself tuning in to the country station when Richard was not even in the car! Today it is my favorite kind of music, offering me everything from soulful ballads that tug at the heart-strings to a boogying beat energizing enough to exercise to.

I am sure these two stories do not represent isolated incidents; exposure can make a difference! So expose your students to a wide variety of music. Show them how much you enjoy it all, and you will open whole new worlds for them!

willingness to participate. Remember, the children learn much from your example.

You must also understand the value of repetition. There will be lots of it, whether you plan it or not, and understanding its importance to children will make it easier to accept! Jarnow (1991, p. 25) writes:

A song or album may sound the same to you every time you hear it, but to [a] child, each listening period is another opportunity

Figure 6-2
It is not necessary to be an expert in the field of music—or have an experienced singing voice—to offer children valuable musical experiences.

to gain mastery of it. By hearing the same music over and over again, she absorbs combinations of tones, rhythms, words, phrases, concepts, and emotions . . . [It] takes on an importance akin to that of an old friend who offers reassurance and comfort at each meeting.

Sometimes, children do not like a song the first time they hear it. Only after repeated exposure does it become familiar and "safe" to

DEVELOPMENTAL STAGES OF MUSICAL EXPERIENCES
As with motor development, every child progresses through the stages of musical development at his or her own pace. Although the sequence of developmental stages remains the same for all children, the ages at which they reach and pass through each stage can vary from child to child.

2-Year-Olds

- Use their bodies in response to music, often by bouncing up and down
- Can learn short, simple songs
- Show increasing ability to follow directions in songs
- Respond enthusiastically to favorite songs, often asking to hear them repeatedly
- May sing parts of songs (often not on pitch), but seldom sing with a group
- Enjoy experimenting with sounds, with everything from household objects to musical instruments
- Can discriminate among songs

3-Year-Olds

- Have greater rhythmic ability
- Can recognize and sing parts of familiar tunes, though usually not on pitch
- Make up their own songs
- Walk, run, and jump to music
- Enjoy dramatizing songs

4-Year-Olds

- Can grasp basic musical concepts like tempo, volume, and pitch
- Show a dramatic increase in vocal range and rhythmic ability
- Create new lyrics for songs
- Enjoy more complex songs

- Love silly songs
- Prefer "active" listening (singing, moving, doing fingerplays, accompanying music with instruments)

5- to 6-Year-Olds

- Can reproduce a melody
- Begin to synchronize movements with the music's rhythm
- Enjoy singing and moving with a group
- Enjoy call-and-response songs
- Have fairly established musical preferences
- Can perform two movements simultaneously (e.g., marching and playing a rhythm instrument)

7- to 8-Year-Olds

- Are learning to read lyrics
- Can learn simple folk dances taught by adults
- Enjoy musical duets with friends
- May display a desire to study dance or play an instrument
- Can synchronize movements to the beat of the music
- Can compare three or more sounds

them, rendering it suitable for their approval. Also, some children—toddlers especially—will not sing a song until they have had many chances to just listen. Finally, there will even be times when you instigate the repetition—for example, when a single tune provides examples of two or more musical elements. With each repetition, you can focus the children's attention on yet another aspect of the composition, changing not only the way the children listen but the way they respond in movement.

MUSICAL EXPERIENCES

Five aspects of musical experiences should be part of every child's life: moving, listening, singing, playing, and creating (Haines & Gerber, 1992; Bayless & Ramsey, 1991; McDonald & Simons, 1989).

Of course, there is considerable overlap and interrelatedness among the five aspects. Listening is a part of all musical experiences, but movement can be too. In Chapter 1, we examined the role of movement in the child's general music education. Now, we will look briefly at the role of the other four aspects of musical experiences and how movement can enhance each of them.

Listening.   As mentioned earlier, there is a difference between listening and hearing. The latter requires no concentration; the former does. To really listen, one must pay attention and focus the mind on what is being heard. As Haines and Gerber (1992) tell us, the ability to pay attention is a learned skill, and "active listening" is required if children are to make sense of their environment and communicate with it.

The examples in Chapter 1 of children tiptoeing to soft music and stamping feet to loud music, swaying to a 3/4 meter and skipping to a piece in 6/8 require active—or focused—listening. They must perceive the different dynamics between soft and loud music and must feel the difference in rhythm between the 3/4 and the 6/8 meter. Having heard and perceived, their bodies respond accordingly.

Singing.   The stages of vocal expression, beginning in infancy, move from cooing and babbling to chanting to singing (although the child's early attempts are rarely on pitch).

Because most children love to sing and often break into spontaneous song, music becomes part of every program where there are children, even when it is not consciously planned.

Adding hand motions and other actions to songs can contribute to singing activities, enhancing listening and adding greater meaning to lyrics. Some children are reluctant to sing but are willing to perform such actions and are thus involved in the activity. You should not be concerned, however, if children are unable to sing and move at the same time. Learning to do both simultaneously is a normal developmental process, and teaching the words before adding the actions can help encourage this process (Bayless & Ramsey, 1991).

Playing.   Playing instruments and exploring environmental sound should occur early and often in a child's life. Both contribute to the child's overall music education and provide an awareness of sound that can enrich daily living.

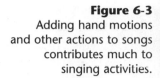

Figure 6-3
Adding hand motions and other actions to songs contributes much to singing activities.

Like singing and moving simultaneously, playing and moving at the same time is more challenging than doing either alone. However, when children reach the stage where they are able to do both, one will enhance the other. For example, marching while playing a rhythm instrument contributes to their enjoyment *and* sense of rhythm.

Creating.   Although others limit this category strictly to the creation of music, Haines and Gerber (1992, p. 13) take a broader view of the creative process in relation to music as a whole. They state:

Figure 6-4
Moving and playing an instrument at the same time is more challenging than doing either alone but children will eventually be able to do both simultaneously.

We believe that every child has the capacity to take the ingredients of music and to make from them a recipe, however simple, that is peculiarly his own, that delights and satisfies him, and that can often be shared with others. To create, the child needs a basic vocabulary of musical experiences and skills. . . . As these are acquired, . . . so the creative acts of music making will appear.

The authors then describe creating through active listening, moving, singing, and playing, lending further evidence to the interrelatedness not only among the five aspects of musical experiences but between the benefits of movement and music education.

LEARNING BY DOING Following a two-hour workshop that was part of a residency at a Maine university, two music majors approached me to say thank you. During the workshop, we had moved to "Robots and Astronauts," contrasting a robot's motions with those of an astronaut floating weightlessly in outer space. It was not until the students had moved to the song, an example of staccato and legato, that they fully understood these two musical terms!

Naturally, I was a bit taken aback by their gratitude. After all, these were music *majors*. They went on to explain, however, that notonly had their professor never asked them to move to examples of staccato and legato (though I cannot imagine why not!), but also she had never even *played* examples. She had merely given them definitions of the terms.

Well, I got over my initial surprise, and I, in turn, have been grateful to those two students ever since. What better testimony could I have received? I then knew for certain if physically experiencing a concept could make such an impression at the university level, then learning by doing was the only answer in early childhood!

MUSICAL ELEMENTS

Some musical concepts are too advanced for young children to grasp. Others are important only to those who go on to study music seriously. But there are many musical elements young children can and should experience, including tempo, volume, legato and staccato, pitch, phrases, form, mood, and rhythm. These can all be explored through movement, offering the children a multisensory approach that gives the concepts greater meaning and makes a longer lasting impression (see Learning by Doing).

A definition of each of these musical elements and a discussion of movement's role in exploring them follows.

Tempo.   Tempo is the speed at which the music is performed, which means this musical element is related to the movement element of time. The best way to introduce tempo is by contrasting the extremes—very slow and very fast. Once children can recognize and move to fast and slow music, you can begin introducing the more challenging concept of the continuum from very slow to very fast and the reverse. *Accelerando* is the term for music that begins slowly and gradually increases in tempo. *Ritardando* indicates a gradually decreasing tempo.

The following are examples of tempo.

Slow.   Possibilities include Pachelbel's *Canon in D-Major,* the first movement of Beethoven's *Moonlight Sonata,* the second movement of Dvorak's *New World Symphony* ("Largo"), and Chopin nocturnes. Also, many New Age recordings consist primarily of slow pieces, as do George Winston's solo piano albums (*Autumn, Winter into Spring, December,* and *Summer*). Another choice is "Slow-Motion Moving," found in the Moving & Learning Series (see Appendix 2).

Fast.   As you know, there is no shortage of fast music. However, if you want to use something other than pop selections, classical pieces include Rimsky-Korsakov's *Flight of the Bumblebee,* Mozart's *The Marriage of Figaro,* and Rossini's *William Tell Overture.* Also, Hap Palmer's *The Feel of Music* includes a song called "Quickly and Quietly."

Slow and Fast.   Several children's recordings offer songs contrasting these two tempos.

1. "Song About Slow, Song About Fast" from Hap Palmer's *Walter the Waltzing Worm*
2. "Fast and Slow March" from Hap Palmer's *Creative Movement and Rhythmic Exploration*
3. "Slow and Fast" from Hap Palmer's *The Feel of Music* (an album that specifically relates the characteristics of music to movement)
4. "The Slow Fast, Soft Loud Clap Song" from *Songs About Me* from Kimbo Records
5. "Moving Slow/Moving Fast" from Rae Pica's *Toddlers Moving & Learning, Preschoolers Moving & Learning, Early Elementary Children Moving & Learning,* and *Let's Move & Learn*
6. "Marching Slow/Marching Fast," also from the Moving & Learning Series

Accelerando.   Strauss' "Acceleration Waltz" is an excellent example of this concept, as are "Beep Beep" (often referred to as "Little Nash Rambler"), a song made popular by The Playmates in the 1950s, and "Getting Fast/Getting Slow" from the Moving & Learning Series. Brahm's "Hungarian Dances" also uses accelerando, ritardando, and abrupt changes in tempo.

Volume. Part of the broader category of dynamics, which also involves the accenting of certain tones, volume refers specifically to the loudness or softness of sounds. According to Haines and Gerber (1992, p. 157), many people incorrectly associate big or high movements with loud music and small, low movements with soft music. However, because volume is better equated with movement's "relative strength or weakness, its firmness or gentleness," this musical element truly goes hand in hand with the movement element of force. When the music is soft, moving with a great deal of muscle tension would be an unlikely response. On the other hand, when the music is loud, it is not likely to conjure up, for example, images of butterflies floating.

Again, the best way to introduce volume is by contrasting extremes. Once the children can move well to loud and soft music, you can begin introducing the continuum from one to the other. *Crescendo* is the term for music that begins softly and gradually gets louder. *Decrescendo* (sometimes called *diminuendo*) refers to a gradually decreasing volume.

Soft. The previous suggestions for slow music are also appropriate here. "Soft Sounds" can be found on *Adventures in Sound,* available from Melody House (Appendix 2). Lullabyes are also excellent examples of soft music, and many recordings available to early childhood professionals are made specifically for "quiet times."

1. "Quiet Times" and "Classical Quiet Times" by Rae Pica and Richard Gardzina (two of the six cassettes in *More Music for Moving & Learning*)
2. Hap Palmer's *Quiet Places* and *Sea Gulls*
3. Joanie Bartels' *Lullaby Magic I* and *Lullaby Magic II*
4. Derrie Frost's *Quiet Time* and *Daydreams*
5. *Quiet Moments with Greg and Steve*
6. *Lullaby Time for Little People, Let's Visit Lullaby Land,* and *Daydreams,* all available from Kimbo Records
7. An entire page of offerings from well- and lesser-known artists in the Educational Record Center catalog

Loud. Again, loud music is easily found. But one piece that children especially enjoy is Tchaikovsky's *1812 Overture.* And *Adventures in Sound* includes "Loud Sounds."

Loud and Soft. Children's songs that offer contrast between these two dynamics include "Soft and Loud," from Hap Palmer's *The Feel of Music;* "Play Soft, Play Loud," from Jill Gallina's *Rockin' Rhythm Band;* "Moving Softly/Moving Loudly," from the Moving & Learning Series; and "The Slow Fast, Soft Loud Clap Song," from *Songs About Me* available from Kimbo.

USING CASSETTES Because teachers can actually see where a song begins and ends, many prefer records to tapes. But there are advantages to using cassettes since records are fast becoming obsolete. Cassettes are sturdier, more child-proof, and last longer. And they are more practical for movement activities because you do not have to worry about a needle jumping or scratching if the movement becomes a bit boisterous. Also, with the advent of dual-cassette players, copying only the songs you need for a particular lesson from a commercial tape to a blank tape is quick and uncomplicated.

Compact discs, of course, are the wave of the future and are the ideal alternative to both records and cassettes. But until they—and their players—become more affordable, most educators will not be using them. Following are some tips to help make using cassettes as painless as possible.

If you are in the market for a new cassette player, be sure to purchase one with a search system (sometimes referred to as cue). With this function, you only have to press "play" and "fast-forward" at the same time and the tape moves quickly ahead to the beginning of the next song. Pressing "play" and "rewind" at the same time reverses the tape to the beginning of the song currently cued-up. Somehow, the cassette player finds the next blank space in the tape! But it is not necessary to understand how it works; you just need to know this feature makes teaching with tapes a lot simpler!

If your tape player does not have the ability to jump to the beginnings or endings of songs but *does* have a counter, you still have an advantage. This feature takes more time initially, but will still make your lessons go smoother.

Once you have selected the songs you want to use for a lesson, rewind the tape(s) they are on. Reset the counter on your player to zero, put the tape in, and fast-forward to the beginning of the first song you plan to use. Write the title of the song on a piece of paper (your lesson plan, if possible), and beside it write the number that appears on the counter and corresponds to the beginning of the song. Then fast-forward (or rewind) to the next song planned for that day's lesson, if it is on the same cassette, once again marking down the number corresponding with its start. If your next song is on a different tape, reset the counter to zero once again before cueing-up the song. You must also remember to reset the counter when it is time to actually play the tapes, or the numbers you have recorded will not correspond to the counter!

One simple—although perhaps not always practical—alternative is to choose only one song per commercial cassette for each lesson and have each song cued-up and ready to play before your lesson begins. This will ensure your students are not standing around, spending valuable time waiting for the music, and becoming more restless by the moment.

Another option, referred to earlier, is copying the songs you need for a single lesson onto a blank cassette, or onto a few, short, blank cassettes. If, for example, you plan to use only two songs in a lesson, you might choose to put them both (one per side) on a five-minute tape (two-and-a-half minutes per side). You could use ten-minute tapes in the same way, or longer cassettes if your lesson plan calls for several songs. (The latter option will only be practical if your tape player has a search system, in which case you will need to leave two to three seconds between songs so the system can find the blank spaces in the tape.) You might even decide to use several five-minute cassettes, each with only one song on it.

If you do your own recording, please remember your children are entitled to *quality* listening experiences. Holding the recorder microphone next to the sound source will *not* suffice, as there will be all kinds of unwanted noise. If you are recording from cassette to cassette, a dual-tape player is the perfect solution. But if you do *not* have a dual-tape player or you are recording from record to cassette, you will have to learn to use the line inputs and outputs on your machines.

Also, name-brand cassettes are worth the additional expense because cheaper tape deteriorates much faster. Sources for short and long blank audio cassettes include the following:

1. Crown Magnetics, Inc.
   1223 Bittner Blvd., Lebanon, PA 17042
   800/736-274-3615

2. Full Compass
   5618 Odana Rd., Madison, WI 53719
   800/356-5844

3. National Audio
   231 West Olive Ave., Burbank, CA 91502
   800/777-3838

4. Polyline Corp.
   1233 Rand Road, Des Plaines, IL 60016
   708/298-5300

5. PolyWest Corp.
   16018 Adelante St., Unit-C
   Irwindale, CA 91702
   818/969-8555

6. Sonocraft
   575 Eighth Ave., New York, NY 10018
   800/274-7666

Finally, although teachers are aware they must occasionally change the needle on a record player and have the player regularly serviced, most are probably unfamiliar with the maintenance required for cassette players.

Since certain parts of the machine are in constant contact with the moving tape, dirt and tape residue accumulate on these parts and decrease the sound quality. To effectively combat this, simply clean the tape heads, pinch roller, and capstans (see Figure 6-5) after ten hours of use, wiping the surfaces over which the tape travels with a small amount of isopropyl alcohol (91%) applied to a cotton swab.

Figure 6-5
Heads, pinch roller, and
capstans should be cleaned
after 10 hours of use.

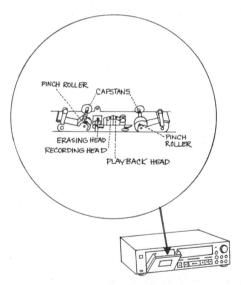

Another option is to buy a commercial cassette head cleaner, available from stores like Radio Shack. Pour the supplied cleaning fluid into a hole on the specially designed cassette and then play and rewind the cassette as you would any other.

Crescendo and Decrescendo.   Ravel's *Bolero* is a classic example of crescendo. From Grieg's *Lyric Suite*, "Norwegian Rustic March" both crescends and decrescends, as does "Getting Louder/Getting Softer" from the Moving & Learning Series.

Staccato and Legato.   Staccato and legato relate to the movement element of flow and are part of the broader category of articulation, which also includes correct breathing, phrasing, and attack. Legato, which corresponds to free flow, indicates the music is to be played without any noticeable interruptions between the notes. In other words, the music flows smoothly. Staccato, on the other hand, is more punctuated and therefore corresponds with bound flow.

Any song you sing with the children can be performed in either manner. You might try a piece like "Twinkle, Twinkle Little Star" to get a feeling for these musical elements. First, sing the song in an easy, flowing manner, demonstrating legato. Then try it in a choppy style, adding brief pauses between syllables, to experience staccato.

Portions of Haydn's *Surprise Symphony* are staccato, while "Aquarium" from Saint-Saens' *Carnival of the Animals* is an example of legato. Pica and Gardzina's "Robots and Astronauts" and "Staccato/Legato," from *Preschoolers Moving & Learning, Early Elementary Children Moving & Learning,* and *Let's Move & Learn* are examples of both elements in one song.

Pitch.   Pitch is the highness or lowness of a musical tone. With this concept the use of high and low movements are most appropriate.

In Haines and Gerber (1992), Haines has written two songs, "High Is Where the Birds Go" and "Low Is Like a Tunnel," to demonstrate the contrast between high and low pitches. The song "High and Low," on cassettes accompanying both *Preschoolers Moving & Learning* and *Early Elementary Children Moving & Learning* moves from low to high pitches and the reverse, and asks children to begin in a crouch, raising and lowering their bodies with the rising or descending pitch.

Phrases.   A phrase is a division of a composition, commonly a four- or eight-measure passage, that represents a musical thought or idea. A musical phrase is similar to a sentence.

Phrases are best introduced to children through listening experiences. By singing a familiar song and pausing between phrases, you can make them aware of this musical concept. Once they grasp it, you can ask them to accompany the song with movement, pausing where you pause. A later, more challenging request would be to have the children change movements or direction at the beginning of each new phrase.

"Row, Row, Row Your Boat" is an appropriate and fairly simple song to begin with, as the first two lines constitute one phrase and the

Figure 6-6
The use of high and low movements are most appropriate for exploring the concept of pitch. Children should first be challenged to raise and lower arms in response to a rising or descending pitch.

second two lines another. Start by singing it at a slow to moderate tempo. Gradually increase the tempo as the children begin to grasp the concept. When the children are ready, play various recordings of the song, finding new ways to challenge your students to match their movements to the phrasing. (Raffi sings this song on *Rise and Shine*.)

Form. Form is the overall design of the phrases that constitute a song's organization and is often designated by letters (e.g., "Row, Row, Row Your Boat," "Pop Goes the Weasel," and "Ring Around the Rosie" are in an AB form; because of its repeating final phrase, "Twinkle, Twinkle Little Star" is in an ABA form). Once young children have become familiar with musical phrases, they will eventually begin to notice repeated or contrasting phrases and to respond accordingly with movement. Repeated phrases call for repeated movements, while contrasting phrases call for contrasting movements (e.g., strong and light, small and large, or forward and backward).

Mood. Feelings are often conveyed by music, and very often, young children are the first to pick up on the mood of a song and to respond to it. This ability seems to be due to the as-yet-undiminished sensitivity of the young child's ear and to her or his as-yet-undiminished willingness to show a physical response.

Children frequently react to happy music by skipping, dancing, running, twirling, bouncing up and down, or performing similar movements. Lively pieces like Bach's "Musette in D-Major" from his *Anna Magdalena Notebook* can evoke such actions. By contrast, Samuel Barber's 20th-century classical piece, "Adagio for Strings," which has a sad feeling to it, usually quiets the children and slows their movements. Brahms' "Lullabye" is a perfect example of a song that conveys a particular mood; it makes its listeners want to sleep!

Your role as teacher is to make the children aware of how different music affects them. Talk to them about how certain songs make them feel, the musical elements involved, and why they think the songs evoke the responses they do.

Rhythm. Rhythm, according to McDonald and Simons (1989, p. 290), is the "organization of sounds, silences, and patterns into different groupings." Within the context of this book, rhythm will consist of the concepts of beat and meter.

The beat in music is the recurring rhythmic pulse that is heard (and felt) throughout a piece. However, very young children are not developmentally ready to match their movements to a beat. Rather, when you first introduce this concept to your students, you should synchronize instrumental accompaniment to *their* rhythm. Watch them walk, run, gallop, and execute other locomotor skills, and then, on a hand drum, beat out a rhythmic pattern that matches their movements. When they change their movements, change the beat. They will soon realize they are responsible for creating rhythm. Eventually, they will be able to move "at one" with the beat of a musical accompaniment.

Meter indicates a basic group of beats. When a meter is stated, the top number refers to the number of beats in a measure; the bottom number indicates the *kind* of note that equals one beat. For example, 2/4 means there are two *quarter*-notes per measure, with 6/8 indicating six *eighth*-notes to the measure.

The four most frequently used meters in Western music—2/4, 3/4, 4/4, and 6/8—were defined in Chapter 2. The 4/4 meter is certainly the most common in Western music, particularly in Top 40 songs. You will find 2/4 used in polkas and many marches, with 3/4 most often found in waltzes but also used for ragtime. Many folk songs and some marches are written in 6/8.

Because some interesting qualities also can result from exposure to less common meters, it is worth the effort to track down pieces in 5/8, 7/8, 5/4, and others. Hap Palmer's "Five Beats to Each Measure," from *The Feel of Music,* and "A Not-So-Common Meter" (in 7/8), from *Preschoolers Moving & Learning,* are examples of lesser used meters.

Figure 6-7
Tapping out the beat with rhythm sticks.

THE COPYRIGHT LAW AND YOU The reproduction of sound recordings is so simple—and is so often done—teachers may not realize that by copying records or tapes (or parts of them), they are sometimes violating the copyright protection granted to the authors of "original works of authorship." In most cases, it is illegal to duplicate sound recordings. There are exceptions, however, and some of them deal specifically with educators.

Section 107 of the Copyright Act covers "fair use." Although the courts have considered and ruled on the doctrine many times, there is still no real definition of fair use. But four factors should be considered in determining whether or not a particular use is fair:

1. the purpose and character of the use, including whether such use is of commercial nature or is for nonprofit educational purposes;

2. the nature of the copyrighted work;

3. the amount and substantiality of the portion used in relation to the copyrighted work as a whole; and

4. the effect of the use on the potential market for or value of the copyrighted work.

Although it may seem, based upon the first point, duplicating recordings can be justified if "for nonprofit educational purposes," it is actually the fourth point teachers must seriously consider. In guidelines established regarding the educational uses of music, copying "for the purpose of substituting for the purchase of music" is specifically prohibited.

In other words, if you are recording musical selections from a previously purchased record or tape onto blank cassettes for teaching purposes (as discussed in Using Cassettes), you are not violating the law. If, on the other hand, you are duplicating music to share it with a friend or colleague so she will not have to buy the record or tape, that is "substituting for the purchase of music." (Artists like Hap Palmer and Ella Jenkins do not earn salaries for the time they spend creating music. Instead, they earn royalties based on the number of their cassettes and records sold. So substituting for the purchase of music does have an effect on the potential market, as stated in 4, above).

Does copying a musical selection or two from a library-owned recording constitute "fair use"? If you have tried and failed to locate a particular recording owned by a library or colleague, is there no possibility of purchase?

These—and others like them—are questions only you can answer, based on your understanding of the copyright law and fair use.

For more information, write Register of Copyrights, Copyright Office, Library of Congress, Washington, D.C. 20559. You can speak to an information specialist by calling 202/707-3000 from 8:30 a.m. to 5 p.m. ET, Monday to Friday. Or you can call the Forms Hotline (202/707-9100) 24 hours a day to request circulars. Circular No. 1 has information pertaining to copyright basics, and Circular No. 21 is entitled "Reproduction of Copyrighted Works by Educators and Librarians."

How can you manage to expose your students to all these musical elements? The answer is simple: When you choose varying styles, periods, nationalities, and textures to play, you will automatically be exposing the children to different tempos, volumes, articulations, pitches, phrases, forms, moods, and rhythms. Think *variety,* and plan to provide your students with a well-rounded music (and movement) education. As pointed out at the beginning of Chapter 6, you do not have to worry if you have never had any music education yourself. As you can see, "There is a great deal that the 'ordinary,' nonmusical caregiver or teacher can do" (Wolf, 1992, p. 56).

Sample Activities

Chapter 1 provided suggestions for exploring rhythmic groupings and common meters. Statues was described as an activity that develops listening skills and helps children differentiate between sound and silence. Because the music stops and starts, Statues also furnishes experience with the movement element of flow. You can also use the activity to explore musical phrases, by always pausing at the end of a phrase. Finally, you can explore the concept of mood with the children by choosing a piece with a different feeling every time you play Statues.

As a movement resource, this text cannot fully develop the subject of music in early childhood. To make music a larger part of your curriculum, refer to the many fine music resources listed throughout the book and in Appendix 2. The following activities, however, can offer you a starting place, provide you with examples of the benefits of using movement and music to enhance one another, and spark ideas of your own.

CONTRASTING ELEMENTS

To provide your students with understanding of the musical element of tempo and the movement element of time, choose one of the songs suggested that contrasts slow and fast music (or choose two separate pieces—one slow and one fast). Challenge the children to move in the following ways to each tempo:

1. Slow
    Gentle swaying
    Walking as though through mud (or deep snow or peanut butter)

Pretending to be a turtle or a snail

Pretending to be on film that is being played in slow motion

2. Fast

Running lightly (in place or around the room)

Skipping

Pretending to be a bumblebee

Pretending to be a race car

You can use a similar activity to enhance understanding of the musical element of volume and the movement element of force. Select a single song that contrasts volumes, or two separate pieces, and ask the children to move in the following ways to each volume:

1. Soft

Tiptoeing

Patting the floor or body with hands

"Floating"

Swaying gently

Pretending to be a cat stalking prey

2. Loud

Stamping feet

Slapping the floor

Marching

Rocking forcefully

Moving like a dinosaur

EXPLORING CONTINUUMS

To familiarize your students with the concepts of accelerando and ritardando, tell the children they are going to play Follow the Leader, with you as leader. Then, accompanying yourself on a hand drum (one beat for every step you take), begin to move very slowly. Gradually accelerate your tempo until you are going as fast as you want the children to go, then begin to gradually slow down—until you are back to the original speed. (Be sure to vary your movements by changing levels, directions, pathways, and if possible, body shape.)

Once the children are familiar and comfortable with this activity, try it to music that accelerates, retards, or does both. Eventually, choose children to act as leaders.

You can explore the concepts of crescendo and decrescendo with this same activity. To do so, your steps and drumbeats will have to be very soft at first, gradually increasing (and then decreasing) in intensity.

DO-RE-MI

Sing the scale to the children, explaining how each successive note is higher in pitch than the previous one. (If possible, also demonstrate on a keyboard, or show the scale written on a staff so the children will *see* as well as hear the rising and descending pitches.)

Ask the children to sing the scale with you. (Depending on your group, you may want to limit their initial experiences to a rising scale only, later exploring it in both directions.) Then ask them to place

Figure 6-8
Once the children can successfully demonstrate pitch with their arms, challenge them to show you a rising or descending pitch with the whole body.

their hands in their laps, raising them a little bit higher with each note you sing (and lowering them if you are also singing the descending scale).

Once the children have grasped the concept, challenge them to demonstrate with their whole bodies, beginning close to the floor and getting as close to the ceiling as possible (and the reverse).

You can vary this activity to also explore other concepts. The simplest variation is to change the tempo at which you sing or play the scale. You can alternately sing or play in staccato and legato styles. You can add the concepts of crescendo and decrescendo by beginning at either a soft or loud volume and gradually increasing or decreasing it. Eventually, if the children have become very familiar with the notes of the scale, you can sing them out of order, challenging them to demonstrate with their arms or whole bodies whether a note was higher or lower than the previous one.

BODY SOUNDS

Children love to make noise, and making noise with their bodies can be a great introduction to rhythm.

Talk to the children about the sounds of a cough, sneeze, yawn, hiccup, giggle, and snore. Then ask them to show you how each sound makes their bodies move. You can ask them either to incorporate the sound into their movement or to perform silently. Also, challenge them to perform repetitions—not just one—of each movement.

Next (or in another lesson), ask them to discover how many sounds they can create with different body parts (e.g., hands, feet, tongue, and teeth). Can they move about the room, accompanying themselves with any of these sounds? Can they use different parts of the room (floor, walls, chalkboard) to create new sounds?

IDENTIFYING HOUSEHOLD SOUNDS

Bayless and Ramsey (1991) suggest making a tape of household sounds, which the children are asked to identify. To vary and extend this listening activity, ask the children to *show* rather than tell you the source of the sound. In other words, they must depict, through movement, the item creating the sound.

Possibilities include keys rattling, washing machine, electric can opener, blender, broom sweeping, clock ticking, toast popping out of the toaster, vacuum cleaner, door closing, garbage disposal, telephone ringing, and water running.

"IF YOU'RE HAPPY"

Teach the children the first verse of "If You're Happy." Then ask them for suggestions of other movements to demonstrate happiness (e.g., tap your feet, wave hello, nod your head, etc.). Do they want to sing about other emotions (e.g., sad, tired, angry, hungry)? What motions and facial expressions go along with them?

The lyrics of the first verse are:

> If you're happy and you know it
> Clap your hands (clap, clap)
> If you're happy and you know it
> Clap your hands (clap, clap)
> If you're happy and you know it
> Then your face will surely show it
> If you're happy and you know it
> Clap your hands (clap, clap).

INTRODUCING INSTRUMENTS

Choose three or four instruments to introduce to the children. Show them one at a time, demonstrating how each is held and played. Then, after producing a sound with each instrument, ask the children for suggestions of a movement to accompany the sound (e.g., they might suggest shaking for a maraca, tiptoeing for a triangle, or stamping feet for a drum). Select one movement for each instrument.

Next, randomly play the instruments one after another, challenging the children to do the appropriate movement with each sound.

When the children are familiar with each instrument's sound, put the sounds on tape, varying the order, so they cannot see the instrument being played. Choosing the correct movement will then require truly focused listening and recognition.

Substitute and add instruments to keep increasing the challenge.

Key Points

- Teachers can make significant, simultaneous contributions to the movement and music education of children.
- Almost any music can be "movement" music.

- Quality and variety must be part of the child's musical experiences, which include listening, singing, playing, creating, and moving.
- Teachers can ensure variety by exposing children to different styles, periods, nationalities, and textures of music.
- Teachers and caregivers do not need a music background to successfully incorporate music into the program.
- Repetition plays a vital role in the music education of young children.
- The musical elements children should explore through movement include tempo, volume, staccato and legato, pitch, phrases, form, mood, and rhythm.

Assignments

1. List typical objects in the children's environment that can serve as sound sources.
2. Watch a group of children during music activities and note your observations regarding the difference between *hearing* and *listening*.
3. Experiment with music of different textures and notice its effect on the movements of a child or group of children.
4. Introduce a new song or style of music to a group of children and note the effect of exposure and repetition upon several individuals.
5. Research the music collection at your local library. What does it offer?
6. Cite an example not given in this chapter of a way in which music and movement enhance each other.

References

Andress, B. (1973). *Music in early childhood.* Reston, Va.: Music Educators National Conference.

Andress, B. (1991). From research to practice: Preschool children and their movement responses to music. *Young Children, 47*(1) 22–27.

Bayless, K. M., & Ramsey, M. E. (1991). *Music: A way of life for the young child.* New York: Merrill.

Church, E. B. (1992). *Learning through play: Music and movement.* New York: Scholastic.

Haines, B. J. E., & Gerber, L. L. (1992). *Leading young children to music*. New York: Merrill.

Jarnow, J. (1991). *All ears*. New York: Penguin.

McDonald, D. T., & Simons, G. M. (1989). *Musical growth and development: Birth through six*. New York: Schirmer.

Schuckert, R. F., & McDonald, R. L. (1968). An attempt to modify the musical preferences of preschool children. *Journal of Research in Music Education, 16*(1) 39–44.

Wolf, J. (1992). Creating music with young children. *Young Children, 47*(2) 56–61.

PART THREE

Facilitating Movement Experiences

Teaching Methods

CHAPTER 7

*T*raditionally, physical education has been taught with a command style of instruction. With this direct style, the teacher decides on the subject matter and how it is to be learned, and demonstration-and-imitation is the primary mode of instruction. When movement education, which calls for more indirect teaching styles, began gaining popularity, many traditional physical education specialists took exception to its philosophy. So, for a long while, the field consisted of two "warring" factions who each believed its was the only way physical education should be taught.

Today as Gallahue (1993) reports, the focus has shifted from the method to the learner. As a result, specialists on both sides of this issue have come to realize the value to learners of both direct and indirect styles of instruction. The question is no longer *Which is the best teaching style?;* rather, it is *Which style is best for the subject matter being taught?* The two styles are now blended into most movement programs, and a striking difference between *physical* education and *movement* education no longer exists.

In Chapter 7, we will review three teaching methods—the direct approach, guided discovery, and exploration—and their roles in implementing movement programs for young children.

The Direct Approach

Some subjects simply lend themselves to a direct method of teaching. In the human movement field, ballet is a prime example. This dance style consists of positions and steps that must be executed exactly;

TEACHING STYLES: ADVANTAGES AND DISADVANTAGES

Advantages of the Direct Approach
• Uses time efficiently
• Produces immediate results
• Produces uniform movement
• Teaches children to replicate movements
• Teaches children to follow directions
• Lends itself to immediate evaluation

Disadvantages of the Direct Approach
• Does not allow for creativity and self-expression
• Does not allow for individual differences in development and ability levels
• Focuses on the product vs. the process

Advantages of Indirect Approaches
• Stimulate cognitive processes and enhance critical thinking
• Develop self-responsibility
• Broaden the movement vocabulary
• Reduce fear of failure and produce a sense of security
• Allow for individual differences among children
• Allow for participation and success for all children
• Develop self-confidence
• Promote independence
• Develop patience with oneself and one's peers
• Lead to acceptance of others' ideas

Disadvantages of Indirect Approaches
• Require more time
• Require patience and practice by the teacher

expecting students to "discover" these positions and steps through exploration is a preposterous notion. A command style that uses demonstration and imitation is the only teaching method that makes sense for ballet.

Although movements as codified as ballet steps are developmentally inappropriate for young children, learning by imitation is sometimes appropriate—and necessary. Modeling is often the best means of helping toddlers and some children with special needs achieve success. Also, as children mature, they have to learn to follow directions and to physically imitate what their eyes are seeing (e.g., when they must print the letters of the alphabet as seen in a book or on a chalkboard). According to Mosston and Ashworth (1990, p. 45), "Emulating, repeating, copying, and responding to directions seem to be necessary ingredients of the early years." They cite Simon Says, Follow the Leader, and songs accompanied by unison clapping or movement as examples of command-style activities enjoyed by young children. Mirroring and fingerplays are among the other activities they suggest fit in the same category.

As mentioned, command-style teaching—the most direct approach—depends on the teacher making all or most of the decisions regarding what, how, and when the students are to perform (Gallahue, 1993). This task-oriented approach requires the teacher to provide a brief explanation, often followed by a demonstration, of what is expected. The students then perform accordingly, usually by imitating what was demonstrated.

One advantage of this approach is that results are produced immediately. This, in turn, means teachers can instantly ascertain if a child is having difficulty following directions or producing the required response. For example, if the class is playing Simon Says and a child

Figure 7-1
One of the advantages of the direct approach is that results are produced immediately, allowing teachers to determine if a child is having difficulty following directions or producing the required response.

repeatedly touches the incorrect body part, the teacher is at once alerted to a potential problem, possibly with hearing, processing information, or simply identifying body parts.

The efficient use of time is often seen as the most significant advantage of the direct approach. Naturally, it takes much less time to *show* the children how movements are to be performed than to let them discover how. And lack of time is a common problem in early childhood and elementary classrooms, where so many subjects must be covered, and in physical education classes.

Mosston and Ashworth (1990) cite achieving conformity and uniformity as two of the behavior objectives—and perpetuating traditional rituals as one of the subject-matter objectives—of the command style. For example, if "rituals" like the Mexican Hat Dance and the Hokey Pokey are to be performed in a traditional manner, with all the children doing the same thing at the same time, the only expedient way to teach these activities is with a direct approach, using demonstration and imitation. Although conformity and uniformity are not

Figure 7-2
Demonstration and imitation are necessary instructional tools in perpetuating traditional rituals like the Hokey Pokey and the Mexican Hat Dance.

conducive to creativity and self-expression, they are necessary to the performance of certain activities. And because such activities are fun for young children and can produce a sense of belonging, they should play a role in the movement program.

Of course, the early childhood years are commonly regarded as the best period for development of creativity. A major disadvantage of this instructional method is that a direct approach fails to allow for creativity and self-expression. Another disadvantage is the failure of the direct approach to recognize individual differences in development and ability among children. Finally, this style focuses on learning certain skills but not on the learning process itself (Gallahue, 1993). The direct approach, therefore, is the teaching method least used in movement education programs.

TO PARTICIPATE OR NOT TO PARTICIPATE When conducting workshops, one of the most common questions I am asked by teachers and caregivers is, "Should I participate in the movement activities myself?"

The question is a logical—and important—one. After all, if diverse responses are the goal of exploration, teachers do not want the children imitating them—which is exactly what the children will do if the teacher models.

My answer, however, is yes and no. As mentioned, modeling can be helpful (even necessary) with toddlers, children with special needs, and some children who are reluctant to participate. And certain activities—like fingerplays and songs requiring identical responses from the children—are meant to be demonstrated.

When self-expression and inventiveness are sought—as when the children are asked to assume crooked shapes—the teacher should refrain from participating so the children can find their *own* responses. Then, by providing feedback that welcomes a variety of responses to every challenge, she can encourage diversity and ensure that even children who were initially afraid of "getting it wrong" or "looking foolish" will realize that it is okay to be themselves.

Exploration is *not* an invitation for teachers to simply sit back and issue challenges. They may not have to model, as required by the direct approach, but they should *always* enthusiastically participate in every activity—even if only with vocal and facial expression.

Guided Discovery

Teaching methods that require students to problem solve are called indirect styles and are typically considered *child-centered,* as opposed to teacher- or task-centered. Movement education incorporates two indirect styles: exploration, which involves divergent problem solving and is discussed in the next section; and guided discovery, which involves convergent problem solving.

With guided discovery, the teacher has a specific task in mind (e.g., teaching the children to perform a step-hop, or that a wide base of support provides the most stable balance). He or she then leads the children through a sequence of questions and challenges toward discovery of the task. This process, while still allowing for inventiveness and experimentation, guides the children as they *converge* on the right answer.

One example (see Cognitive Development, Chapter 1) is a series of questions that leads the children toward discovery of a forward roll. As another example, if a teacher wanted primary-grade children to learn to execute a step-hop, he or she would first have to choose how to accomplish this: either use the direct approach and simply *show* the children how to do it, or help the children discover it for themselves. With the latter approach, he or she might issue the following challenges:

- Practice walking forward and in place with short springy steps.
- Hop in place and forward, first on one foot and then the other. Change feet often.
- Make up your own combination of walks and hops, using any number of each. Try it first in place and then moving forward.
- Make up a combination of walks and hops that fits into 2 counts, slightly accenting the first count.

The only correct response to the last challenge is a step-hop, as the step is more accented than the hop. Once some students have discovered this, they can be used for demonstration purposes, with the rest of the class asked to try it that way. They will then have successfully "discovered" the step-hop.

Although guided discovery does take longer than the direct approach, many educators feel its benefits far outweigh the time factor. With problem solving in general (convergent or divergent), the children are not only learning skills but are learning *how* to learn. Critical thinking skills are enhanced as the children make choices and decisions (Buschner, 1990; Kirchner et al., 1970). And, according to Klein (1990, p. 27), "Most learning takes place when young children are actively engaged in . . . experimenting, experiencing, and raising their own questions and finding answers."

Self-responsibility is another positive result of indirect teaching styles. Students are involved in the learning process and, therefore, acquire a sense of self-direction. They are able to take ownership of their responses and, ultimately, to develop confidence in their ability to discover and solve problems (Gallahue, 1993; Pica, 1993; Klein, 1990).

Problem solving also helps broaden the children's movement vocabulary. In addition, it reduces fear of failure and thus produces a sense of security that motivates the children to continue experimenting and discovering. Guided discovery, specifically, enables children to find the interconnection of steps within a given task.

When using guided discovery with children, it is important to accept all responses—even those considered "incorrect." For example, if you have asked a series of questions designed to ultimately lead to execution of a forward roll and some children respond with other rolls, these responses must also be recognized and validated. They can then be given more time to "find another way"; or the teacher can continue, asking even more specific questions, until the desired outcome is achieved.

One important tip is the teacher should never provide the answer (Graham, 1992; Mosston & Ashworth, 1990). If the answer is given in the beginning, the discovery process is no longer possible (one cannot discover what one already knows). If, following a convergent problem-solving process in which the children do not discover the expected solution, the teacher ultimately gives the answer anyway, the children will expect this and will be less enthusiastic about exploring possible solutions themselves. Graham (1992, p. 129) also maintains that, because "wonder and curiosity are valuable mental processes," there is no harm in concluding a lesson in which the children have yet to discover the solution.

Two valuable problem-solving tools (whether it be convergent or divergent problem solving) are demonstrations and verbalization, which give the children two other ways to experience movement. Although demonstrations should not be overused, selecting some children to occasionally demonstrate, or asking half the class to perform for the other half (thus alleviating self-consciousness), gives them the opportunity to *see* movement as well as experience it physically. Also, as in the step-hop, demonstrations can be used in guided discovery to help lead the children toward the solution.

Verbalization is a tool you will use more often than the children do, since you should teach them the names of the movements and the movement elements *as they are experienced*. However, you can also occasionally ask the children to evaluate what they have seen during a demonstration (ensuring a positive evaluation by asking what they *liked* about what they saw) or to describe a movement they have just

Figure 7-3
Occasionally selecting children to demonstrate can help lead toward the solution sought in guided discovery and offers children the opportunity to see movement.

performed or a body position they have just assumed (e.g., "I'm sitting cross-legged, and my hands are on my shoulders"). This technique gives them a chance to form mental images of what they are doing.

For the teacher, of course, the most difficult part of guided discovery is designing the questions and challenges that will lead students to the desired outcome. Mosston and Ashworth (1990) suggest two

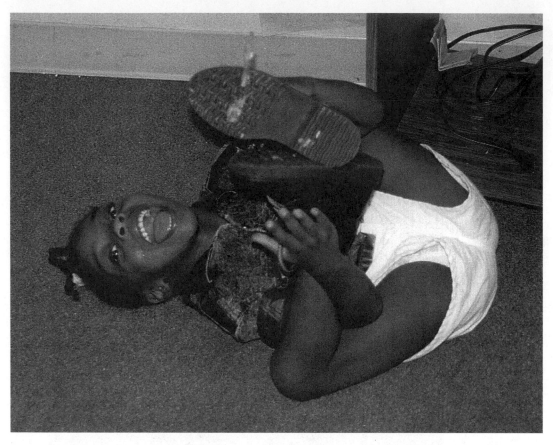

Figure 7-4
Children should occasionally be asked to describe a movement they have just performed or a body position assumed. This child might describe herself as being in a small round shape.

techniques for achieving this. One is to work backward, beginning with the final question—the one that will produce the targeted answer. The preceding question can then be identified, and so on, back to the first question. The second technique is to write a series of commands, as though a direct approach were going to be used. The commands can then be converted to questions.

Although the direct approach is perhaps more appropriate for the youngest of young children, because it relies on convergent problem solving, guided discovery is most suitable for older preschoolers and primary-grade students.

THE SLANTED ROPE Mosston (1966) introduced the Spectrum of Teaching Styles, a model of instructional styles based on the premise that the teaching/learning process involves decisions made by the teacher and the learner before, during, and after learning. Since then, he and his colleagues have continued to expand, modify, and improve his original ideas (Franks, 1992). Mosston's Spectrum is now accepted and applied throughout the United States and throughout the world in gymnasiums and classrooms, and is the model for the teaching styles described in Chapter 7.

Mosston and Ashworth (1990) present an example of guided discovery that has become so well known most physical educators need only to hear "slanted rope" to recognize the principle being discussed. The example is repeated here to help you better understand guided discovery.

In the episode cited, the "target," or the principle the teacher wishes the students to discover, is *inclusion* (how to include everyone in the same task). The teacher begins by asking two children to hold a rope for the others to jump over. They respond by holding the rope horizontally at about hip level. The teacher then asks them to decrease the height so everyone can be successful.

When all the students have jumped the rope, the teacher wonders aloud what they should do with it now. Inevitably, the children clamor to raise it. The rope is raised a little, and the jumping resumes. Again, the teacher asks what they should do, and again the answer is the same.

This process continues until some children become unable to clear the height of the rope. Instead of eliminating these children, as would have been the case in traditional situations, the teacher stops the process and explains the result here has been *exclusion* rather than inclusion. "What can we do with the rope," he asks, "to include everyone?"

Usually the children offer two possible solutions: (1) hold the rope high at the ends and let it dip in the middle; and (2) slant the rope so one end is high and the other is low. The teacher encourages them to try the second alternative. The rope is slanted, and the students prepare to jump over it—with each student selecting the height at which he or she can jump successfully! The guided discovery process has led the children to the solution sought: inclusion for all.

Exploration

Exploration is developmentally appropriate for young children and, therefore, should be the teaching method most widely used in their movement programs. Because it results in a *variety* of responses to each challenge presented, it is also known as divergent problem solving. For example, a challenge to demonstrate crooked shapes could result in as many different crooked shapes as there are children responding. A challenge to balance on two body parts can result in one child balancing on the feet, another balancing on the knees, and still another—who may be enrolled in a gymnastics program—performing a handstand.

This approach to instruction is perhaps best described by Halsey and Porter (1970, p. 76):

Figure 7-5
Exploration or divergent problem solving results in a variety of responses being given to each challenge.

[Movement exploration] should follow such basic procedures as (1) setting the problem, (2) experimentation by the children, (3) observation and evaluation, (4) additional practice using points gained from evaluation. Answers to the problems, of course, are in movements rather than words. The movements will differ as individual children find the answer valid for each. The teacher does not demonstrate, encourage imitation, nor require any one best answer. Thus the children are not afraid to be different, and the teacher feels free to let them progress in their own way, each at his own rate. The result is a class atmosphere in which imagination has free play; invention becomes active and varied.

In other words, you will present your students with a challenge (e.g., "show me how tall you can be," or "find three ways to move across the balance beam in a forward direction"), and the children will offer their responses in movement. You can then issue additional challenges to continue with and vary the exploration (*extending* the activity), or you can issue follow-up questions and challenges intended to improve or correct what you have seen (*refining* responses).

Extending exploration is a technique that requires time, patience, and practice by the teacher—and therein lies one drawback to this instruction method. When teachers are not yet comfortable with all the aspects of exploration, they may hurry from one movement challenge to the next. Not only does this leave the class with too much time and nothing left to do, but also it fails to give children ample experience with the exploration process and with the movements being explored.

Generally, three aspects comprise extending activities. The first involves using the elements of movement to vary the way skills are performed. As discussed in Chapter 3, the elements of space, shape, time, force, flow, and rhythm are considered adverbs used to modify the skills, which are regarded as verbs. An example was given there of using the movement elements to change the locomotor skill of walking. As another example, if the children are asked to make themselves tall, the teacher might challenge them to change the body's *shape* while still being tall. If the children are challenged to move across the balance beam in a forward direction, the teacher could suggest they try it at different levels (the element of *space*), to encourage them to consider forms of locomotion other than walking.

Second, extending movement experiences, as you might assume, entails reacting to the children's responses. In the last example, the teacher simply may have wanted the children to experiment with different levels in space. *Or* he or she may have seen they were walking across the beam and, based on that, chose that particular question to inspire other forms of locomotion. Another possible follow-up is the simple challenge to "find another way."

Figure 7-6
A challenge to move across the balance beam in a forward direction is likely to result first in a simple walk. The teacher can elicit more creative responses by suggesting the children find another way or by encouraging them to use specific elements of movement. For example, the teacher might suggest this child make a different body shape the next time she moves across the beam.

Mosston and Ashworth (1990) recommend that finding new ideas continue until a pause occurs. Until then, they assert, even though participants are producing divergent responses, they are mainly "safe," or "common," responses—the product of recalling past experiences. Less common responses begin to appear after the first pause. If the teacher persists in encouraging additional exploration beyond the second and third pauses, learners may often appear physically uncomfortable but eventually cross the "discovery" or "creativity threshold." New solutions evolve as divergent production continues.

The third aspect of extending responses puts parameters on the exercise. For instance, again using the example of children crossing the beam in a forward direction, the teacher can further limit the possible responses by suggesting they do so with more than two body parts touching the beam, or in a rounded shape. Mosston and Ashworth (1990, p. 252) write:

> As the new combinations evolve, cognitive inhibition is reduced and often disappears in such episodes. It changes to joyful production. Episodes like this often evoke laughter, enjoyment, and intense interest in the process. . . . People realize in a very short time that they can, indeed, produce new ideas in an area in which they were not accustomed to do so.

Of course, teachers must design problems and suggest extensions that are developmentally appropriate and relevant to the subject matter and to the children's lives (Cleland, 1990). They must also provide the encouragement children need to continue producing divergent responses. Encouragement should consist of *neutral* feedback (e.g., "I see you're moving across the beam on your tummy," or "your three-point balance uses two hands and a foot").

Although teachers must be careful to accept all responses, there will come a time when they wish to help the children improve, or refine, their solutions. If, for example, the teacher has challenged the children to make themselves as small as possible and some children respond by lying flat on the floor, he or she should not observe aloud that this response is incorrect. In fact, it is not necessarily incorrect; it is simply another way of looking at things (see sidebar Expect the Unexpected). But the teacher, wanting the children to truly experience a small shape, might issue the further question, "Is there a way you can be small in a rounded, or curled, shape?" Although the teacher has helped the children improve their responses, individuality is not stifled, as diverse solutions are still possible (e.g., some will make a small rounded shape in a sitting position, some will lie on their sides, others on their backs, etc.).

Too often in the past, physical education was taught "to the middle." In other words, teachers chose activities that could be handled by children of average ability. Though the system worked well for these children, students who were not as skilled were constantly lagging behind, resulting in a vicious cycle of failure that eroded their confidence and led to more failure. Highly skilled children, on the other hand, were not sufficiently challenged and became increasingly bored.

EXPECT THE UNEXPECTED As pointed out in Chapter 2, children do not think the same way adults do. First, their cognitive processes differ from ours. But they also tend to be much more creative than we are—perhaps because their creativity has yet to be invalidated, or perhaps because they have yet to experience situations in life that limit their idea of how things should be! Whatever the reason, adults conducting movement activities with young children should be aware of this so they can expect the unexpected!

Graham (1992) offers examples of what I mean. He warns teachers that while some children count a single foot as a one-part balance, some count each toe, meaning a balance on one foot is actually a balance on *five* body parts. Some children count the bottom as one body part; others count it as two.

He relates the story of asking a class to make narrow shapes with their bodies and questioning the response of one child who was standing with feet and arms spread wide. He was looking at it the wrong way, the child informed him, and instructed him to look at it from the side. He did and discovered that, from the side, her shape was indeed narrow!

I once asked a class to make themselves as tall as possible. Some children stretched tall, but did not rise onto the balls of their feet. I wanted to encourage them to try *all* of the possibilities, but did not want to state specifically that they should get on tiptoe. Instead, I asked, "Is there some way you can use your feet to make you even taller?" In my mind, there was only one possible response to this question. But one little girl did not see it the way I did: She lifted her entire leg as high as she could and called out, "I don't think so!"

But a story from a first-grade teacher perhaps best demonstrates the uniqueness of each child's interpretation of our world and words. Christmas was approaching, so this teacher had asked the children to draw pictures of someone associated with the holiday. As she walked up and down the aisles, glancing admiringly at the children's works, she came across one she found puzzling. The drawing was of a heavy-set man, but he was obviously not Santa Claus. "And who is this?" she asked the boy who had drawn him. "That's round John virgin," he replied.

Exploration allows *every* child to participate and succeed at her or his own level of development and ability. In addition to the self-confidence and poise continual success brings, this process promotes independence, helps develop patience with oneself and one's peers and allows the acceptance of others' ideas. Perhaps most importantly for young

OBSERVATION AND EVALUATION Because movement education primarily uses indirect approaches to instruction, teachers often believe observation and evaluation are not critical because students have little chance of responding incorrectly. But the efficient execution of motor skills is the ultimate goal of any movement program and the determining factor in deciding how far and how fast to progress through the program.

Evaluation methods vary greatly and are essentially a matter of personal choice. Some teachers feel more comfortable with checklists; others, with rating scales. Godfrey and Kephart (1969) created checklists for 18 movement patterns. Schurr (1980) provides her own example of a skill checklist based on the identification of the presence—or lack thereof—of pattern elements and possible deviations. Most major physical education textbooks include descriptions and/or illustrations of the progression of motor skills from initial to elementary to mature stages.

Using these resources as guides, you can devise your own checklists or rating scales to evaluate the motor patterns of the children in your movement program.

children, exploration leads them to the discovery of the richness of possibilities involved in the field of human movement.

Key Points

- Today's physical and movement education programs consist of a blend of direct and indirect teaching styles.
- The three teaching methods most appropriate for use in movement programs for young children are the direct approach, guided discovery, and exploration.
- The direct approach is also referred to as the command style of teaching. In this task-oriented approach, the teacher tells the

children what to do and how to do it, and the children comply. This method is most appropriate when working with toddlers and special-needs children requiring modeling and when uniform movement is the goal.

- Guided discovery engages the learner in convergent problem solving and is most appropriate for older preschoolers and primary-grade students.
- Stimulation of cognitive processes and an enhanced sense of self-responsibility are two benefits of problem solving in general. Problem solving also helps broaden the movement vocabulary, reduces fear of failure, and motivates children to continue.
- In guided discovery, the teacher should never provide the answer.
- Demonstrations and verbalization offer children other ways in which to experience movement and are two valuable tools in the problem-solving process.
- Exploration should be the teaching method most widely used in movement programs for young children. It is also known as divergent problem solving because it results in a variety of responses being given to each challenge.
- The three aspects of extending activities are (1) using the elements of movement to vary the way in which skills are performed, (2) reacting to the children's responses, and (3) putting parameters on the exercise.
- Teachers must design problems and suggest extensions that are developmentally appropriate and relate to the subject matter and to the children's lives.
- Because it allows every child to participate and succeed, exploration increases self-confidence and poise, enhances feelings of independence, helps develop patience with oneself and one's peers, and leads to acceptance of others' ideas.

Assignments

1. List at least five activities, in addition to those cited in this chapter, that are best presented with a direct approach. Write an explanation of why these particular activities lend themselves to a direct approach.
2. Choose a movement skill that could be taught to young children using guided discovery, and prepare a list of questions (working backward or beginning with commands, if necessary)

that can guide the children to the "discovery" of the skill. Justify in writing your choice of guided discovery as the method for teaching this skill.

3. Choose a movement theme that lends itself to exploration and create a set of challenges and questions that encourage the children to fully explore it. Justify your choice of exploration as the teaching method for this theme.

4. Imagine that you have asked the children to explore moving through general space in a backward direction. Create a list of common responses and then devise follow-up questions and challenges that extend the activity and encourage uncommon solutions. What if some children were actually demonstrating *sideward* movement instead? What questions and challenges could you pose to correct (refine) that response?

References

Buschner, C. A. (1990). Can we help children move and think critically? In W. J. Stinson, ed., *Moving and learning for the young child* (pp. 51–66). Reston, Va.: American Alliance for Health, Physical Education, Recreation, and Dance.

Cleland, F. (1990). How many ways can I . . . ? Problem solving through movement. In W. J. Stinson, ed., *Moving and learning for the young child* (pp. 73–76). Reston, Va.: American Alliance for Health, Physical Education, Recreation, and Dance.

Franks, B. D. (1992). The spectrum of teaching styles: A silver anniversary in physical education. *Journal of Physical Education, Recreation, and Dance, 63*(1), 25–26.

Gallahue, D. L. (1993). *Developmental physical education for today's children.* Dubuque, Iowa: Brown & Benchmark.

Godfrey, B. B., & Kephart, N. C. (1969). *Movement patterns and motor education.* N.Y.: Appleton-Century-Crofts.

Graham, G. (1992). *Teaching children physical education.* Champaign, Ill.: Human Kinetics.

Halsey, E., & Porter, L. (1970). Movement exploration. In R. T. Sweeney, ed., *Selected readings in movement education* (pp. 71–77). Reading, Mass.: Addison-Wesley.

Kirchner, G., Cunningham, J., & Warrell, E. (1970). *Introduction to movement education.* Dubuque, Iowa: Brown.

Klein, J. (1990). Young children and learning. In W. J. Stinson, ed., *Moving and learning for the young child* (pp. 23–30). Reston, Va.: American Alliance for Health, Physical Education, Recreation, and Dance.

Mosston, M. (1966). *Teaching physical education.* Columbus, Ohio: Merrill.

Mosston, M., & Ashworth, S. (1990). *The spectrum of teaching styles: From command to discovery*. White Plains, N.Y.: Longman.

Pica, R. (1993). Responsibility and young children: What does physical education have to do with it? *Journal of Physical Education, Recreation, and Dance, 64*(5), 72–75.

Schurr, E. (1980). *Movement experiences for children*. Englewood Cliffs, N.J.: Prentice-Hall.

CHAPTER 8

Creating and Maintaining a Positive Learning Environment

Many teachers and caregivers hesitate to make movement part of their programs because, when they think of *children* and *movement* in the same sentence, they immediately form a mental image of children "bouncing off the walls." It is certainly a realistic concern. Movement activities can generate a lot of energy, and unless the instructor has some idea of what to expect and how to deal with all that potential energy, the "walls" will certainly see much action.

Managing the movement session must be handled with special care. You do, however, have a few factors in your favor from the outset. Most important, a success-oriented program is likely to have few behavioral problems. After all, a child who is experiencing success is not likely to want to wreak havoc on the class. The same is true of the child who is actively involved and interested (Fowler, 1981). Movement exploration lends itself to successful, active involvement.

Common sense also plays a vital role. Beginning at the beginning (wherever the children are, developmentally) and building from there with a logical progression of skills will ensure the children are challenged yet not overwhelmed. Not only can we expect greater success from children who are asked merely to build on their earlier successes, but also we can expect greater *response* from them as well.

Another commonsense guideline offered by Cherry (1971), is planning movement activities when the children are well rested and not overstimulated from another activity. She suggests immediately following rest or story time, or shortly after their arrival in the morning.

Because success is always the goal in movement exploration, the class atmosphere is critical. As Miller (1995, p. 267) points out, "It is more nurturing and less stressful for everyone involved if adults focus on setting the stage for proper behavior, rather than on reprimanding children after they behave improperly."

Chapter 8 focuses on teaching tips that can help set the stage for what can be stress-free movement experiences. There are no surefire recipes for success, however. So, should you find yourself doing everything right and still running into occasional stumbling blocks, we also examine dealing with the nonparticipant and with disruptive behavior. Finally, we conclude with a discussion of the role of relaxation in the movement program.

Tried and Tested Teaching Tips

If you have conducted movement sessions with young children, you may have had an experience or two when a group became so unmanageable you wondered if there was not an easier way to make a living! These suggestions (offered in no particular order) cannot guarantee you will never again be tempted to look for a less challenging job, but they can help make the task easier and more satisfying for you and your young students.

ESTABLISH RULES

Creating and maintaining a positive learning environment does not mean an absence of ground rules. Children need rules and guidelines and, once established, they must be enforced consistently.

Most rules for young children are related to safety (Essa, 1995)—certainly true where movement is concerned. At the beginning of the movement program, you must determine what guidelines are needed to keep the children safe (e.g., no participating in stocking feet, no gum allowed during movement). However, you (with help from the children) may want to establish additional guidelines to ensure movement activities run smoothly. Graham (1992) suggests, once you have outlined these "protocols" you *practice* them with the children just as you would practice other skills.

The next two rules should have a place in every movement program.

Rule #1: We will respect one another's personal space.   At first, this may be difficult to enforce, especially with the youngest students because they generally enjoy bumping into one another. So it is your challenge to make it a goal for the children to avoid colliding or interfering with one another.

You can accomplish this by practicing the personal space activities outlined in Chapter 3. Also, ask the children to space themselves evenly at the beginning of every movement class. Reinforce the idea of personal space, encouraging the children to imagine they are each surrounded by a giant bubble. Whether standing still or moving, they should avoid causing any bubbles to burst.

Another image that works quite successfully is that of dolphins swimming. Children who have seen these creatures in action, either

Figure 8-1

Carpet squares provide tangible evidence of personal space and, placed strategically throughout the room, can help the children develop a respect for one another's space.

at an aquarium or on television, will be able to relate to the fact that dolphins swim side by side but never get close enough to touch one another. The goal, then, is for the students to behave similarly. (Showing pictures of dolphins swimming together could be helpful.)

Rule #2: We will participate with as little noise as possible.
Naturally, you cannot expect movement exploration to take place in silence. But you should not have to raise your voice or shout to have your challenges, directions, and follow-up questions heard.

Establish a signal to indicate it is time to stop, look, and listen ("Stop, look at me, and listen for what comes next"). Choose a signal the students have to watch for (two fingers held in the air or the time-out sign from sports) or something they must listen for (a hand clap, a strike on a triangle, or two taps on a drum).

With some classes, either possibility works well. With other, more challenging groups of children, you will probably find an audible signal more effective than a visual one. After all, children can avoid looking if they want to, but they cannot avoid hearing! If you do choose an audible signal, you should be aware your voice may not be the best choice because it is heard so often by the children. Also, be sure your signal is a quiet one. A whistle, for example, is generally not suitable because it can be heard above a great deal of noise. (It also has certain authoritative connotations.)

Whatever the signal, it is not unreasonable to expect the children to be stopped, looking, and listening within two to four seconds of having seen or heard it. And you should have to give the signal only once (Graham, 1992).

Children are generally willing to follow rules as long as they know what is expected of them and the rules have significance for them (Woods, 1993; Essa, 1995; Miller, 1995). Do not simply tell the children what the rules are; tell them why the rules are necessary.

ESTABLISH BOUNDARIES

A movement space needs to be open and uncluttered if the children are to participate without distraction or injury. Although a spacious gymnasium is the ideal location for movement, such a space is not always (or even often) available.

If you are working in a classroom, the space must be prepared in advance and clearly defined. Helping prepare the space can be part of the protocol you establish with the children, who are usually quite happy to lend a hand. (Clements and Schiemer [1993] suggest asking the children to pretend to be construction workers, Santa's elves, or Snow White's dwarves as they help rearrange the furniture.) Certain areas and objects (the art corner or the piano, for instance) should be designated as off-limits.

Boundaries are still required even if you have access to a gym or an exceptionally large room, as *too much* space can be overwhelming to some children. You also do not want the children roaming so far from you and the group they are either unable to hear you or no longer seem to be part of the activity. Masking tape, rope, or plastic cones (available from suppliers like Flaghouse and Bell [Appendix 2]) are examples of materials that can be used to outline the boundaries.

Figure 8-2
Use items like plastic cones to mark boundaries in an especially large area. And do not hesitate to ask the children to assist you in helping to prepare the space.

USE POSITIVE CHALLENGES

If you assume the children are capable of handling your challenges, they are more likely to *be* capable. For example, "Find four ways to . . ." assumes students can find several ways to respond. Similarly, "Show me you can . . ." implies you *know* they can. Conversely, if you present challenges by asking, "Can you . . . ?" you are implying a choice, and many preschoolers will simply say no.

Also, young children love to show off—to display their abilities—especially for their teachers. Therefore, if you introduce challenges with phrases, "Let me see you . . ." or "Show me you can . . . ," the children will *want* to show you they can. Positive challenges are a simple technique but amazingly effective, especially when used in tandem with positive reinforcement.

MAKE CORRECTIONS CREATIVELY

Singling out children who have responded incorrectly (for, say, *hopping* when the challenge was to *skip*) causes embarrassment and self-consciousness. And those feelings do not lead to future success. On the other hand, you cannot help children improve if you simply ignore their incorrect responses.

The alternatives are to (1) ask children responding correctly to demonstrate, (2) describe the differences between skipping and hopping, and (3) reissue the challenge to give them another chance to succeed. If the same children still respond incorrectly, you are alerted to an area requiring attention. However, you should offer the attention when it is possible to provide it privately and positively. (Do not forget some children will be unable to perform certain skills because they are not developmentally ready.)

Not squelching the children's creativity and self-expression is also extremely important. When you have asked the children to create new words to a song, for example, you must accept their creations even if they do not rhyme or fit the rhythm of the melody. Correcting and adjusting their lyrics will invalidate their offerings and give them the sense they can succeed only with adult intervention.

In a similar vein, Sullivan (1982, p. 18) gives the example of a child who responds to a challenge to make a high shape by climbing onto a table. She suggests, "Rather than negate the inventiveness, you can acknowledge the cleverness and add '. . . with both feet on the ground' to the next instruction."

USE HONEST PRAISE AND POSITIVE REINFORCEMENT

Praise the children freely, but only when it is deserved. Children can sense when adults are not being honest, and the praise will cease to have any meaning for them if it is not sincere. On the other hand, an overabundance of praise can turn children into praise addicts who need more and more every day to maintain their self-esteem (Miller, 1995).

Perhaps one of the most difficult habits to overcome is moralizing. We often say, "Good girl" or "Good boy," which implies the child is good because she or he is doing what we asked. We might also say, "That was a good jump," when it would be more appropriate to describe the jump as high, low, light, or heavy.

Miller (1995) suggests *recognition* and *encouragement* as alternatives to false praise and value judgments. By *describing* the children's responses with enthusiasm and respect, we validate them and encourage original solutions.

THE POWER OF POSITIVE REINFORCEMENT Everyone who has spent any time working with young children has seen evidence of the power of positive reinforcement. Young children thrive on praise and positive reinforcement from adults; and if you offer it honestly (while simultaneously ignoring negative behavior), all your students will strive to hear it from you.

I once had a 5-year-old vehemently balk at my suggestion that the children stand straight and tall, loudly proclaiming that she was not "in the army!" I was stunned by her statement, and my initial, gut reaction was to confront her. Instead, I regained my composure, looked quickly at another child who was complying with my suggestion, and praised that child's excellent posture. When I looked back at my little "dissenter," she was also standing straight and tall, wanting to receive the same congratulations—which I, of course, sincerely offered!

USE YOUR VOICE AS A TOOL

This is a straightforward, commonsense suggestion. If you want the children to move slowly, *speak* slowly. If you want them to move quietly, *speak* quietly. Also, just as it is possible to catch more flies with honey than vinegar, you can attract and maintain more attention with a lower volume than with a higher one. Children are far more likely to react to a whisper than to a yell.

Remember, too, although you should present your challenges enthusiastically (and with the proper *facial* expressions as well), if you maintain a fever pitch of enthusiasm, the children will become overstimulated.

One additional thing you can do with your voice is to say the children's names often. A child's name is special; when a child hears it being said in a positive way by an adult, he or she receives recognition and reassurance (Essa, 1995).

USE FAMILIAR IMAGERY

If you ask a group of 4-year-olds to walk as though anxious or disillusioned, you will probably get no response. But if you ask them to walk as though mad or sad, you *know* they are able to respond because every 4-year-old has felt those emotions! Similarly, if you ask preschoolers to walk like different animals, you know an elephant is more familiar than, for instance, an anteater.

This is not to say, however, your children must be *personally* acquainted with every object, creature, or situation you ask them to portray. Young children enjoy pretending to walk weightlessly on the moon because they have witnessed such scenes on television and in the movies, they have heard about it in books and discussions with their teachers, and they have wonderful, vivid imaginations. So if you want to use imagery with which the children are not personally familiar, you must first *make* it familiar to them. Otherwise, your challenges will be met with blank stares.

MONITOR ENERGY LEVELS

As mentioned, movement activities can generate an abundance of energy, and too much energy can result in frustrating, unproductive, unmanageable movement sessions. Too little energy can have comparable results, as tired children tend to display irritability and off-task behavior.

Alternating lively and quieter activities usually is enough to ensure against frenzy and fatigue. Sullivan (1982) suggests other contrasts: difficult movements with easy movements, high with low, loose with tight, and big with little to keep everyone involved. She also proposes bringing the children to the ground with commands to freeze and collapse or sit to achieve a calming effect.

Whether you choose to alternate contrasting activities, channel excess energy into gross motor activities (Cherry, 1971), use grounding techniques, or simply stop at the first sign of fatigue, having some plan beforehand can help guarantee you will not have to end your movement sessions abruptly, feeling helpless and frustrated.

Figure 8-3
Alternating lively and quieter, difficult and easy, or high and low movements can help ensure against both frenzy and fatigue.

BE FLEXIBLE

Dancers and gymnasts, of course, are known for the flexibility of their bodies. But that is not the flexibility being referred to here. Rather, you need a flexibility of mind and spirit to accept that your lessons will not always go exactly as you have outlined them on paper. We are, after all, talking about young children and movement exploration.

In monitoring the class' energy levels, for instance, you may suddenly find it necessary to veer from your original course to either excite or calm the children. Perhaps nothing you planned is interesting to a particular class on a particular day, forcing you either to improvise or go to another lesson plan entirely. Also, young children have wonderful ideas of their own—ideas that would never occur to you. If you can be flexible enough to sometimes explore the possibilities presented by the children, not only will this help personalize the lessons for them but also they will gain greater confidence in their creative abilities.

What About the Nonparticipant?

Sometimes, especially at the beginning, some children do not want to participate in the movement program. There can be several reasons for this and you must determine why they choose to sit out, initially eliminating any physical problems as the cause.

Although sad, some children refuse to take part out of a fear of looking foolish or "being wrong." Even at a very young age, not only is this fear already instilled in some preschoolers but also it is quite powerful.

For these children, observing your success-oriented movement experiences is the key to unlocking their fear. They *will* notice, for example, that eight of their classmates have responded to your challenge in eight different ways—and you are praising each and every response. They will begin to realize that there is no right or wrong; and with a bit of gentle coaxing and positive reinforcement, these children can eventually be encouraged to join in.

Some children are genuinely shy and only need time to get used to the idea of moving with the rest of the group, while others will require specific encouragement from you or another adult. Essa (1995, pp. 325–27) outlines a series of steps to help children overcome shyness at group time:

- sitting with the child for a few minutes at least once a day and reading her a story,
- inviting another child to join the activity,

- gradually adding more children to the small group,
- continuing the daily small-group activities while also making an effort to involve the child in total group times, and
- reinforcing any involvement in group activities.

Sometimes merely standing near the shy child as you facilitate movement activities, offering occasional smiles or gentle touches, is the only encouragement you need to offer. At other times, you may have to physically (but gently) initiate the child's participation by taking his hands in yours and moving them accordingly, or sitting behind the child and rocking her with you to the rhythm of the music. Positive reinforcement of any level of participation will do much to contribute to the shy child's confidence. For example, if you have asked the children to freeze and the nonparticipant is sitting particularly still, you can use him as an example of stillness. If you have

Figure 8-4
Sitting and reading with a child for a few minutes a day and gradually adding more children to the small group can help children overcome shyness at group time.

Figure 8-5
Sometimes the close proximity and participation of an adult can encourage reluctant children to join in.

asked the children to move just one body part and the nonparticipant raises an eyebrow, you can acknowledge her "response."

At the other extreme is the child who uses nonparticipation as a way of getting adult attention. If that is the case, Essa (1995) suggests ignoring all nonparticipation and offering reinforcement only when the child is involved in group activity, using a process of "successive approximations." At first, you reinforce the child when he is observing the activity of others. When the child consistently watches, you move on to the next step, which is reinforcement as the child moves physically *closer* to the group. Once the child is fully involved, you can gradually decrease the amount of reinforcement, offering only as much as you offer the children who are participating.

Whatever the reason for the lack of involvement, nonparticipants must not be forced to join in, as this can place undue emotional stress on them. You can insist, however, that they not be allowed other classroom activities, like reading or playing with blocks, during the movement session. Instead, they must take on the role of audience. Not only does this involve them to a certain extent, but also it ensures they are gaining something from the experience as children can absorb much from watching movement. Occasionally, you may even be pleasantly surprised to learn from a parent that a child who is

Figure 8-6
Whatever the reason for the lack of involvement, nonparticipants should not be forced to join in. Instead, they can take part as members of the "audience."

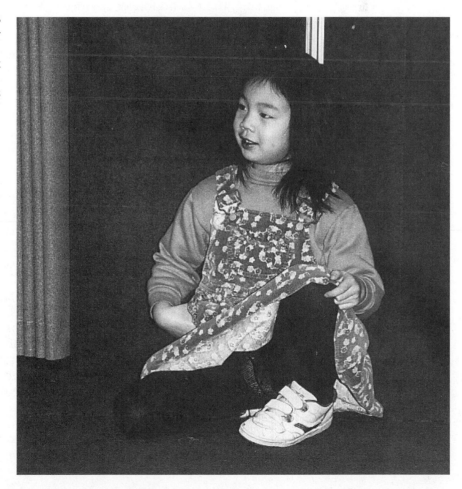

merely watching at school or day care is imitating everything she sees in the privacy of her own home.

What About Disruptive Behavior?

Disruptive behavior is another tactic children use to receive attention from adults; for some, even negative attention is better than none at all. And, unfortunately, because disruptions are annoying, distracting, and sometimes harmful, children causing them often do get more attention than those who are behaving well.

Essa (1995) and Miller (1995) agree ignoring the behavior is generally an effective policy when it is simply annoying or mildly distracting. Because the child does not receive the attention he or she is seeking, there is no longer any need to continue the behavior. Sometimes the child's focus can be redirected elsewhere; for instance, a child making noise stamping her feet can be asked to demonstrate tiptoeing or other substitutes for the stamping.

Essa and Miller believe, however, when the disruptive behavior is harmful to the child or others, it must be stopped immediately. Sometimes a single warning, issued firmly but gently, is enough to end the behavior. Miller (1995, p. 269) suggests undivided attention involving eye contact, a body position at the child's level, appropriate touch, and use of the child's name: "A half-hour of nagging and threatening from across the room will not have the impact of one quiet statement made eye-to-eye, using the child's name."

If, after one such warning, the harmful behavior continues, the child should be removed from the group (calmly and without anger) to allow for a cooling-off period (for the child and the teacher).

Philosophies regarding time-out specifics vary. Graham et al. (1993) suggest the time out last until the child comes to you and explains why he was asked to sit out; Gallahue (1993) suggests questioning the child about the reason for the isolation and how it can be prevented in the future. Essa (1995), on the other hand, contends the child knows the reason and no further discussion is necessary. Graham et al. (1993) also recommend time out for the remainder of the class should the child misbehave again, but French et al. (1990) feel exclusion for longer than five minutes is less effective than shorter periods. (Also, be aware some children will be disruptive to get out of class; thus, time out gives them exactly what they wanted.)

How you handle time out has to be a personal choice. Experts generally agree, however, once a child is asked to sit out she should be ignored. Also, time out must be used *sparingly* or it becomes an ineffective management technique.

Figure 8-7
Although philosophies regarding the use and specifics of "time out" vary widely, the experts all agree this management technique must be used sparingly.

The Role of Relaxation

Teachers are often surprised by the idea of relaxation as part of a *movement* program. But there are many good reasons why every movement session should include relaxation exercises.

When used alternately with vigorous activities, quieter activities can help establish a pace that assures there will be no "wall-bouncing." Relaxation gives children the opportunity to experience motionlessness and an understanding of its contrast to movement. It helps prepare children for slow and sustained movement, which requires greater control than fast movement. And whether the children are going to another subject, to lunch, or home at the end of your movement session, it is always a good idea to wind them down a bit before sending them on their way.

Relaxation exercises offer many other benefits to young children. If you use imagery to promote relaxation, you enhance their ability to imagine. If you use music, you expose them to the world of quiet, peaceful music. Most important, relaxation is a learned skill; and with stress so much a part of our society and our children's lives today, it is a greatly needed skill. Jacobsen (1973), a leading authority in relaxation techniques, believes tension control can help children learn better. Cherry (1981, Preface) says simply that relaxing can make "serenity" a part of children's lives, helping them learn "they can be in control of their own bodies and feelings rather than having to let their bodies and feelings control them."

Following are four suggestions for promoting relaxation. Cherry (1981) offers dozens of others.

Images.   What comes to mind when you think of rag dolls, cooked spaghetti, or soggy dishrags? Limp! Show the children a rag doll or a

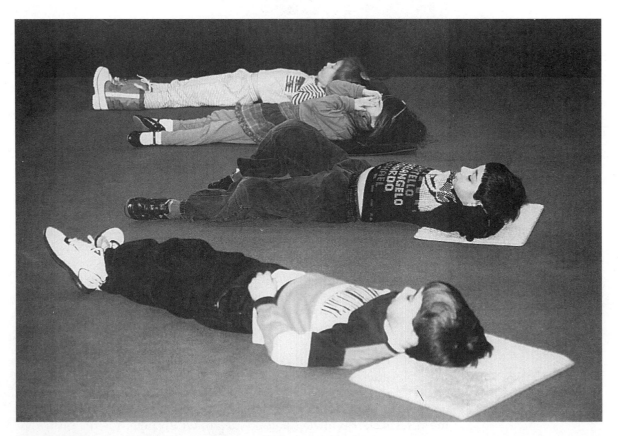

Figure 8-8
Relaxation exercises will benefit both the children and the movement program.

wet dishrag. Talk to them about the difference between uncooked and cooked spaghetti. Then ask them to pretend to be one of these objects.

You can also paint a picture in their minds. Ask them to lie on the floor and imagine, for example, they are at the beach. Talk to them (softly!) about the warmth of the sun, the cool breeze, and the gentle sounds of the waves and the gulls circling overhead. Do not be surprised if a few of them drop off to sleep.

Melting.   Melting is a wonderful slow-motion activity with which to end a movement session. Discuss how slowly ice cream cones, snow sculptures, or ice cubes melt. Then ask the children to stand and demonstrate one of these possibilities.

Balloons.   To promote deep breathing, you can ask the children to expand (by inhaling) and contract (by exhaling) like balloons, alternately (and slowly) inflating and deflating. Initially, you can demonstrate with an actual balloon to help make this image more vivid.

Feeling Calm/Feeling Nervous.   This activity (from Pica, 1991, pp. 12–13) is appropriate for early elementary children.

Background Information.   *Calm* . . . is a very relaxed feeling—like that experienced just before falling asleep at night. At those times, muscles feel loose and "liquid." Other times when children might have experienced calmness include while sitting by a lake, observing a bird soar through the sky, or watching the sun set.

What are some times when the children have felt nervous? Nervous is a combination of scared and worried. Have they ever worried it might rain on the day of a big outing? Have they ever lost sight of parents in a big store and felt nervous until spotting them again? How did their muscles and bodies feel at those times? Were they loose or tense? Ask them to show you.

Activity.   The children are going to experience the differences between feeling calm and feeling nervous at various levels in space. They begin standing. When you say *calm,* the children should make their bodies as relaxed as possible. When you say *nervous,* they should tense up. (Vary the time between verbal cues. Also, remember the quality of your voice is very important; it should sound like the word you are saying.) Repeat this process with the children kneeling, sitting, and finally, lying down.

Using Music.   Because music is mood-altering, it offers wonderful possibilities for relaxation. Chapter 6 lists examples of slow and soft pieces, as well as children's recordings made especially for resting or quiet times. These are some of your best choices for relaxation, along with certain classical and New Age compositions.

Choose only those selections you have previously heard and found to be suitably relaxing, asking the children to lie or sit comfortably with eyes closed, sometimes listening to the music in general and at others listening specifically for sounds or elements you have asked them to identify.

Of course, you can also use peaceful music in conjunction with imagery or deep-breathing exercises.

Key Points

- A success-oriented movement program has fewer behavior problems because children experiencing success are less likely to want to disrupt the class.
- The two rules that should be part of every movement program are (1) we will respect one another's personal space; (2) we will participate with as little noise as possible.
- Boundaries are necessary in small, cluttered spaces as well as large, open spaces.
- Positive challenges and creatively offered suggestions contribute to the children's confidence.
- Describing the children's responses with enthusiasm and offering positive reinforcement are more meaningful and encouraging to the children than insincere or vague praise.
- Too little, as well as too much, energy can result in off-task behavior. Alternating contrasting activities helps keep the pace manageable.
- The first step in dealing with the nonparticipant is determining why the child is not taking part. Different measures are taken for the shy child and the child using nonparticipation to get adult attention.
- Ignoring disruptive behavior is the most effective technique.
- Relaxation has many benefits to offer the movement program and children in general.

Assignments

1. List the rules you feel would be especially important in conducting a successful movement program. Provide justification for each.

2. List phrases (e.g., "Well done!") that do not include the word *good* and can be used for positive reinforcement.
3. Observe a movement session, noting the pace and the participation level. Are all the children taking part? If there are nonparticipants, are they observing? Can you get a sense of the reason(s) for their lack of participation? Are some children displaying disruptive behavior? What do you think is the cause? How does the instructor handle it?
4. Determine a policy for time out. Cite the reasons behind your decisions.
5. Create four or five activities you could use to promote relaxation.

References

Cherry, C. (1971). *Creative movement for the developing child.* Carthage, Ill.: Fearon.

Cherry, C. (1981). *Think of something quiet.* Carthage, Ill.: Fearon.

Clements, R. L., & Schiemer, S. (1993). *Let's move, let's play: Developmentally appropriate movement activities for preschool children.* Montgomery, Ala.: KinderCare Learning Centers.

Essa, E. (1995). *A practical guide to solving preschool behavior problems.* Albany, N.Y.: Delmar.

Fowler, J. S. (1981). *Movement education.* Philadelphia: Saunders College.

French, R., Silliman, L., & Henderson, H. (1990). Too much time out. *Strategies, 3*(3), 5–7.

Gallahue, D. L. (1993). *Developmental physical education for today's children.* Dubuque, Iowa: Brown & Benchmark.

Graham, G. (1992). *Teaching children physical education.* Champaign, Ill.: Human Kinetics.

Graham, G., Holt/Hale, S., & Parker, M. (1993). *Children moving: A reflective approach to teaching physical education.* Mountain View, Calif.: Mayfield.

Jacobsen, E. (1973). *Teaching and learning new methods for old arts.* Chicago: National Foundation for Progressive Relaxation.

Miller, D. F. (1995). *Positive child guidance.* Albany, N.Y.: Delmar.

Pica, R. (1991). *Special themes for moving & learning.* Champaign, Ill.: Human Kinetics.

Sullivan, M. (1982). *Feeling strong, feeling free: Movement exploration for young children.* Washington, D.C.: National Association for the Education of Young Children.

Woods, A. M. (1993). Off to a good start: Establishing a productive learning environment. *Teaching Elementary Physical Education, 4*(4), 8–9, 11.

PART FOUR

Movement and Music
Through the Day

Movement Across the Curriculum

*A*lthough, technically, the phrases *whole language, integrated curriculum, interdisciplinary approach,* and *child-centered teaching* have different meanings, they do have several things in common. They are among the most often used buzzwords in the educational field today—frequently the topics of sessions at educational conferences and articles appearing in professional publications. All, essentially, call for the teaching of concepts as part of a *whole,* rather than as separate pieces of information under segregated study units; and all embrace the idea of the whole child.

What is meant by the "whole child?" Simply put, children are thinking, feeling, moving human beings who learn through their senses. An increasing knowledge of learning styles has made us aware some children grasp concepts most easily through sounds and words (auditory learners), others through what they see (visual learners), and still others through bodily experiences (kinesthetic learners).

Perceptual-motor theorists feel certain movement is essential to a child's learning process. Unlike cognitive development, which requires children to use and process abstract information (using words and/or numbers), perceptual-motor development involves "the concrete, physical dimensions of the environment" (Williams, 1983, p. 10), as when a child is asked to deal with pencils, scissors, balls, bats, and so forth.

In addition, Gardner (1983) has helped us recognize the variety of intelligences each individual possesses: linguistic, logical/mathematical, musical, spatial, interpersonal, intrapersonal, and *bodily/kinesthetic.* The last, involving movement, is the intelligence that allows our bodies—or parts of our bodies—to solve problems, create, and

MORE ABOUT PERCEPTUAL-MOTOR FUNCTIONING Williams (1983) defines the focus of perceptual-motor development as "the development of the child's capacity to make sensory and motor decisions and to use feedback to modify and/or eliminate errors from his behavior and from these decision-making processes" (p. 9).

A typical example of perceptual-motor functioning is that of a child preparing to catch an approaching ball. The first thing the child must do is receive and process sensory information. In this case, the child takes in information through the eyes (the visual sense) regarding factors such as the size and distance of the ball and the speed of its approach. This information is then integrated with knowledge acquired from similar past experiences, enabling the child to decide what needs to be done to catch the ball. Once the decision is made, a motor response follows. The final step in the process involves information feedback that tells the child whether or not the motor response was appropriate. If the ball was caught successfully, this feedback will help ensure success in later catches. If the attempt was unsuccessful, the feedback will inform the child that some modification must be made next time. In either instance, learning will have taken place.

This same process occurs anytime a child is asked to deal with his physical environment, whether it is catching or kicking a ball or cutting out or coloring pictures in a book. But it also teaches the child not to touch a hot stove more than once and that lemons are sour. For example, in the latter case, the child could not know for certain lemons are sour unless she physically experienced it; in this instance, the sensory information would have been received through the mouth (the sense of taste). Once this sensory information reaches the brain, it is given meaning, based on previous information, and called perception. Thus, a link exists between perception and cognition. Perceptual-motor theorists believe, though it may be indirect, there is also a link between moving and learning—"that how an individual moves, how he perceives his surroundings, and his ability to learn are all somehow interrelated and interdependent" (Lerch et al., 1974, p. 5).

discover. Gardner suggests that the "whole person" possesses all seven intelligences in varying degrees.

Unfortunately, although the concept of the whole child has existed for years, many teachers still fail to acknowledge the *moving* part of the child—the kinesthetic mode of learning, or the bodily/kinesthetic

SEVEN KINDS OF SMART An excellent introduction for the general reader, to Gardner's theory of multiple intelligences, is Armstrong (1993). This easy-to-read book begins with a basic overview of the multiple-intelligence theory and then defines each of the seven primary intelligences first identified by Gardner. The book also includes checklists for determining strongest and weakest intelligences and practical suggestions for developing all seven.

In the preface, Armstrong says his interest in exploring the seven kinds of smart began after he had worked for several years as an elementary school teacher and became "disenchanted with the way parents and teachers all too often plucked the learning potential from blossoming children by focusing too much attention on words and numbers at the expense of other gifts and talents" (p. 5). It's his hope that knowledge of the various intelligences can help prevent the loss of further potential!

intelligence. Methods abound for learning through the eyes and ears—discussion, books, chalkboards, audiovisual equipment, and, more recently, videos and computers. But little planning and few equipment purchases serve the physical senses (Hendricks & Hendricks, 1983; Rowen, 1982; Werner & Burton, 1979). As Hendricks and Hendricks so aptly put it, "Kinesthetic learners have typically gotten the short end of the slide rule in schooling" (p. 4).

To help correct this imbalance, movement must become a greater part of the learning process. If education is to serve all children, *movement* education must play a role in whatever approach is adopted, whether it is considered whole language, integrated, interdisciplinary, or simply child-centered.

Making movement part of the learning process, however, does not serve only kinesthetic learners. Every child has the capability for multimodal learning; many, in fact, including those thought to be low-achieving, retain more information when it is introduced through multiple senses (Isenberg & Jalongo, 1993; Fauth, 1990). Likewise, Gardner (1983) contends, although individuals have their strengths and weaknesses among the seven intelligences, each person does possess—and can further develop—all seven.

Werner and Burton (1979, pp. 1–2) offer six reasons why physical activity is an effective learning medium.

1. Children more readily attend to the learning task. . . . When children are physically active, they tend to be totally involved

in the learning experience. This assists them in focusing on the relevant attributes of the learning task and helps prevent their attention from being distracted by extraneous factors.

2. The children are dealing with reality. The facts are tangible. An action-oriented learning task provides direct rather than vicarious experience. The children actually manipulate objects or situations. This enables them to see the facts applied and the principles in operation. They do not just read about the content—they experience it.

3. It is a process approach in which development of the affective domain is a primary concern. Affective development is enhanced because the children must closely attend to the stimulus message and actively respond to it. The movement response is both natural and pleasurable and therefore acts as a positive reinforcer. This promotes development of positive attitudes toward the learning process and the particular content being learned.

4. Action-centered learning helps compensate for some of the sensory deficiencies inherent in sedentary activities in which only cognitive operations are employed. When children are physically active, they receive sensory input from their tactual and kinesthetic senses. This makes learning a multisensory experience in which they are feeling as well as observing.

5. It is results-oriented. Each learning activity culminates in an observable goal having been attained. Thus the children experience immediate rather than delayed gratification.

6. It provides an incentive for self-directed learning. The learning process is exciting and satisfying. This has a tendency to promote participation in learning activities that are self-initiated.

Movement also facilitates class management. Children are not known for their ability to sit still, yet in most elementary schools (and even in some preschools), they are expected to remain motionless at desks for lengthy periods. Not only does this make concentration difficult, but also it often causes children to act out—if not in the classroom then on the playground, when the long-awaited recess presents an opportunity to break free. At the other extreme, Hendricks and Hendricks (1983) and Gilbert (1977) attest to the "sense of community" and the "atmosphere of cooperation" generated by allowing children to move in the classroom.

Furthermore, movement activities provide teachers an effective means of evaluation. While the traditional question-and-answer method does not always reveal those students who have failed to grasp the concept under discussion, movement experiences allow the teacher to immediately detect those students who do not understand (Gilbert, 1977).

Typically, early childhood and early elementary curriculum includes experiences in seven content areas: art, language arts, mathematics, music, physical education, science, and social studies (see Figure 9-1). Since music has already been covered in Chapter 6 and this entire text focuses on physical education experiences, Chapter 9 examines the five remaining subjects and the themes they traditionally cover. Following a brief discussion of each subject are recommendations for exploring the content of each through movement. The final section, Putting It All Togehter, provides an example of how one topic can be explored through experiences in all the content areas, employing a multisensory, integrated, developmentally appropriate approach to learning.

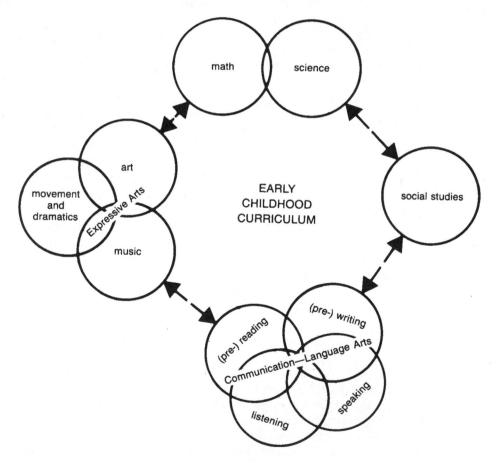

Figure 9-1
Model of early childhood curriculum demonstrating seven major content areas. From Schirrmacher, *Art and Creative Development for Young Children,* 2nd edition, copyright 1993 by Delmar Publishers Inc.

Whether incorporating into the curriculum full-fledged movement sessions requiring desks be pushed aside, short movement breaks at desks, or occasional physical demonstrations to help make concepts clearer, classroom teachers can use these activities—and others like them—to enhance learning, develop rapport among children, gain immediate feedback, and promote a positive attitude toward education that can influence future learning. Similarly, physical education specialists can use these activities to augment the cognitive and affective aspects of physical activity and relate their programs to those taking place in the classroom. When both classroom *and* physical education teachers decide to use a multisensory approach that has an impact on the cognitive, affective, and physical domains, then and only then can we truly educate the whole child.

Art

Art and movement have a number of things in common—particularly where young children are concerned. Art, because it involves movement, helps develop motor skills. Gross motor skills are used in such art activities as painting on an easel, creating murals, body tracing, and working with clay. Fine motor control, which is refined later than gross motor control, is practiced during such art activities as working with small paintbrushes, cutting with scissors, and pasting. Both art and movement also help develop eye-hand coordination (Schirrmacher, 1993; Mayesky, 1995).

But perhaps the most significant common factor between art and movement is that self-expression is encouraged. When given ample opportunity to explore possibilities—whether through movement or a variety of art materials—children make nonverbal statements about who they are and what is important to them. Through both mediums, they can express emotions and work out issues of concern to them and achieve the satisfaction that comes from experiencing success. These results can only occur, however, when the child's movement responses and artwork are not censored by adults and when they are accepted and valued as evidence of the child's individuality. With such acceptance, children gain confidence in their abilities to express themselves, solve problems, and use their creativity. (See The Lost Art of Self-Expression in Chapter 1 for examples of what happens when adults invalidate children's artistic efforts.)

Finally, concepts like shape, size, spatial relationships, and line are also part of art and movement education. Even such artistic concepts as color and texture can be explored and expressed through movement. It makes sense, therefore, to explore these concepts through both mediums.

SUGGESTED ACTIVITIES

Whenever children arrange their bodies in the space around them, they are exploring artistic as well as physical concepts. With their bodies, they are creating lines and shapes. When they move into different levels, in different directions, along different pathways, and in relation to others and to objects, they are increasing their spatial awareness. All these concepts are ingredients in art and movement education—and in bodily/kinesthetic intelligence.

Figure 9-2
Whenever children arrange their bodies in the space around them it can be said that they are exploring artistic concepts as well as physical ones.

To explore shape with the youngest children, begin with simple comparisons between straight and round. Show the children straight objects (e.g., rulers, the lines on ruled paper, etc.) and round objects (e.g., a ball or a globe); ask them to create these opposite shapes with their bodies. Later, you can ask them to form bridges and tunnels with their bodies or body parts. Play a mirror game by facing them and creating different shapes and challenging them to match each shape, as though they were your mirror reflection. When the children are developmentally ready, you can challenge them with an activity like Making Shapes (see Chapter 1), later adding more difficult shapes (e.g., pointed, angular, or oval). With older children, you can explore the possibilities for symmetrical and asymmetrical shapes.

To focus on the concept of lines, use a jump rope or something similar to demonstrate the difference among vertical, horizontal, diagonal, curved, and crooked lines. Can the children use their bodies to replicate the line you have created with the rope?

Shapes and colors can be explored in tandem by providing pictures or examples of objects in various colors (e.g., a yellow banana; a red apple; a green plant) and asking the children to demonstrate the shape of each object. An alternative is to mention a color and ask them what it brings to mind. The children can then either take on the shape of the objects mentioned or become them (e.g., if the color green reminded some children of frogs, they could depict the movement of frogs).

An appropriate activity for early elementary children is Primary Colors (Pica, 1991, pp. 146–147). For this activity, you discuss—or, better still, demonstrate—the primary colors red, yellow, and blue. The children should know red and yellow combine to make orange, yellow and blue combine to make green, and red and blue give us purple.

Then divide your class into three groups and assign each group a primary color. Ask the members of each group to pretend to be as many different things in their color they can think of. (They can perform these examples either individually or with others in the group.)

The next phase is to assign one child from each group to pair with a child from a different group. Each pair must then depict something in the color they have created with their joining. For example, if a child from the red group and a child from the blue form a pair, they should create something purple. You can ask the pairs to work simultaneously; or you can ask one pair at a time for a solution, which it demonstrates for the rest of the class and the class must guess.

As mentioned, you can even explore the concept of texture through movement by gathering items of various textures (e.g., rope, satin, burlap, feathers, a beachball, seashells, a stuffed animal, a carpet square) for the children to see and feel. Talk to them about how each item feels or *makes them feel* (i.e., feathers might make them feel ticklish). Then ask them to demonstrate through movement.

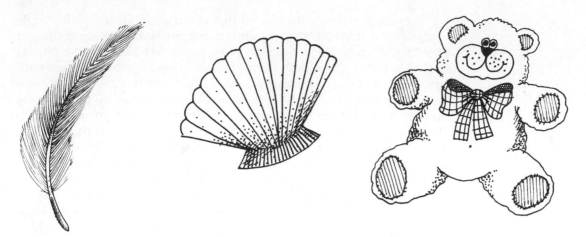

Figure 9-3
A feather, a seashell, and a stuffed animal all have different textures.

Of course, the simplest combination of art and movement is to ask the children to draw pictures of something they experienced during a movement session—immediately following the session is best while the images are still fresh in their minds. Figures 9-4 and 9-5 are examples of the drawings of kindergarteners and second-graders, respectively, following movement sessions.

Because these activities involve more than one sense, they are valuable learning experiences for young children. You can incorporate other senses by using books and/or recordings to expand these experiences. For example, after reading a story to the children, you can ask them to draw something related to the story and to act out or dance about what they drew. (You can extend the experience even further by asking older children to write about what they drew.)

ADDING LITERATURE AND MUSIC

Many children's books are available that deal with artistic concepts. Tana Hoban's books, for instance, include *Circles, Triangles, and Squares* (also appropriate for mathematics); *Is It Red? Is It Yellow? Is It Blue?, Round, Round, Round, Is It Larger? Is It Smaller?* (again, also appropriate for mathematics); and *Shapes, Shapes, Shapes*. Other possibilities are Eric Carle's *My First Book of Colors, My First Book of Shapes;* John Reiss' *Colors* and *Shapes;* and Joanne and David Wylie's *A Fishy Color Story* (also appropriate for science).

To make music part of the experience, you can ask the children to paint to the accompaniment of different styles of music, perhaps

Figure 9-4
The kindergarteners who drew these two pictures especially enjoyed moving to the song "Robots and Astronauts."

Figure 9-5
Second graders created thank-you cards for me after I visited their school for a special movement session on Earth Day. The combined activities integrated physical education, music, science, art, and language arts.

suggesting they change colors every time the music changes. Also, many songs can be found that relate to the concepts of color and shape. Among them are Hap Palmer's "Colors," from Volume I of *Learning Basic Skills Through Music;* and from Volume II, "Parade of Colors," "Triangle, Circle, or Square" (also for mathematics), and "One Shape, Three Shapes." Derrie Frost's *Color Me a Rainbow* and Mr. Al's *Mr. Al Sings Colors and Shapes* offer two albums devoted to artistic concepts.

Language Arts

Because the language arts comprise listening, speaking, reading, and writing, this content area is an intrinsic part of every individual's life. It is about communication—imparted or received. It is tied to linguistic intelligence, which has enormous validation in our society. And it is part of every curriculum, in one form or another, from preschool through advanced education.

In early childhood programs, language arts traditionally receive the greatest concentration during daily group or circle times. During these periods, teachers and caregivers read stories or poems to the children who sit and listen. Sometimes discussion precedes or follows the reading. In elementary schools, reading and writing have commonly been handled as separate studies, with the children focusing on topics like phonics, spelling, and grammar.

The whole-language approach to children's emerging literacy, which has received increasing attention during the past decade, recognizes that listening, speaking, reading, and writing overlap and interrelate, each contributing to the growth of the others. This approach also acknowledges children learn best those concepts that are relevant to them; therefore, their language acquisition and development must be a natural process that occurs over time and relates to all aspects of the children's lives (Sawyer & Sawyer, 1993; Raines & Canady, 1990).

Movement, like language, plays an essential role in life and is also a form of communication. Thus, the two are naturally linked. Teachers who adopt a whole-language, or integrated, approach to literacy soon realize movement is a vital tool in the acquisition and development of the language arts.

SUGGESTED ACTIVITIES

The possibilities for exploring language arts through movement are inexhaustible. Consider the simple act of children forming letters of the alphabet with their bodies or body parts—individually or with a partner. Such an activity leads to greater awareness of the straight and curving lines that comprise each letter and the difference between upper- and lowercase letters.

Talking about experiences, depicting them through movement, and then discussing the movement contribute to language development by requiring children to make essential connections between their cognitive, affective, and physical domains.

Rhythm is an essential ingredient in words and movement. The rhythmic patterns of poetry, in fact, often make it difficult for young children to just sit and listen (Rowen, 1982). Therefore, when children clap the rhythm of words or rhymes, or move to the rhythm of a poem, they are increasing their knowledge of both rhythm and language. Clapping, stamping, or stepping to the rhythms of words can also familiarize them with syllables.

Figure 9-6
One child demonstrates the letter "I" with his body as a friend looks on. When the children are developmentally ready, partners can work together to form letters of the alphabet.

Fingerplays are basically poems or word plays in which movement has a critical function—to make the words more meaningful. Raines and Canady (1990, p. 178) write, "The complementary rhythms and movements of fingerplays and action songs incorporate language, symbolism, and perception, which help children to remember them." Omitting lines from familiar fingerplays (while still performing the actions) tests the children's memories and listening abilities. (See Chapter 10 for more about fingerplays.)

Any listening or sound identification activity (see suggestions in Chapter 6) helps develop auditory discrimination. Auditory sequential memory can be improved by giving the children a sequence of movement instructions to follow. You might, for example, present a challenge to clap twice, blink eyes, and turn around, lengthening the sequence as they are ready. (Begin by performing the actions as you say the words; when the children are ready, eliminate the actions.)

Acting out fairy tales and nursery rhymes increases the children's comprehension and helps them recall the order of events (Rowen, 1982). And it is fun! Nursery rhymes like "Jack and Jill," "Humpty Dumpty," and "Jack Be Nimble" (which also provides practice with jumping) are perfect for dramatization, as are such classic tales as "Jack and the Beanstalk," "Henny Penny," "Hansel and Gretel," "The Three Billy Goats Gruff," and "Goldilocks and the Three Bears."

Children's stories like "The Little Engine That Could" and, more recently, "Rosie's Walk" are among those that also lend themselves to movement. Raines and Canady's (1990) series of *Story S-t-r-e-t-c-h-e-r-s* books offer hundreds of activities—among them movement and music activities—for "expanding" children's favorite books. Or you can simply ask the children to show you their interpretations of the story's characters and action. Rowen (1982, p. 43) suggests the following criteria for determining whether or not a story is appropriate for dramatization:

1. The story must have action.
2. There must be changes in feeling.
3. It can have many characters, but only two or three should be involved in the action at the same time.
4. Characters with differing qualities make good dramatization.

Acting out the meaning of individual words from stories, poems, or even spelling lists can lead to greater understanding. Through movement, children can begin to comprehend suffixes and, thus, the distinction between words like *frightened* and *frightening*. They can better grasp the meaning of action words like *slither, stalk, pounce,* or *stomp*—or descriptive words like *graceful, smooth,* or *forceful*. Preschool children can work in pairs to demonstrate the meanings of simple opposites like *sad* and *happy*, or *up* and *down*, with primary-grade partners challenged to demonstrate possibilities like *tight* versus *loose* or *open* versus *closed*.

Gilbert (1977) suggests reading-readiness activities involving movements that go from left to right—like turning the head, slowly and quickly, and drawing a line on the floor with a leg.

ADDING MUSIC

Music can also become a component in an integrated language arts approach. Songs like "The Eensy Weensy Spider" and "Where Is Thumbkin?" can sometimes be substituted for nonmusical fingerplays. You can familiarize the children with the lyrics of songs by introducing them first without music—as though they were poems—asking children to depict the actions suggested by the lyrics or the meaning of individual words. Also available are song picture books—illustrated versions of children's songs—some with the music notation and some with a recording.

Isenberg and Jalongo (1993) recommend musical storytelling—for example, using a slide whistle to represent Jack's ascent and descent of the beanstalk and drums of different sizes to depict Jack's and the giant's footsteps. When the children are developmentally ready, you can challenge them to use rhythm sticks or other instruments to mark the rhythms of words, rhymes, or poems. Children should also be encouraged to invent new lyrics to familiar melodies—with or without your help, depending on their level of development.

Finally, songs and albums are also available that emphasize the language arts. Hap Palmer's *Ideas, Thoughts, and Feelings* includes the song "Letter Sounds (A–M) and (N–Z)," and Volume I of *Learning Basic Skills Through Music* contains "Marching Around the Alphabet." Palmer also has an album called *Classic Nursery Rhymes;* and Rosemary Hallum and Henry "Buzz" Glass offer *Children's All-Time Mother Goose Favorites,* both of which are available from Educational Activities. Available from Kimbo are *ABC's in Bubbaville* (26 careers based on the letters of the alphabet, so also appropriate for social studies); *Singable Nursery Rhymes;* and *Nursery Rhymes for Little People.*

Mathematics

To many adults, math is the most abstract of the content areas. We may have an aversion to this content area because we have failed in the past to do well in subjects like algebra and calculus or on standardized tests (I.Q. tests or SATs), which concentrate heavily on areas related to the logical/mathematical intelligence (Gardner, 1983; Armstrong, 1993). Or we may consider balancing a checkbook or staying within a budget complicated processes.

But children do not view math the same way we do; for them, it is not abstract. As Essa (1992, p. 370) explains, "The foundations of math are grounded in concrete experience such as the exploration of objects and gradual understanding of their properties and relationships. The cognitive concepts . . . of classification, seriation (ordering), numbers, time, and space all contribute to the gradual acquisition of math concepts."

Thus, children are acquiring mathematical knowledge (Mayesky, 1995; Essa, 1992) when they sort, stack, and compare manipulatives;

Figure 9-7
When children sort, stack, and compare manipulatives, they're acquiring mathematical knowledge.

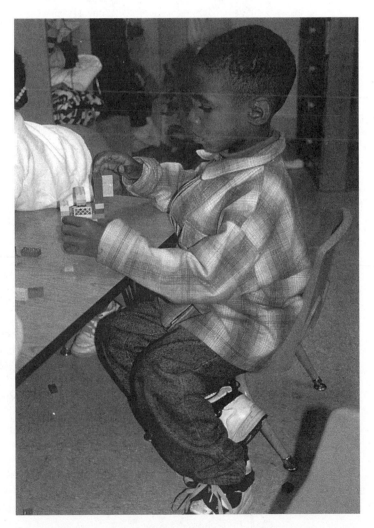

play with sand and water; measure or set the table in the housekeeping center; or learn nursery rhymes and stories like "The Three Little Kittens" and "Goldilocks and the Three Bears."

Quantitative ideas are also part of the language of mathematics. Mayesky (1995) recommends the following words be incorporated into the children's daily routine:

big and little	few	bunch
long and short	tall and short	group
high and low	light and heavy	pair
wide and narrow	together	many
late and early	same length	more
first and last	highest	most
middle	lowest	twice
once	longer than	

Obviously, physical activity can help children attach meaning to these words, as well as to numerals and other mathematical concepts—so math can continue to be a concrete, rather than an abstract, subject.

The mathematical concepts appropriate for exploration with young children include quantitative ideas, number awareness and recognition, counting, basic geometry, and simple addition and subtraction.

SUGGESTED ACTIVITIES

With one look at the above list of quantitative words, it is easy to see movement is an ideal, tangible means of conveying most of these ideas to children. Activities involving levels and body shapes can demonstrate the concepts of *big and little, long and short, high and low, wide and narrow, tall and short, highest, lowest,* and even *same length,* and *longer than.* The movement element of force is about *light and heavy.* Children can form *pairs* and *groups,* or a *few* children can work *together.* Throughout the movement activities, teachers can pose questions and challenges: "Which body part has the *most* possibilities?"; "How *many* ways can you find to . . . ?"; "Show me you can you do it *twice*"; or "Repeat the action *once more.*"

The poem "Giants and Elves" (Pica, 1990a, p. 23) is an example of quantitative concepts in action.

> See the giants, great and tall
> Hear them bellow, hear them call
> Life looks different from up so high
> With head and shoulders clear to the sky
> And at their feet they can barely see

Figures 9-8 and 9-9
Movement activities can help children attach meaning to quantitative concepts. The child in Figure 9-8 is demonstrating high, long, and tall while the child in Figure 9-9 displays an example of low, long, and wide.

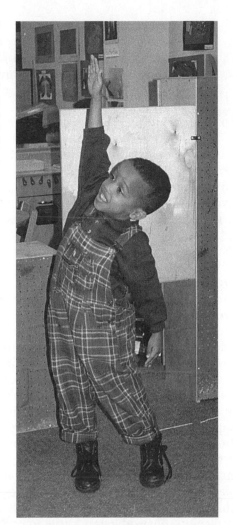

The little people so very tiny
Who scurry about with hardly a care
Avoiding enormous feet placed here and there
But together they dwell, the giants and elves
In peace and harmony, amongst themselves.

Positional concepts can be demonstrated by asking the *first* or *last* child in line to perform an action. You can ask children to stand *in front of* or *behind* a person or object, or *between* or in the *middle* of others. Props and obstacle courses are excellent for demonstrating such positional concepts as *over, under, around,* and *through.*

To develop number awareness and recognition, the children must hear the numerals often. The simple activity Blast Off is appropriate for even the youngest children and can help them advance from rote memorization of numbers to actual comprehension. With this activity, the children squat low, pretending to be spaceships on their launching pads as you count backward from ten (with as much drama as you can muster). When you say, "Blast off!" the children "launch" themselves upward.

Children can also form the shapes of numbers with their bodies or body parts. To begin, assign numbers they must replicate, challenging them to try it at varying levels (i.e., standing, kneeling, sitting, lying). When the children are developmentally ready, you can ask them to choose numbers, say, between zero and four or five and nine. You can ask them to form the shapes of numbers with jump ropes and to trace those shapes with locomotor skills. Challenge them to show you their ages with their bodies, to form numbers in pairs or trios, or to draw invisible numbers in the air or on the floor with different body parts. Can their classmates guess the numbers drawn?

Although an activity like Blast Off can begin to familiarize children with counting backward, the process will have little meaning for them until they fully understand how to count forward. You can help them develop this understanding by counting beats clapped (e.g., clapping and counting 1-2-3 and asking them to echo); steps taken (giving the class a number and asking the children to take that many steps or hop that many hops); or repetitions performed (asking children to repeat a movement two more times).

Other possibilities include asking children to place a certain number of body parts on the floor or to balance on so many parts. Challenge them to count the number of times they are able to bounce a ball, the number of seconds they can hold a static balance, or the number of ways they can find to move the head, for example. With all these activities, you can instantly ascertain which children are having trouble counting.

Chapter 9 has already discussed shape as part of the subject of art, but shape is also a component of math—especially geometry. Simple

Figure 9-10
Simple geometry includes vertical, horizontal, diagonal, curved, and crooked lines. Children can be challenged to replicate these lines with their bodies and body parts.

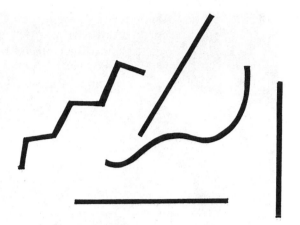

geometry includes straight, curved, vertical, horizontal, crossed, and diagonal lines, as well as circles, squares, triangles, and rectangles (Werner & Burton, 1979).

You can begin acquainting children with geometric shapes by giving them blocks and puzzles and other manipulative materials. If the children's environment contains foam wedges, cubes, balls, crawl-through boards with geometric shapes cut out, or geometrically shaped beanbags to throw through geometrically shaped holes in target boards, they will begin to attach a meaning to such words as *circle, square, triangle,* and *rectangle.*

The children can form lines, curves, points, and angles with the body or body parts and later advance to forming geometric shapes— alone or with others, at various levels in space. They can move in straight, curving, zigzag, and diagonal lines and advance to moving in circular, square, rectangular, and triangular patterns on the floor.

Computation is much less abstract when human bodies are used for addition and subtraction. Fingers and toes have always been the perfect tools for adding and subtracting, but whole bodies can also be used. Acting out the song "Roll Over" ("there were ten in the bed, and the little one said . . .") makes subtraction very clear—and lots of fun. (Merle Peek has illustrated this song in the book *Roll Over: A Counting Song.*) By asking one child to stand at the front of the room and then adding (later subtracting) one child at a time, you can help children learn both processes. Similarly, when three bodies are lying on the floor and one rolls away, it is quite easy to see three minus one leaves two.

Cambigue (1981) suggests using the arms as a means of helping children understand the plus and minus signs. When the children form a plus sign with their arms, you should point out they are putting two things together; and whenever they see this sign, they should

Figures 9-11 and 9-12
By crawling through geometric cut-outs, children begin to attach meaning to such words as circle and rectangle.

Figure 9-13
The arms can be used to help children remember the difference between plus and minus signs.

remember to put the things or numbers together (addition). Then ask them to take away the vertical arm and put it behind the back. This leaves the horizontal arm demonstrating the minus sign, which should remind them they must always take something away from something else when they see this sign (subtraction).

ADDING LITERATURE AND MUSIC

Children's books that emphasize early mathematics and can serve as "jumping-off points" for movement activities include Molly Bang's *Ten, Nine, Eight* (counting backward from ten); Laurent de Brunhoff's *Babar's Counting Book;* Susanna Gretz's *Teddy Bears One to Ten;* Tana Hoban's *1, 2, 3;* Lois Ehlert's *Fish Eyes;* and Scholastic's *My First Look at Sorting.*

As with art and the language arts, you can purchase musical selections to help make mathematics more concrete and enjoyable for the children. Among them are the shape songs mentioned under Art, as well as "The Number March" from Volume I of Hap Palmer's *Learning Basic Skills Through Music* and "Lucky Numbers" from Volume II. He also has three albums dedicated to mathematics: *Math Readiness:*

Vocabulary and Concepts, Math Readiness: Addition and Subtraction, and *Singing Multiplication Tables,* available from Educational Activities. Alan Stern's *Sing a Sum . . . or a Remainder,* for first and second grades, is also available from Educational Activities. Melody House offers an album called *Number Fun.*

Science

The word *science* reminds us of such topics as chemistry, physics, biology, botany, and astronomy. We can imagine men and women in lab coats, poring over facts and figures or measuring strange concoctions into test tubes and beakers. Since none of this is relevant in the lives of young children, you might wonder—rightly—how science fits into the early childhood curriculum.

Science, however, is also about exploration, investigation, problem solving, and discovery—all of which *are* relevant for young children. A child's whole life, from its very beginning, is exploring, investigating, solving problems, and discovering!

The principal difference between these two views of science is much of the former deals with the theoretical and the abstract, while the latter, as far as young children are concerned, deals with the concrete and the tangible—with what can be easily observed. For example, children discover what objects will float or sink by actually placing objects in water. They discover different floating by blowing bubbles through a wand and watching them drift through the air. Balls, however, will not float when sent into the air; this is due to gravity, a concept the children may not grasp but one they can witness firsthand.

In other words, science for young children is learning by doing—just as movement is.

Naturally, this text cannot begin to cover the endless possibilities for exploring science themes through movement. For a multitude of ideas and activities, you should refer to the many excellent resources cited at the end of the chapter. Remember, too, almost every theme and movement activity has corresponding music; it is just a matter of looking for it.

SUGGESTED ACTIVITIES

Many themes typically explored in classrooms and child-care centers fall in the science category, including such themes as the human body

(body parts and their functions, the senses, hygiene, and nutrition); seasons; and other topics related to nature—weather, animals, plants, and the ocean.

Of course, anytime children perform movements—locomotor, non-locomotor, manipulative, gymnastic, and dance—they are learning something about the functions of the human body. However, you can be more specific simply by focusing on certain functions. You can ask them to concentrate on the muscles, for example, by suggesting they think about the amount of muscle tension used to perform a movement, or the shape of the muscles when they freeze in different

Figure 9-14
Every time children move they are learning something about the functions of the human body.

positions. Relaxation exercises that require the children to contract and relax the muscles are also excellent for developing an awareness of these important body parts.

Similarly, relaxation exercises focusing on the breath can create an awareness of the lungs. You can introduce the function of the heart by asking children to find their pulse at rest and after strenuous activity. Can they match their pulse's rhythm with the tapping of a hand or foot?

Listening activities focus on the sense of hearing; asking children to try various nonlocomotor movements with their eyes closed draws attention to the sense of sight. The texture activity suggested under Art can be used to concentrate on the sense of touch. And taste and smell, which are also part of a nutrition unit, can be explored by challenging children to demonstrate with faces or bodies how various flavors and odors make them feel.

Nutrition can be further explored by challenging children to take on the shapes of various fruits and vegetables. You can also ask them to show you the difference between, say, an apple hanging from a tree and applesauce simmering on the stove (especially if the class has visited an orchard and then made applesauce!). Cathy Slonecki's album *Eat Well! Feel Well!* (available from Educational Activities) is dedicated to nutrition and includes such songs as "The Vegetable Rock" and "I Am What I Eat."

Even hygiene can be less abstract and more fun by exploring it through movement and music. Children can pretend to perform many hygienic activities—brushing teeth, washing hair, bathing, and caring for clothes—and nursery rhymes like "Rub-a-Dub-Dub, Three Men in a Tub" can lead in to such activities. Also, a number of musical selections can accompany your explorations, including "Take a Bath," "Cover Your Mouth," "Keep the Germs Away," and "Brush Away" from Volume II of Hap Palmer's *Learning Basic Skills Through Music*. Joe Scruggs offers "Even Dragons Brush Their Teeth" on his album *Even Trolls Have Moms;* Raffi sings "Brush Your Teeth" on *Singable Songs for the Very Young* and "Bathtime" on *Everything Grows;* and "The Wash Song" can be found in Rae Pica's *Toddlers Moving & Learning*.

Animals are tremendously appealing—and therefore relevant—to young children. Moving like different animals can contribute not only to knowledge about them but also to the development of empathy and a proficiency with various movement skills and elements. It is not enough, however, to merely ask the children to pretend to be different animals. You must create a greater awareness by discussing pertinent characteristics of the animals they are to portray. Cats, for example, can move very slowly and quietly. What is it about the way they use their muscles and paws that makes this possible? What is it about their spines that makes them able to twist, stretch, and arch so easily?

Numerous possibilities for exploring the study of animals with music are available. Pica and Gardzina's *More Music for Moving & Learning* includes a cassette entitled *All About Animals*. Educational Activities offers *Animal Antics;* Kimbo, *Animal Walks* and *Walk Like the Animals;* Educational Record Center, *Save the Animals, Save the Earth;* and Derrie Frost presents *A Zippity Zoo Day,* available from Melody House.

Virtually every aspect of nature can be explored in innumerable ways through movement and music. You can even promote an early and much needed awareness of the environment by asking children to portray insects, ocean creatures, plants, weather conditions, and more. Jane Murphy's *Insects, Bugs and Squiggly Things,* Lois Skiera-Zucek's *What's in the Sea?,* and Sally Rogers' *Piggyback Planet,* all available through Educational Record Center, can make musical contributions to these science activities.

EXPLORING SCIENTIFIC CONCEPTS

Specific scientific concepts appropriate for exploration with early elementary children include flotation, gravity, balance and stability, action and reaction, magnetics, machinery, and electricity. Balance and stability, gravity, and even flotation are naturals for exploring through movement.

For the latter, children can watch bubbles, feathers, and chiffon scarves drift through the air and then attempt to simulate the movement. Does floating require light or strong movement? Little or much muscle tension?

Is it possible for human beings to really float? No—because of gravity. When we jump, hop, or leap in the air, the force of gravity pulls us back down, just as it pulls down any object (e.g., a beanbag or ball) we toss in the air. But the higher we toss the object, the longer it takes to reach the ground. Challenge the children to discover how many times they can clap or turn around before the beanbag or ball returns to their hands or to the ground.

Gravity is also a factor when we attempt to balance. Challenge the children to balance on their knees or seat, lean in any direction as far as they can before falling over, and then return to their original positions. This is called balance and recovery. Now ask them to lean again, this time going beyond the point of recovery. What happens? Gravity causes them to fall over! You can also help the children discover balance is easier when the body's center of gravity is lowered and there is a large, rather than a narrow, base of support.

Weightlessness (lack of gravity) is a concept you cannot actually explore, but one children love to imagine. Children are fascinated by outer space—a topic that "addresses the child's innate sense of wonder at the universe . . . [and] promotes a better understanding of our own planet" (Weimer, 1993, p. 1). Weimer, at the encouragement of NASA, created *Space Songs for Children,* a cassette with 12 songs written from a child's perspective and an accompanying 104-page book with lyrics and suggestions for related activities to extend the ideas in each song. The project was created for children ages 3 to 8.

Other scientific concepts may be less obvious candidates for movement exploration, but that does not mean movement cannot be used—or that movement cannot make these ideas less abstract.

For example, children are familiar with most, if not all, of the six simple machines: lever, wheel, pulley, inclined plane, screw, and wedge (Gilbert, 1977). They can roll like wheels and twist like screwdrivers—and they may have had experience with inclined planes and wedges meant specifically for movement. Levers with which the children are familiar—and which they can imitate—include scissors, wheelbarrows, and seesaws.

Children can also depict the movement of such household machines as washing machines, dryers, vacuum cleaners, dishwashers, and blenders. An activity called The Machine can not only begin to develop their understanding of machinery but also is an excellent exercise in cooperation. In this activity, one child begins by repeatedly performing a movement that can be executed in one spot. A second child then stands near the first and contributes a second movement that relates in some way to the first. For example, if the first child is performing an up-down motion by bending and stretching, the second child might choose to do the reverse, standing beside his or her classmate. A third child might choose an arm or leg motion timed to move between the two bodies bending and stretching. As these movements continue, each remaining student adds a functioning part to the machine. They may choose any movements, as long as they do not interfere with the actions of others and they contribute in some way to the machine. Once all the parts are functioning, you can ask each child to make a corresponding sound.

All the aforementioned household machines require electricity to operate. What other machines or appliances can the children think of—and show you—that use electricity? You can also introduce the idea of electricity being *conducted* by asking the children to hold hands in a line or a circle and to pretend electricity is flowing from one body to the next.

Rowen (1982) suggests the children discover action and reaction (every action force has an equal and opposite reaction force) by sitting on the floor in pairs with legs straddled, feet touching, and hands held. As one child pushes forward, the other pulls back—and then the reverse. (Remind the children to move *slowly* for this activity.)

Magnets are always fascinating for children. Once you have demonstrated opposite poles attract (stick together) and identical poles repel, turn the children themselves into magnets. Ask them to move around the room as though they were magnets with only north or south poles. What happens when two such magnets (children) approach each other? Then assign half of the class to act as north poles and the other half as south poles (or ask them to decide themselves which they would like to be). The "north poles" should point a finger or hand toward the ceiling, while the "south poles" point toward the floor. Now what happens when two magnets get close to each other? (If two identical poles meet, they repel; if opposite poles meet, they stick together.)

To add a literature component to science/movement activities, teachers can choose from a great many children's books focusing on early science concepts. In addition to the seemingly endless number of books about animals and seasons, many science series are available. Among them are Scholastic's First Discovery Books, which include *Weather* and *The Ladybug and Other Insects;* and David Evans and Claudette Williams' Let's Explore Science series, consisting of *Make It Balance, Make It Go, Make It Change,* and *Me and My Body.* And do not forget Eric Carle's *The Very Hungry Caterpillar, The Very Busy Spider,* and *The Tiny Seed.*

Although this is only a small sample of the possibilities for exploring science concepts, any teacher with a little imagination and a strong desire to educate the whole child can devise countless others.

Social Studies

Lessons in social studies for young children begin with the children themselves—because that is where their world begins. Self-concept, therefore, is a logical starting point in the early childhood social studies curriculum. The child's world then extends, respectively, to family, friends, neighborhood, and the community in general (Mayesky, 1995; Raines & Canady, 1990).

As children learn about themselves and about each other, they discover how they are alike and different. They explore feelings, rules for living (particularly with regard to safety), holidays and celebrations, traditions and cultures, and the jobs that keep a community functioning. In early childhood settings, these topics generally fall under the themes of self-awareness, families and friends, holidays and celebrations, occupations, transportation, and multicultural education.

Under Science, we considered how movement develops an understanding of the body and its parts, functions, senses, and care. Obviously, movement contributes greatly to self-awareness. In addition, a positive self-concept is promoted through the successful experiences movement education offers. In Chapter 1, we looked at some ways social develoment, in general, is enhanced through movement. Based on the information in Chapters 1 and 9 alone, we can easily argue every movement activity is an exercise in social studies. However, the following section will offer specific recommendations for exploring topics that typically come under the heading of social studies with young children.

SELF-CONCEPT

Emotion is one aspect of self-awareness that fits better under social studies than under science. If a young child is to have a positive self-concept, he needs to accept his feelings as a part of himself to later gain greater understanding of them. She must also learn others have feelings, too.

Activities in which children pretend to walk as though sad, mad, proud, scared, tired, or happy are a good place to start because they give them permission to express themselves. Children can also show you with their hands or faces alone how these emotions look (see "A Face Has Many Roles in Life" in Chapter 1).

Songs like "If You're Happy" can get children thinking about their feelings, especially if you add other emotions to the lyrics. Some children's albums dedicated to self-concept are *Mr. Al Sings Friends and Feelings* and Hap Palmer's *Getting to Know Myself* and *Ideas, Thoughts, and Feelings.* Children's books related to self-concept include Nancy Carlson's *I Like Me,* Marissa Moss's *Regina's Big Mistake,* Norma Simon's *I Was So Mad!,* and Aliki's *Feelings.*

The concepts of families and friends are explored in such children's books as James Marshall's *George and Martha One Fine Day,* Jackie Carter's *Knock, Knock,* Harriet Hains' *My Baby Brother,* Anne and Harlow Rockwell's *When I Go Visiting,* and many more. Tonja Evetts Weimer's two-volume set, *Fingerplays and Action Chants,* comes with accompanying cassettes, the second volume of which is Family and Friends. All these materials can be lead-ins to activities in which the children demonstrate what it means to have a younger or older sibling, pretend to be a parent or grandparent, or depict some things they do with family and friends.

HOLIDAYS AND CELEBRATIONS

Possibilities abound for exploring holidays and celebrations through movement, music, and literature. Catherine Stock's *Christmas Time,*

Figure 9-15
Ask children to demonstrate various emotions with faces or hands alone before challenging them to show you with the whole body. This preschooler is displaying his best "angry" face.

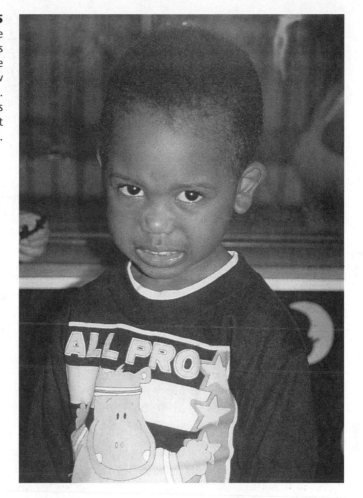

Jeanne Titherington's *Pumpkin Pumpkin* (also science), Thacher Hurd's *Little Mouse's Big Valentine,* and Jean Marzollo's *In 1492* are just a tiny sample of the variety of children's books about holidays and celebrations. Musical selections include Steve and Greg's *Holidays and Special Times,* Jill Gallina's *Holiday Songs for All Occasions,* Tickle Tune Typhoon's *Keep the Spirit,* Hap Palmer's *Holiday Songs and Rhythms* and *Holiday Magic,* and Pica and Gardzina's *Moving Through the Holidays* (from Pica & Gardzina, 1990).

Holidays offer a multitude of images that inspire movement. Children can move like black cats and ghosts at Halloween, turkeys at Thanksgiving, flickering flames and melting candles at Hannukah, elves and reindeer at Christmas, and on and on. For specific ideas, refer to Pica (1991), Wnek (1992), and thematically organized curriculum resources that include movement.

OCCUPATIONS AND TRANSPORTATION

Field trips, in conjunction with books like Rachel Field's *General Store* and Margret and H. A. Rey's *Curious George at the Fire Station,* are perfect for stimulating movement experiences related to occupations. The children can impersonate everyone and everything they have seen and heard. You can also use an album like Kimbo's *ABCs in Bubbaville* to inspire discussion and movement experiences about lesser-known occupations. Or ask early elementary children to demonstrate three actions performed by someone in the occupation of their choice, with the rest of the class challenged to guess the occupation.

Naturally, because transportation is specifically about movement, there is no lack of ideas for matching these two fields. (Several activities related to transportation can be found in Chapter 10.) To make problem solving part of your exercises, you can ask children to think of and depict modes of transportation found mainly in cities, on water, and in the sky or ones that are motorless. To add a literature component to the activities, incorporate books like Donald Crews' *Flying* and *Freight Train,* Helen Oxenbury's *The Car Trip,* and Diane Siebert's *Truck Song.*

Under transportation, you may also want to deal with traffic safety. *Safe Not Sorry* is an album from Melody House that deals with safety, including traffic. Volume III of Hap Palmer's *Learning Basic Skills Through Music* has a song called "Buckle Your Seat Belt." You can introduce the children to traffic lights by playing a movement game with three sheets of paper—one red, one yellow, and one green. When you hold up the green sheet, the children walk. They walk in place when they see the yellow sheet and come to a complete stop when you hold up the red.

MULTICULTURAL EDUCATION

As mentioned in Chapter 1, using the music and learning the dances of other cultures and countries can aid in multicultural education, but only if the activities are accompanied by discussion and related learning experiences. A good first step is inviting family members of children representing various cultures to visit the classroom and share something of their heritage—particularly as it relates to movement and music. Use books like Marie Hall Ets' *Gilberto and the Wind,* Phil Mendez' *The Black Snowman,* Verna Aardema's *Bringing the Rain to Kapiti Plain,* and Tomie dePaola's *The Legend of the Indian Paintbrush* to stimulate discussion and movement activities.

Children's recordings of multicultural music include Georgiana Stewart's *Children of the World,* available from Kimbo; Cathy Slonecki's

Children's Songs Around the World, available from Educational Activities; and *Moving Through the World* (Pica & Gardzina, 1990). Remember, too, you can find collections of folk songs not specifically intended for children but still perfectly suitable for listening and moving at your local public library.

Putting It All Together

Throughout Chapter 9, suggestions have been made as to how you can use movement, music, and literature to explore the major content areas of art, language arts, mathematics, science, and social studies. These suggestions have specifically linked the content area under discussion with the three content areas of physical education (movement), music, and language arts (literature). However, there is no need to stop there if you want a truly integrated, cross-curricular program.

An example of how one topic can be studied through experiences covering all seven content areas follows. We will use a nutrition theme, which falls under the general heading of science. If nutrition were the weekly, monthly, or quarterly unit, it would be logical to spend some time studying breads.

Scientific explorations concerning bread would, of course, depend on the developmental stage of the children. However, an explanation that breads and grains comprise one of the food groups would be appropriate for all stages. The basic ingredients of bread should be discussed, as well as the various kinds of bread and their common elements. And an excursion to a local bakery would be an appropriate and enlightening field trip. Naturally, at some point, the class would make some bread—and sorting and measuring the ingredients would fall under the content area of mathematics.

Ann Morris' *Bread, Bread, Bread,* with photos by Ken Heyman, adds literature, art, and multicultural (social studies) components to our hypothetical study. Published by Scholastic and suitable for children ages 3 to 8, it contains photographs of people throughout the world eating different breads. The index identifies the countries and breads shown in the photos. Because bread is something every child is familiar with, this multicultural aspect of nutrition is relevant to them. The children can then talk or write about the bread their families eat (language arts) and draw pictures of their favorite bread (art).

You could choose a familiar melody and create new lyrics about, for example, kneading bread—to add a musical component (also language arts). Or you could select from the surprising number of bread-related songs on children's recordings. Possibilities include the following, which are available from Edcuational Record Center:

- "Biscuits in the Oven" on Raffi's *Baby Beluga*
- "Peanut Butter Sandwich" on Raffi's *Singable Songs for the Very Young*
- "The Muffin Man" on Steve & Greg's *We All Live Together #2* and Sharon, Lois & Bram's *Singing 'n Swinging*
- "Pizza" on Rosenshontz's *Family Vacation*
- "Animal Crackers" on Ann Murray's *There's a Hippo in My Tub*

Of course, our study would be incomplete if we failed to incorporate movement (physical education) into the "recipe." Bread-making can become much more understandable—and memorable—to the children if they themselves depict, first, the ingredients and, then, the bread itself. Following is an activity called In the Beginning (Pica, 1991, p. 18).

Background Information.   Where does bread come from? Why, the supermarket of course—although some "enlightened" children might say the bakery. But back in the "olden days," children knew where bread really came from: Their mothers made it from flour and water and yeast, and it filled the house with a most wonderful aroma.

Talk to the children about this basic food, explaining that it does not originate on the grocer's shelves. Describe the process of mixing flour and water and yeast into dough, kneading the dough, letting it rise, rolling it out with a rolling pin, shaping it to fit a bread pan, and baking it.

Activity.   Tell the children you are going to be the baker and they are going to be the ingredients. And when you are through with them, they are going to be loaves of bread all ready to eat.

Use the appropriate hand and arm movements for each step of the process, as you pretend to do to the children the steps listed. They, in turn, will pretend to have the following *done* to them. The process is as follows:

Stir the flour and water and yeast together.
Knead the dough.
Cover the dough with a cloth and let it rise.
Punch the dough down.
Roll the dough out.
Shape the dough into a loaf.
Let the dough rise again.
Bake the dough; it rises even more and becomes firm.
Remove the bread from the pan.
Slice the bread and eat it!

Alternate Activity.   Ask the children to take on the shapes of other types of dough, including the following:

A pretzel   A gingerbread man
A muffin   A round loaf

INTEGRATION IS EASY Integrating content areas is easier than you might imagine. Take for example, a simple activity like Ducks, Cows, Cats and Dogs, adapted from Docheff (1992).

This activity, which is fun for groups of all ages, requires children to close their eyes or wear blindfolds. Once all eyes are closed or covered, the teacher whispers the name of an animal in each player's ear. For the youngest children, the animals should be limited to two or three of those cited in the title of the game (their sounds are most familiar to young children). To make the activity more challenging for older children, use all four animals (ducks, cows, cats, and dogs); perhaps, if the group is large enough, adding others with familiar sounds, like pigs, chickens, donkeys, or birds.

When each child has been assigned an animal, he or she gets on hands and knees and, at the teacher's start signal, begins to move, making the sound of his or her animal. The object of the game is for like animals to find one another. When they have done so, they stop making their sounds and sit and watch the others who are still trying. (Once the teacher sees all the dogs, for example, have found each other, she can let that group know they have succeeded in their goal.)

Obviously, this exercise provides experience with the locomotor skill of creeping, making it a physical education activity. However, because it is also a listening—or sound discrimination—activity, it falls under the headings of music and language arts; and by requiring cooperation, in the category of social studies. Because the topic of animals and the sense of hearing are emphasized, the content area of science is involved, too. The children can even be asked to count the numbers of animals in each group, making it a mathematics experience as well!

And there you have it: one topic explored through experiences covering all seven major content areas. And these are just *some* of the possibilities!

In the words of Susan Griss (1994):

> Children exposed to creative movement as a language for learning are becoming more aware of their own natural resources. They are expanding their concepts of creativity and of how they can use their own bodies. They are learning through their own creations. The combination of discipline and imagination is an invaluable foundation for creative thinking. Encouraging children to work both alone and with others, to give and to take, to evaluate and to edit, to feel and to think, proves to be empowering to students, and ultimately, therefore, to teachers. (p. 80)

Key Points

- The philosophy of the whole child embraces the theory that children are thinking, feeling, moving human beings who learn through all their senses.
- Although there is no shortage of materials and planning in the schools for teaching children through the eyes and ears (for visual and auditory learning), little thought has traditionally been given kinesthetic learners—those who learn through physical experiences.
- Movement can help *all* children learn and better retain information through its use of multiple senses.
- In addition to enhancing learning, movement facilitates class management, provides an effective means of evaluation for teachers, and promotes a positive attitude toward education.
- Art, like movement, contributes to fine and gross motor control, eye-hand coordination, and self-expression.
- Movement can be used to explore the artistic concepts of shape, size, spatial relationships, line, color, and texture.
- The language arts involve listening, speaking, reading, and writing, all of which overlap and interrelate. The whole-language approach to emerging literacy recognizes this and calls for learning experiences that are relevant to children and develop naturally over time. Movement is a vital tool in the natural acquisition and development of the language arts.
- The mathematical concepts appropriate for exploration with young children—all of which can be explored through

movement—include quantitative ideas, number awareness and recognition, counting, basic geometry, and simple addition and subtraction.

- Science, for young children, deals with the concrete and the tangible and is a process of exploration, investigation, problem solving, and discovery—just as movement is. Many early childhood themes—the body, seasons, weather, animals, plants, and the ocean—fall under the category of science. Specific scientific concepts appropriate for exploration with early elementary children include flotation, gravity, balance and stability, action and reaction, magnetics, machinery, and electricity. All these topics lend themselves to movement exploration.
- Social studies for young children begins with self-concept and extends to family, friends, neighborhood, and the community in general. In early childhood settings, these topics typically fall under the themes of self-awareness, families and friends, holidays and celebrations, occupations, transportation, and multicultural education.
- With a little effort and creativity, almost any topic can be explored through experiences covering the seven major content areas: art, language arts, mathematics, music, physical education, science, and social studies.

Assignments

1. Based on the information in Chapter 9, write a rationale of why movement, when used as a teaching tool, can promote a more positive attitude toward learning.
2. Find at least four poems and/or stories not cited in this chapter that lend themselves to movement experiences. Write brief descriptions of the movement activities that could accompany the literature.
3. List action and/or descriptive words movement can help young children better comprehend.
4. Provide at least one additional example of how movement can help children better understand quantitative ideas.
5. Find five songs or albums not cited in this chapter appropriate for use in studying aspects of art, language arts, math, science, and social studies.
6. Create at least one movement activity for each of the five content areas covered in Chapter 9.
7. Choose a topic (like the nutrition/bread example) and describe experiences that cover the seven major content areas.

References

Armstrong, T. (1993). *Seven kinds of smart*. New York: Penguin.

Cambigue, S. (1981). *Learning through dance/movement*. Los Angeles: Performing Tree.

Docheff, D. M. (1992). *Hey, let's play!: A collection of P.E. games and activities for the classroom teacher*. Elma, Wash.: Dodge R Productions.

Essa, E. (1992). *Introduction to early childhood education*. Albany, N.Y.: Delmar.

Fauth, B. (1990). Linking the visual arts with drama, movement, and dance for the young child. In W. J. Stinson, ed., *Moving and learning for the young child* (pp. 159–87). Reston, Va.: American Alliance for Health, Physical Education, Recreation, and Dance.

Gardner, H. (1983). *Frames of mind: The theory of multiple intelligences*. New York: Basic Books.

Gilbert, A. G. (1977). *Teaching the three Rs through movement experiences*. Minneapolis: Burgess.

Griss, S. (1994). Creative movement: A language for learning. *Educational Leadership, 51*(5), 78–80.

Hendricks, G., & Hendricks, K. (1983). *The moving center: Exploring movement activities for the classroom*. Englewood Cliffs, N.J.: Prentice-Hall.

Isenberg, J. P., & Jalongo, M. R. (1993). *Creative expression and play in the early childhood curriculum*. New York: Macmillan.

Mayesky, M. (1995). *Creative activities for young children*. Albany, N.Y.: Delmar.

Pica, R. (1990a). *Preschoolers moving & learning*. Champaign, Ill.: Human Kinetics.

Pica, R. (1990b). *Toddlers moving & learning*. Champaign, Ill.: Human Kinetics.

Pica, R. (1991). *Special themes for moving & learning*. Champaign, Ill.: Human Kinetics.

Pica, R., & Gardzina, R. (1990). *More music for moving & learning*. Champaign, Ill.: Human Kinetics.

Raines, S. C., & Canady, R. J. (1990). *The whole language kindergarten*. New York: Teachers College.

Rowen, B. (1982). *Learning through movement*. New York: Teachers College.

Sawyer, W. E., & Sawyer, J. C. (1993). *Integrated language arts for emerging literacy*. Albany, N.Y.: Delmar.

Schirrmacher, R. (1993). *Art and creative development for young children*. Albany, N.Y.: Delmar.

Weimer, T. E. (1993). *Space songs for children*. Pittsburgh: Pearce-Evetts.

Werner, P. H., & Burton, E. C. (1979). *Learning through movement*. St. Louis: Mosby.

Wnek, B. (1992). *Holiday games and activities*. Champaign, Ill.: Human Kinetics.

Using Movement and Music for Transitions

CHAPTER

10

A transition, according to *Webster's Third New International Dictionary*, is "a passage or movement from one state, condition, or place to another" or "a passing from one subject to another especially without abruptness." In early childhood and school settings, transitions often involve moving from one place to another *and* from one subject to another. And, to occur without abruptness is certainly one of the goals for transitions.

Although generally not given as much thought as other facets of the curriculum, transitions absorb a good part of the children's day, especially in early childhood settings, and therefore merit equal consideration (Isenberg & Jalongo, 1993; Essa, 1992; Feldman, 1991; Allen & Hart, 1984; Hildebrand, 1980). If they are to take place without chaos—another goal—they must be planned, as are other daily components of the program.

A few general tips for ensuring smooth transitions include the following:

- Remain calm and collected. If you appear unhinged during transitions, the children become unhinged, too. On the other hand, if you move slowly and speak softly, they respond in kind.
- Make necessary preparations in advance. If the children are transitioning to lunch, for instance, they should not have to sit at the table waiting; the meal should be ready as the children are concluding their prior activity.
- If the transition involves taking turns (as do those involving toileting or donning outerwear), be sure the same children are not always chosen to go first. Hildebrand (1980, p. 97) writes,

285

"Children learn to wait their turns when they know from experience that they'll get a turn." One day, you can assign brown-eyed children to go to the coatroom first. The next day, all children wearing blue shirts can go first, with children born in January asked to lead on the following day.

An important benefit of planning transitions, which often represent an accumulation of wasted time (Davidson, 1982), is they can be used as yet another opportunity for learning. Not only will children learn to bring satisfactory closure to activities, but also successful transitioning teaches them to move easily into and out of group situations. These dynamics naturally entail cooperation and consideration. Furthermore, children learn to follow directions "from the simple to the complex and concerned with locations, object descriptions, and sequences of actions" (Allen & Hart, 1984, p. 104). Transitions can also be linked to curriculum content, adding continuity and more opportunity for learning to the day's components. (Chapter 10 uses a transportation theme to show how transitions can be connected to the curriculum.)

Because transitions usually require moving from one place to another—and music is a common partner of movement, as well as being mood-altering—movement and music are the perfect instruments for transition times. Children naturally enjoy movement and music, so transitions can become pleasurable experiences—even something to be looked forward to. Movement activities, songs, and fingerplays (all of which should be in a teacher's ready repertoire) provide a focus for the children during transitions, hold the attention of waiting children, and are easily tied to curriculum content. And transitions present opportunities for additional experience with movement and music—two subjects teachers often have trouble finding ample time for.

Typical transitions in the early childhood setting entail arrival, group time to free time (or the reverse), cleanup, snacks and lunch, rest or nap time, outdoor time, and departure (see Figure 10-1). The elementary school setting is similar, except nap time is not included in the schedule and there may or may not be group and free times. The rest of Chapter 10 reviews typical transitions and offers suggestions for making movement and music an integral part of them.

Arrival

Everybody, at any age, likes to be welcomed; it makes them feel special. Teachers and caregivers can make the children in their program feel

Half-Day Toddler Program

9:00–9:30	Greet Children
	Inside Activities
	• playdough and art/easel
	• home living
	• blocks and manipulatives
	• books
9:30	Door to outdoors opens
9:45–10:20	Outdoor Play
	• large motor
	• social play
10:20	Music/movement outdoors
10:30	Snack/"Here We Are Together" song
	• washing hands
	• eating/pouring/cleanup
10:45–11:15	Outside
11:15	"Time to Put Our Toys Away" song
	• all encouraged to participate in cleanup
11:20	Closure (indoors)
	• parent-child together
	• story or flannelboard

Full-Day Program for Preschoolers

7:00	Arrival, breakfast
7:30	Inside free play
	• arts/easels
	• table toys/games/blocks
	• dramatic play center; house, grocery store, etc.
9:00	Cleanup
9:15	Group time: Songs/fingerplays and small-group choices
9:30	Choice Time/small groups
	• discovery/math lab/science activity
	• cooking for morning or afternoon snack
	• language art/prereading choice
10:00	Snack (at outside tables/cloths on warm days) or snack center during free play
10:15	Outside free play
	• climbing, swinging; sand and water, wheel toys, group games
12:00	Handwash and lunch

12:45	Get ready: toileting, handwashing, toothbrushing, prepare beds
1:15	Bedtime story
1:30	Rest time
2:30	Outdoors for those awake
3:30	Cleanup outdoors and singing time
4:00	Snacktime
4:15	Learning centers; some outdoor/indoor choices, field trips, story teller
5:30	Cleanup and read books until going home

Half-Day Kindergarten Plan

8:15–8:30	Arrival:
	Getting ready to start
	• checking in library books, lunch money, etc.
8:30	Newstelling
	• "anything you want to tell for news"
	• newsletter written weekly
9:00	Work assignment
	• write a story about your news *or*
	• make a page in your book (topic assigned) *or*
	• work in math lab
9:30–10:15	Choice of indoors (paints, blocks, computer, table toys) *or*
	second grade tutors read books to children
	• when finished, play in loft *or* read books until recess
10:15	Snack
10:30	Recess
10:45	Language: chapter in novel read *or* other language activity
11:15	Dance *or* game *or* visitor and snack
11:45	Ending: Getting ready to leave
	• check out library books
	• gather art and other projects
12:00–1:30	For part of group each day:
	Lunch, then:
	• field trips
	• writing lesson
	• math or science lab

Figure 10-1
These sample schedules excerpted from *Beginnings and Beyond,* Gordon and Browne (1993), p. 297 show the many transitions that occur during a typical day. From Gordon and Browne, *Beginnings and Beyond: Foundations in Early Childhood Education,* 3rd edition, copyright 1993 by Delmar Publishers Inc.

special—and get the day started right—by providing a warm welcome for each and every arriving child.

Especially warming is the sound of one's own name, which children love to hear. But simply saying, "Good morning [Tony]" may not be enough to generate enthusiasm and make the child feel glad to be there. Instead, adults greeting children at the door can use songs or chants that include their names. One possibility is simply to sing "Good morning to you. . ." to the tune of "Happy Birthday." Another example, sung to the tune of "London Bridge," is

> [Marianne] is here today
> Here today, here today
> [Marianne] is here today
> I'm (we're) so glad to see you!

Performing fingerplays is a pleasant way to come together and to transition into the rest of the day. Teachers should acquire a collection of fingerplays and keep a card file of favorites (the teacher's enjoyment will help ensure the children's) and memorize several so they are ready to use whenever the need or opportunity arises.

Children love and need repetition, so it is not necessary to learn *dozens* of fingerplays. Hamilton and Flemming (1990, p. 50) suggest these guidelines for choosing the most appropriate ones:

1. Select one or two fingerplays for each subject, making certain they teach *best* the concept to be learned.
2. As with books, poems, and songs, watch for difficult vocabulary, the length of verse, the concept to be learned, and the maturity level of your group.
3. Use the simplest fingerplays with the youngest or least mature group; increase the complexity as the group shows readiness.
4. Select fingerplays carefully with a sensitivity for *all* people. Consider your group's age, understanding and experience, and the appropriateness for its use that day.
5. Adapt when one word, adjective, or action spoils an otherwise good rhyme or action game. Some descriptive words can be alternately exchanged. "Boys" or "girls" or a nonsexist term can be exchanged for one given in a book. Verses that stereotype or ridicule a race, cultural group, type of physical disability, or refer to violence (guns, soldiers) in any form should be avoided. For example, the words "gymnasts" or "band" can be exchanged in a fingerplay for a more military reference to soldiers marching in a parade.
6. Fingerplays at best can be vehicles for teaching good English. Watch out for misuse of verbs and adverbs. Books such as *Move*

Over, Mother Goose . . . offer imaginative fingerplays and poems that consider the broader need to explore language while many other books of fingerplays only rhyme.*

A number of other books of fingerplays include

- *Move Over, Mother Goose* by Ruth Dowell (available from Gryphon House)
- *Finger Frolics: Fingerplays for Young Children* by Liz Cromwell and Dixie Hibner (published by Partner Press and available from Gryphon House)

Figure 10-2
Performing fingerplays is a pleasant way to come together and to transition into the rest of the day.

---

* "A Few Guidelines When Selecting Fingerplays." Copyright © 1990 by Harcourt Brace & Co., reprinted by permission of the publisher.

- *Mitt Magic: Fingerplays for Finger Puppets* by Lynda Roberts (Gryphon House)
- *Ring a Ring o' Roses* by Flint Public Library (Redleaf Press).

Musical versions of fingerplays can be found on the following recordings:

- *PreSchool Action Time* by Carol Hammett (Kimbo)
- *Fingerplay Fun!* by Rosemary Hallum (Educational Activities)
- *Fingerplays and Footplays for Fun and Learning* by Rosemary Hallum and Henry "Buzz" Glass (Educational Activities)
- *Clap, Snap, and Tap* by Ambrose Brazelton (Educational Activities)
- *Finger Games* by Liz Williams and Donna Wemple (Educational Activities)
- *Let's Sing Fingerplays,* a collection from Tom Glazer's book, *Eye Winker, Tom Tinker, Chin Chopper* (Educational Record Center).

According to Hamilton and Flemming (1990), some fingerplays date back almost 2,000 years; and although they originally used only the fingers and hands to teach various concepts (like perhaps the most famous musical fingerplay, "Where Is Thumbkin?"), today's fingerplays sometimes use the entire body. These authors suggest teaching fingerplays to children by demonstrating the actions while speaking or singing the words. The process is then repeated, with the children being encouraged to perform only the actions. On the next repetition, children who want to can participate with both actions and words.

As the children are arriving at the school or center, one adult could serve as the official greeter while a second sits on the floor and performs fingerplays with those children who have shed their outerwear and are ready to begin their day.

When all the children have arrived and are gathered together, an activity like This Is My Friend (adapted from Orlick, 1978) is a wonderful way for the children to welcome one another. They stand in a circle holding hands, and one child raises the arm of the child to her right or left, saying "This is my friend [Ahmad]." The process continues around the circle, in the same direction until each child has been introduced and all arms are in the air. The children can then take a deep bow for a job well done.

Finally, before proceeding, you can talk with the children about what to expect that day and then perform a relevant song or movement activity. If you are working with a theme, the song or activity should definitely be related to it. For instance, if the theme is transportation, you might sing "Wheels on the Bus," with or without the accompaniment of a recording. (For those who want to use a recording, this song is on Raffi's *Rise and Shine,* Hammett and Bueffel's *Toddlers on Parade,* and Sharon, Lois, and Bram's *Elephant Show.*)

Figure 10-3
An activity like "This Is My Friend" is a wonderful way for teachers and children to welcome each other.

Transitions Within the Classroom

Among transitions within the classroom are moving from group time to free time, from free time to group time, and to snacks or lunch—all of which can easily be tied into the current classroom theme.

Continuing with the transportation theme, you might ask the children to move from place to place as though rowing a boat, riding a horse, or another familiar mode of transportation. The children can sing an appropriate song (e.g., "Row, Row, Row Your Boat"), or you could create and teach them a short chant involving a form of transportation.

These transitions also offer a means to reinforce something experienced during a movement session. The children can be asked to perform their favorite movement from the most recent session or to execute a specific skill—locomotor, nonlocomotor (e.g., turns), or manipulative (e.g., pretending to pull something)—as they move from place to place. Movement elements can also be explored; if you have been working on the element of force, you could ask the children to make the transition as lightly as possible, like a butterfly, or as though weightless in outer space.

In addition, opportunities for problem solving present themselves here. Gordon and Browne (1993), referring to it as a "creativity question," suggest asking the children to move while using only one foot and one hand in some way. Other possibilities include asking them to move like any four-legged animal, in a particular shape, at the highest or lowest level, in a backward or sideward direction, using only curving or zigzag pathways, or using any locomotor skill but walking or running.

Figure 10-4
Use transitions to reinforce something experienced during a movement session. These children have been asked to move like robots.

If the children are going to or from snack or lunch, you can ask them to move like juice being poured, moving through peanut butter or marshmallow fluff, the odor of food floating through the air, or in the shape of a food served—perhaps, a carrot stick or a cookie. In keeping with the transportation theme, ask them to move like trucks, trains, tractors, or wheelbarrows transporting food.

When leaving story time, the children can pretend to move like their favorite character in the story. A song performed to the tune of "London Bridge" can help transition children from other group times to free time.

> Now we go our separate ways, separate ways,
>   separate ways
> Now we go our separate ways
> We'll come back together soon.

To dismiss a few children at a time from the group, you could point to individual children as you sing the following, to the tune of "Ten Little Indians":

> One little, two little, three little children
> Four little, five little, six little children
> Seven little, eight little, nine little children
> Off to learning centers (leaving from our circle).

If you want the children to transition from free to group time and to form a circle, you can ask every child to take the hands of two other children, with all tummies facing the center of the room, and to meet in the middle of the room (or the movement space, etc.). Or you could use the following chant:

> Come together, come together
> Come together now
> Stand together in a circle
> Take a great big bow!

Transitions to Outside the Classroom

This section discusses transitions that involve, among others, going outdoors for play time or recess, leaving for field trips, or simply going to another area within the building (e.g., the gym, library, or cafeteria).

When preparing to leave the room in single file, you might use some of the suggestions mentioned earlier, such as asking all children

Figure 10-5
Children are willing to wait their turn as long as they know they will get one. Vary the methods you use to form lines so the same children are not always first or last.

wearing a certain color shirt to line up at the door, followed by all those whose names begin with the letter B, etc. Or, if the children have been working individually at learning centers, you can move from center to center, inviting the children to join you with a chant such as the following:

> Take my hand
> Come take my hand
> We're going on a journey.

You can then lead the children, with a spirit of adventure, toward the door.

Follow the Leader is an excellent activity for these transitions. Leaders should use the elements of movement to vary how they transport the group (e.g., slowly, quickly, lightly, strongly, at various levels, in different shapes, etc.). Or they can relate the activity to the current theme. Using transportation, for instance, the leader can pretend to be an airplane, a train engine, riding a horse, or rowing a boat. Initially,

adults should act as leaders; but once the children have gained ample experience, they can take turns handling the responsibility.

Problem solving is appropriate here also. You can use the examples given in Transitions Within the Classroom, as well as the following possibilities:

- Move to the playground (library or cafeteria) like the occupation (character, animal) you would most like to be.
- Find a way using only one foot (or three body parts, etc.).
- Move in the most crooked shape possible.
- Move in a sideward direction, using any method of locomotion but walking or running.
- Find a way to move that involves a preposition (e.g., over, under, around, between, or through).

If you need to be especially quiet during a transition, as when going down a hallway with other classes in session, you can ask the children to pretend to be turtles, weightless astronauts, butterflies, eagles soaring, or mimes. They can also imagine they are moving through peanut butter, deep snow, or waist-high water.

Finally, if your class is going on or coming from a field trip, you can make the transition more relevant by relating it in some way to the trip. If, for example, the field trip were to the fire station, ask the children to move like water flowing through a hose or the hose being unwound from the truck and stretched out. (Can they create a single hose with their bodies?) If the field trip were to the public library, they can pretend to move like a bookworm, a quiet librarian, or a whisper.

Cleanup

Cleaning up is a fact of life for adults. Many do it grudgingly, only because it must be done. But perhaps that would not be true if cleanup had been an enjoyable experience during early childhood. Teachers and caregivers can ensure cleanup is pleasant for young children. And by making it agreeable *and* a necessary routine, they can help children learn self-responsibility.

Although experts vary in their suggestions regarding the length of notice to be given prior to cleanup time, they agree it is important to give children notice of forthcoming shifts in activity. Isenberg and Jalongo (1993) suggest ten-, five-, and one-minute warnings to begin cleanup; Gordon and Browne (1993) suggest a five-minute warning;

and Essa (1992)—because older children are more product-oriented—recommends one minute of warning for each year of the child's age (e.g., three minutes for three-year-olds). Whatever time you determine is most appropriate, you should establish a signal, such as a flick of the lights, to indicate it is time to begin wrapping up. A chant can also serve as a signal that warning time has elapsed and the actual cleanup must begin.

> It's time to clean up
> It's time to clean up
> It's time to clean up right now.

Figure 10-6
The experts agree that it is important to give children notice of forthcoming shifts in activity.

Once cleanup starts, a number of possibilities can make it both fun and expedient. Music can certainly be valuable. Beaty (1984) suggests playing a favorite recording and challenging the children to finish before the song ends. You might choose Mr. Al's "It's Clean-Up Time," from *Sing Me Some Sanity,* a collection of transition songs available from Melody House. Any lively song is fine as long as it is one with which the children are very familiar, so they can anticipate the ending.

You can encourage the children to sing or hum "Whistle While You Work." For recorded accompaniment, *Homemade Games and Activities* is available from Kimbo. Or you could put your own words to the melody.

> Singing while we work
> We're happy to be neat
> We pick up here and pick up there
> Until our job's complete.

Imagery can also do the job. Children enjoy pretending to be vacuum cleaners, elves, robots, construction workers, homemakers, and custodians. Other images, again using the transportation theme, include pretending to be trains or garbage trucks transporting materials where they belong. They should also learn walking while carrying things is a form of transportation.

Nap Time

As mentioned in Chapter 8, relaxation is a learned skill. Nap time offers a daily opportunity to help children acquire this skill.

To bring closure to any activity going on and alert the children that nap time has arrived, dim or turn off the lights and play a recording of some soft, slow, instrumental music. Several possibilities, including children's recordings for quiet times, are listed in Chapter 6. Then, to assist the children make the transition from activity to inactivity, ask them to move to their mats or cots like any of the following:

- deflating balloons coming down from the sky,
- wind-up toys winding down,
- the melting witch in the *Wizard of Oz,*
- turtles,
- snails, or
- bears lumbering to their caves for hibernation.

If you are using a theme, incorporate it into the imagery. For a transportation theme, you could ask children to imagine they are hot air balloons or airplanes coming in for a gentle landing, motorboats or cars running out of gas, or trains chugging into the station.

Once the children are in their places, some of the relaxation exercises suggested in Chapter 8 can help them unwind. You could sing a favorite, slow-paced song or do a fingerplay. "Tony Chestnut" and "Eensy Weensy Spider" cover both bases and should be familiar enough to the children to be relaxing. Or teach the children a fingerplay specifically related to rest that can become a part of their nap time routine, like the following, excerpted from Cherry (1981, p. 79):

> It's time to rest, to rest your head
> (Put right forefinger in left palm.)
> Snuggled down in your own little bed.
> (Rock finger back and forth.)
> Covered up tight in blankets so warm,
> (Cover with left fingers.)
> Safe and cozy and away from all harm.
> (Bring hands to cheek, bend head against
>   hands, close eyes.)

Create chants and songs using the children's names, which you can sing from your place in the center of the group, looking at each child as you sing his or her name; or you can sing as you quietly move from cot to cot. Following is one possibility, sung to the tune of Brahms' "Lullabye":

> Rest your eyes, rest your eyes
> Rest your eyes, little [Sarah]
> Let your body relax
> Feel the peace that it brings.

Later, waking children can stretch like waking cats or bears coming out of hibernation. They can then go quietly to prepared learning centers or into a group led by a teacher doing fingerplays, songs, or quiet movement activities. Since children (all people, in fact) have varying body rhythms, they should be allowed 15 to 20 minutes following nap time for quiet activities (Cherry, 1981).

Those children still asleep after the majority are up and about should be woken *gently*. You might place a hand on the sleeping child, quietly singing "Are You Sleeping?" and substituting the child's name for Brother John.

Figure 10-7
Create quiet chants and
songs using the children's
names. The personal touch
is always appropriate.

Departure

Because achieving closure brings such satisfaction, the transition to departure is an important one. It can help children feel good about their day, good about you, and good about returning in the morning.

"Ring Around the Rosie" is a fun, familiar activity to bring the children together in a circle on the floor. Once they are sitting down, you can sing an uplifting song like "If You're Happy," asking those who are developmentally ready to suggest motions, in addition to clapping, that demonstrate happiness.

An activity that reviews what was experienced or learned during the day (about transportation, for example) is appropriate for closing the day. "Punchinello," for instance, is an excellent end-of-the-day activity. The children form a circle, with one child in the center ("Punchinello") and chant or sing: "What can you do, Punchinello, funny fellow? What can you do, Punchinello, funny you?" The child in the center chooses one of the day's activities to demonstrate. When she is through, the group sings: "We can do it, too, Punchinello, funny fellow. We can do it too, Punchinello, funny you." And they do! Each child, in turn, has a chance to be Punchinello.

Then, just as each arriving child was welcomed individually, so should each departing one be individually acknowledged. The following is a chant you and the remaining children can offer to each child as he or she leaves:

> It was good to have you with us today
> It was good to have you, [Kara]
> It was good to have you with us today
> I'll (we'll) see you in the morning.

Or you and the children could sing this song to the tune of "Goodnight, Ladies":

> Goodbye, [Michael], goodbye, [Michael]
> Goodbye, [Michael]
> We'll see you tomorrow.

Obviously, many activities suggested in Chapter 10, though listed under one category, can work equally well for other transitions. Use these examples as a starting point, creating and collecting other ideas as you work with the children. If you plan for transitions, using movement and music to add personality, warmth, learning opportunities, and fun to parts of the day that might otherwise be routine and dull, you will know you and the children are making the most of every day.

Key Points

- Because they comprise a large part of the children's day, transitions should be planned as are other components of the program.
- Among the goals for successful transitions are that they occur without abruptness and without chaos. These goals can be

achieved with advance preparation and by notifying children of upcoming shifts in activity.

- In addition to the learning opportunities presented by tying transitions to curriculum content, transitions teach children to bring closure to activities, to move into and out of group dynamics, and to follow directions. Also, when linked to curriculum content, transitions add continuity to the day and give children more on-task time.
- Movement and music can help make transitions smooth, fun, and educational.
- Transitions typically occur on arrival and departure and when children move to or from group time, free time, snacks and lunch, nap time, and the outdoors. Cleanup is also considered a transition in early childhood and elementary programs.
- Teachers and caregivers should have a repertoire of memorized fingerplays, songs, and movement activities to use whenever the need or opportunity arises.

Assignments

1. Create at least one original activity with movement and/or music for each of the transitions described in Chapter 10.
2. Choose a well-known song and write new lyrics to its melody that can help bring the children from free time to group time.
3. Write a rationale for planning transitions as other parts of the daily program are planned.
4. Produce a collection of at least eight songs, movement activities, and fingerplays (not including those you created for assignment 1) that could be routinely used for transitions.

References

Allen, K. E., & Hart, B. (1984). *The early years: Arrangements for learning.* Englewood Cliffs, N.J.: Prentice-Hall.

Beaty, J. J. (1984). *Skills for preschool teachers.* Columbus, Ohio: Merrill.

Cherry, C. (1981). *Think of something quiet.* Carthage, Ill.: Fearon.

Davidson, J. (1982). Wasted time: The ignored dilemma. In J. F. Brown, ed., *Curriculum planning for young children* (pp. 196–204). Washington, D.C.: National Association for the Education of Young Children.

Essa, E. (1992). *Introduction to early childhood education.* Albany, N.Y.: Delmar.

Feldman, J. R. (1991). *A survival guide for the preschool teacher.* West Nyack, N.Y.: Center for Applied Research in Education.

Gordon, A., & Browne, K. W. (1993). *Beginnings and beyond.* Albany, N.Y.: Delmar.

Hamilton, D. S., & Flemming, B. M. (1990). *Resources for creative teaching in early childhood education,* 2d ed. Fort Worth, Texas: Harcourt Brace Jovanovich.

Hildebrand, V. (1980). *Guiding young children.* New York: Macmillan.

Isenberg, J. P., & Jalongo, M. R. (1993). *Creative expression and play in the early childhood curriculum.* New York: Merrill.

Orlick, T. (1978). *The cooperative sports and games book: Challenge without competition.* New York: Pantheon.

CHAPTER 11

Bringing Movement Education Outdoors

*T*ime spent outdoors has traditionally been considered "break" time—an opportunity for children to play without interference from adults and for teachers and caregivers to relax a bit. More and more early childhood professionals, however, are realizing the potential of the outdoors as an extension of the indoor setting, with that time viewed as yet another opportunity to enhance the children's development. And the experts agree.

Gordon and Browne (1993), Isenberg and Jalongo (1993), Shipley (1993), Essa (1992), and Frost (1992) are just some of the authors who maintain the outdoor space should be used not only for the enhancement of physical skills, but also for children's social, emotional, creative, and cognitive development.

This is not to say teachers must go to the extreme of preparing structured lesson plans for every outdoor session. But many activities begun indoors can certainly be continued and extended outdoors, including movement activities. (Batteries in the cassette player and hand-held instruments like guitars, recorders, and autoharps, mean even music can be a part of outdoor movement experiences.) Also, during free play time, adults *can* and *should* interact naturally and informally with the children, offering guidance and suggestions that extend the children's play.

The fact is, traditional playgrounds and their traditional uses do little to stimulate the children's development. Curtis (1982, p. 107) says,

---

Portions of Chapter 11 were adapted from Pica, R. (1991). By permission of *Early Childhood News*.

"[Playgrounds] fall short of providing the impetus for movement that is essential to a child's development because they are static. Children cannot change the equipment to challenge themselves and practice specific movements."

Bowers (1992, p. 158) concurs, stating:

> The natural play of all young children, which is characterized by exploration, creativity, and gaining mastery over new physical challenges, is in direct conflict with the limited ways traditional play equipment can be used. Play equipment which . . . demands that these activities be performed in a singular prescribed way severely limits the imaginative play of children.

Although some modern, multiple-function structures (both wooden and modular plastic ones) lend themselves to divergent play experiences, not every playground has such equipment. And even on those playgrounds that do, children may still view these structures as having limited uses, and thus require adult assistance in discovering more creative possibilities.

Figure 11-1
Some modern multi-function playground structures lend themselves to divergent play experiences, but the children may still require adult assistance in discovering creative uses for the equipment.

The playground is the obvious and natural choice for many facets of the movement program. Unless you are fortunate enough to have the necessary equipment indoors, such gymnastic skills as climbing, hanging and swinging, and balancing can be experienced best on outdoor equipment. The playground can be the most appropriate area for the practice of manipulative skills; not only is it conducive to the performance of such ball-handling skills as throwing, catching, and striking, but also here children have opportunities to perform such actions as *pushing* a swing, *pulling* a wagon, and *lifting and carrying* movable objects. And, of course, it is in the outdoors that children can fully and freely experience gross motor skills like running, leaping, and jumping (including jumping *off* things).

The remainder of this chapter looks at how teachers and caregivers can encourage children to use the playground space and some typical equipment in varied and creative ways. Not only do the suggested activities promote motor learning in ways the basic, obvious uses of swings, slides, and sandboxes simply cannot, but also they provide the children a much needed outlet for creativity, self-expression, and problem solving. In other words, the playground—an area already synonymous with movement—can become an arena for movement *education*.

Note that some of the following activities require adult supervision and/or assistance. Caution the children they should have an adult helper if they try these activities at home or at the park.

Playground Space

As mentioned, the playground is a great place to practice manipulative skills. On paved areas, children can work on their bouncing and ball-rolling abilities. Grassy areas are perfect for practicing dribbling (the grass helps keep the ball under control). And any open area is great for throwing, catching, kicking, volleying, and striking.

These, of course, are typical playground activities. However, you may not have considered the open areas of your playground for movement experiences—like large-group activities—that are inconvenient or impossible indoors due to lack of space. Games like Follow the Leader can be more challenging and more appealing when there is ample space to explore and obstacles to have an impact on the courses taken. Shipley (1993, pp. 346–47) suggests a game called Cross Over in which children form a large circle and note those standing on either side of them. On a signal from the teacher, the children try to cross through the circle to the opposite side without bumping into or touching one another. When they have crossed over, they should be

Figure 11-2
Open areas naturally lend
themselves to the practice
of a number of manipulative
skills. From Pugmire-Stoy,
*Spontaneous Play in Early
Childhood,* copyright 1992
by Delmar Publishers Inc.

standing next to the same children as they were when on the other
side. This excellent activity reinforces the concept of personal space,
and whole-group activities such as this further social development.

Cherry (1976, p. 71) proposes teachers construct "skinny paths" by
laying "unit blocks or pieces of rope, wood, or board in parallel rows
that allow just enough space for the children to move cautiously
between them." These narrow walkways provide balancing challenges
unlike those fostered by beams or planks raised off the ground.

Parachute, hoop, and ribbon activities are often more practical outdoors (ribbon activities are certainly safer in a large, open area). And
the possibilities for obstacle courses, using small and large equipment,
are endless. Start small, changing the course often (even daily) and
gradually increasing the challenge. The course should give the children a great deal of experience with such concepts as over, under,
through, around, and between. Eventually, they can even help you
design the courses.

Climbing Structures

Cherry (1976, p. 53) writes, if she had room for only one piece of equipment, it would definitely be something to climb on. In addition to the physical benefits derived from the practice of climbing (and hanging and swinging), she believes that "few experiences can make a child feel so important as sitting on top of a jungle gym."

Whether your climbing equipment consists of a jungle gym, monkey bars, or cargo nets, you can help the children view it in new and exciting ways. Suggestions for exploring climbing structures using imagery and elements of movement follow.

Figure 11-3
Climbing, hanging, and swinging are the obvious possibilities for climbing structures, but teachers can help the children view it in new ways too. From Pugmire-Stoy, *Spontaneous Play in Early Childhood,* copyright 1992 by Delmar Publishers Inc.

IMAGERY

Children can pretend they are ivy growing and spreading, snakes slithering and wrapping themselves around tree limbs, clothes hanging on a line and drying in the breeze, Tarzan, mountain climbers, squirrels, firefighters at work, birds perched on branches, lookouts in a watchtower, and chimps and gorillas.

ELEMENTS OF MOVEMENT

Questions and challenges to pose include the following:

- Can you climb using just one leg and one arm?
- Can you climb up by rocking from one foot to the other?
- Can you climb up and down on tiptoe?
- Climb up quickly and down slowly.
- Add pauses to your climbing (climb and pause, etc.).

Balance Beams

Balancing is a skill children simply cannot practice too often. You can purchase a commercial balance beam from suppliers like Flaghouse and J. L. Hammett (Appendix 2), or ask a parent to construct one for you. Or use narrow planks—placed either on or slightly above the ground, depending on the children's developmental levels. The edge of a sandbox, if wide enough, can also encourage other balancing activities.

Balancing, however, is not the only function of a balance beam. You can explore the concept of *over* by asking children to find how many ways they can get over the beam. (Possibilities include jumping, hopping, leaping, and crawling.) Also, challenge them to discover how many ways they can get *onto* and *off* the beam.

IMAGERY

To explore travel *along* the beam, challenge the children to move across like a tightrope walker; a gymnast (can they make up Olympic routines?); a butterfly, inchworm, spider, or bumblebee; a cat stalking its prey; or an elephant, penguin, turtle, kangaroo, or snake. How

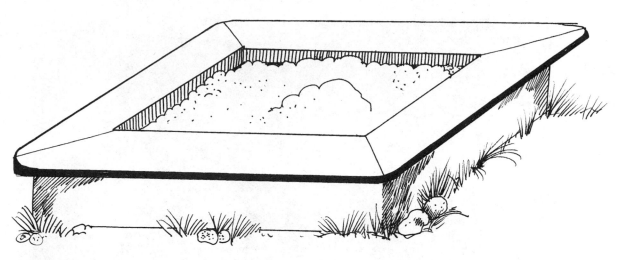

Figure 11-4
The edge of a sandbox, if wide enough, can be used in place of a balance beam.

might a circus clown move from one end to the other? A ballet dancer? A giant or an elf?

ELEMENTS OF MOVEMENT

Possibilities for travel along the beam include moving forward, backward, and sideward (trying it with right and left sides leading); on one foot; in slow motion and as quickly as possible; being as tall (small) as possible; on tiptoe or heels; taking tiny or giant steps; moving as lightly or strongly as possible.

Also, walking is not the only locomotor skill that should be practiced. How many others can the children execute on a balance beam? Which are the easiest? Which are the hardest? How many can be performed backward or sideward?

Tunnels

Most children love tunnels; and, when concrete conduits or plastic culverts or modular playground structures are not readily available, they will create them from rows of upright tires, wooden crates, or large cardboard boxes. Tunnels are especially suitable for exploring

Figure 11-5
Children enjoy practicing balancing skills. Here a plank has been placed between cable spools. From Frost, *Play and Playscapes,* copyright 1992 by Delmar Publishers Inc.

the concepts of *through* and *inside,* but can also be used for experiencing *over, around,* and *under* (when inside, children are also under the roof of the tunnel).

IMAGERY

Children can imagine they are hiding from someone or looking for buried treasure, water flowing through the tunnel, space travelers, cave dwellers, bears in hibernation, and trains or subway cars.

Figure 11-6
Empty large appliance boxes and rows of upright tires can be used to create tunnels.

ELEMENTS OF MOVEMENT

Challenge the children to travel through the tunnels in the following ways:

Backward
Being as round (flat) as possible
On hands and feet
On feet and bottom and hands (or in an upside-down way)
Slowly (quickly)
Lightly (heavily)
Occasionally pausing to look back over the shoulder
Using the arm and leg on one side of the body only

Platforms

Platforms can be part of playground superstructures or constructed with upright telephone cable spools; sturdy tables (e.g., picnic tables); solid wooden crates; or large tree stumps—all of which can also serve as support for bridges or high-wire acts for those children developmentally ready to move above the ground.

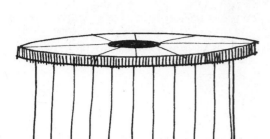

Figure 11-7
Telephone cable spools and large tree stumps can serve as platforms or "stages."

IMAGERY

Children can use their imagination to move on top of whatever platforms are available. Frost (1992, p. 106) describes the playground as a "stage where children can act out, spontaneously and freely, the events that touch their lives." When the children are on outdoor platforms, you can encourage them to think specifically of being "on stage." Ask them to imagine they are

a singer
a dancer
someone making a speech
a model in a fashion show
an actor
a performing seal
a musician playing an instrument
a magician

ELEMENTS OF MOVEMENT

Just being above the ground, even on a wide, stable base, can add an extra challenge to balance activities. Ask the children to try balancing on tiptoes, one (the other) foot, one foot on tiptoe, one foot while leaning in different directions, one hand and one foot, one hand and one knee, one knee only, bottom only, and tummy only.

Imagining the platform is their very own personal space, how many ways can the children find to move in personal space? (This can lead to a thorough exploration of nonlocomotor skills.) How many body shapes can they find to fill the space? How many ways can they find to fill very little of the space? How many ways can they find to move around the space?

Tires

Tires have so many uses! As mentioned, they can be placed upright in rows to create tunnels. They can also be stacked, rolled, crawled through, and used as targets to throw balls and beanbags through. When laid flat, they can be grouped in different patterns (e.g., in a single-file line or in a pattern resembling hopscotch), inviting the children to explore possibilities for moving from one end to the other

Figure 11-8
Among other things, tires make great swings.

(by stepping either inside of or on top of the tires). They also make great swings.

IMAGERY

An automobile or bicycle tire lying flat on the ground can be a small boat being tossed at sea; a flying carpet; a cloud floating across the sky; a sled sliding down a steep, snowy hill; a hot air balloon; or any mode of transportation they can imagine.

Tires also make excellent cauldrons for stirring up a witch's brew, a giant pot for cooking a crowd-size batch of spaghetti, or the world's largest bowl of cereal. And when the children are done cooking, they can pretend it is a pool and wade in it.

ELEMENTS OF MOVEMENT

Many of the activities described for platforms can be explored inside a tire. Because the area is smaller, the challenge of finding diverse ways to move can be even greater. Moving forward, backward, and sideward around the edge of the tire provides additional practice with balance. And how many ways can the children find to get into and out of the tire? (Possibilities include jumping, hopping, and leaping.) Can they get into and out of the tire in forward, backward, and sideward directions? Quickly and slowly? Lightly and heavily?

Sand

First and foremost, sand, with digging and pouring materials, is great for constructive play. It also lends itself to science experiments. What happens when a little water is added to sand? How about a lot of water? Does dry or wet sand weigh more? What would happen if a tunnel were dug into the sand and water poured into the tunnel? Does the water follow its path? Can the children show you with their bodies what water looks like when it travels through a tunnel?

To demonstrate art experiences, what shapes can the children mold with sand? Can they show you those shapes with their bodies?

Sand is also effective for fantasy play. Ask the children to pretend to be digging for buried treasure at the beach or in the desert, chefs or bakers mixing a famous recipe, scientists working on an experiment, gophers burrowing, or dogs burying bones.

Riding Toys

Maneuvering a riding toy along pathways and around corners and obstacles does much to develop visual-motor skill and laterality. But riding itself may not be enough of a challenge for some children. The following recommendations can add to the challenge.

IMAGERY

Children can pretend to be absolutely anyone they would like to be, traveling on anything they would like to ride. Possibilities include Santa on his sleigh, cowhands riding the range, a circus acrobat atop an elephant, an astronaut in a spaceship, a jockey, or a race car driver. Less dramatic but equally valid are situations in which they pretend the riding toy is a tractor, bulldozer, fire engine, or police car. Perhaps it is a tow truck. What can the children find to tow? If it were a piece of construction equipment, what could they find to haul? What if several children formed a parade with a line of riding toys? What modes of transportation are often seen in parades? (Possibilities include floats, fire engines, cars with convertible tops, and horses.)

ELEMENTS OF MOVEMENT

Challenge the children to ride in straight, curving, and zigzag pathways. Set up an obstacle course with these three pathways. Can the children ride both quickly and slowly? (Which requires the most force?) Can the children ride backwards?

Slides

Slides are perhaps the most static pieces of equipment on a typical playground; they have so few functions. But you can introduce your

Figure 11-9
A slide is perhaps the most static piece of equipment on a typical playground, but you can introduce the children to some nontraditional ways of using it.

children to some nontraditional ways to use this traditional piece of equipment, opening their minds to the possibilities brought about through imagination and problem solving.

IMAGERY

Children can use the ladder of the slide as a piece of climbing equipment and thus imagine they are all the people and things listed earlier. The ladder can also be part of a hook-and-ladder truck, a piece of equipment used by a painter or carpenter, or a life-saving fire escape.

The slide itself does not have to be only a slide. It can be a laundry chute, a water slide, or the side of a steep mountain that must be climbed.

ELEMENTS OF MOVEMENT

Challenge the children to climb the ladder in the same ways suggested for the climbing structures. For the slide itself, the possibilities include going down backward, lying on the tummy, in the smallest shape possible, as flat as possible, as crooked as possible, with one leg bent and the other straight; and with both legs bent. (Most of these require adult supervision to prevent mishaps.)

Swings

Shipley (1993, p. 339) contends swings promote "coordination, muscle development, and a sense of freedom and emotional release. Through learning to pump the swing to gain momentum, children develop a sense of the mid-line of the body. . . ." You can ensure the swing sets on your playground have even more to offer the children.

IMAGERY

Swinging is probably the closest to flying most children ever get. Ask them to imagine they are on a flying trapeze, or any flying creature or superhero they would like to be. They can pretend to be the pendulum on a grandfather clock, a windshield wiper, or a tolling bell. The swing can be any mode of transportation imaginable, from a covered wagon to a space shuttle.

ELEMENTS OF MOVEMENT

Challenge the children to swing with one leg bent and the other straight; with both legs remaining straight, with both legs bent, as slowly (quickly) as possible, gradually increasing speed and then gradually slowing, while nodding the head up and down or turning it from side to side, while kneeling, stopping on cue and starting again, and with as much force as possible.

Although the ideas presented in Chapter 11 certainly do not cover the full range of possibilities, they can begin to help you—and, in turn, the children—view some common playground equipment in uncommon ways. Children are naturally inventive and, with some initial enthusiasm from you, can create uses for the equipment beyond your wildest imaginings.

PLAYGROUND EQUIPMENT LIST When selecting playground equipment for children, teachers and caregivers must choose only those materials that are age-appropriate and safe. For example, many early childhood professionals consider trampolines inappropriate for young children. When available, they should only be used with supervision. Also, if items like rakes, spades, and hoes are not child-sized, they should be used only by adults and kept in storage, inaccessible to children.

The following is excerpted from Shipley (1993, pp. 344–345) and reprinted by permission of Nelson Canada.

Large Muscle

climbing structure or A-frame

jungle gym

securely suspended rope
   to climb and swing on

tire or bucket swings

rope ladder

firefighter's pole

triangular ladder

slide with 15- to 20-cm drop at
   end

spring-based seesaw

trampoline

ramps for sliding and jumping

bowling set

snow shovels

baseball bat and ball

7-, 10-, and 18-inch balls

large hoops

punching ball or bag

skipping ropes and hoops

rowboat

beanbags and target

balance beams or interlocking boards

balance blocks

stilts

pogo stick

skate boards with helmets and shin
   pads

stationary-spring riding animals

horizontal ladder

simple playhouse or house frame

stick horses

tree house

steering wheel on wooden frame

large hollow wooden building blocks

Vehicles and Accessories

gas station fuel pump

tricycles

wagons or carts

pedal cars

wheelbarrow

tractor

bicycle pump

hard hats

cargo for wagons and carts

Loose Materials

painted wooden boxes

barrels and kegs

large packing boxes and crates
  (e.g., appliance cartons)

sawhorses

short wooden ladders

lumber in 2- and 1-m
  lengths

rocks and boulders

workbench

softwood supplies

tool kit and tools

tires

logs

tree stump

telephone cable spools

weather-treated large blocks

rope

milk crates

tarpaulins

clothesline and pulleys

large and small paint brushes

pails

water-soluble paint

old shirts and dropsheets

surplus building materials

Gardening

hose and tap or pump

rakes

sterilized manure

string or rope

spades

hoes

hand shovels

claws

bags and baskets

sprinkler

watering cans

seed packets

flats for seeds

peat moss

wooden stakes

rubber gloves

gardening gloves (for the teacher)

overalls

old fabric and rags (for a scarecrow)

jiffy starter kits

gardening books

Sand and Water

buckets

scoops

shovels

sieves

steam shovels

heavy-duty trucks and cars

hose and tap

construction hats

camp stools

fishing rods and nets

tackle box

plastic wading pool

air mattress

diving mask

paddles

small sailing boats

inflatable raft

jugs and plastic pails

funnels and siphons

pup tent

flashlight

sleeping bag

knapsack

tin lunch boxes

canteen

tin pots and pans

saddle bags

Storage and Furniture

storage sheds with locks

benches

picnic table and umbrella

lawn chairs

barbecue or hibachi

firewood and grate

fire pit

prop box

Frost (1992, p. 336) asserts, "[The] adult who remains aloof from play misses opportunities for engaging with and learning from children." Further, such an adult will be unable to enrich the children's outdoor experiences, offering them opportunities to express themselves creatively, stretch their imaginations, and be continually challenged. On the other hand, teachers and caregivers who interact with the children on the playground can make certain the outdoors becomes an extension of the indoors and movement education is taking place in *both* settings.

Key Points

- Early childhood professionals should not hesitate to interact with the children outdoors due to concern regarding interfering with their play. Rather, they should consider the outdoor setting an extension of the indoors, providing opportunities for children's physical, social, emotional, creative, and cognitive development.
- Due to their static nature, traditional playgrounds and their traditional uses do little to stimulate children's development and seriously limit their imaginative play.
- Divergent play experiences that allow children to adapt equipment and materials to their own needs and to find more than one way to use equipment and materials are developmentally appropriate for young children.
- The playground is the natural choice for many facets of the movement program, including the practice of manipulative and gymnastic skills. However if weather permits, many other movement activities can also be conducted outdoors. The playground is especially appropriate for large-group activities;

obstacle courses; and practice with parachutes, hoops, and ribbons.
- Teachers and caregivers can use imagery and movement elements to encourage varied uses for such common equipment as climbing structures, balance beams, tunnels, platforms, tires, sand, riding toys, slides, and swings.

Assignments

1. Think about your beliefs regarding the adult's role on the playground. Justify your position in writing.
2. Cite examples other than those listed in Chapter 11 of ways the outdoor setting can enrich learning begun indoors, particularly in regard to movement education.
3. Using early childhood catalogs, create your own wish list of playground equipment and materials. Justify your choices in writing, keeping in mind creativity and safety.
4. Design an obstacle course. Determine how it can be made both less and more challenging to suit different developmental levels.
5. Using imagery and the elements of movement, create new uses for two pieces of equipment not described in Chapter 11.

References

Bowers, L. (1992). Playground management and safety. In C. M. Hendricks, ed., *Young children on the grow: Health, activity, and education in the preschool setting* (pp. 157–65). Washington, D.C.: ERIC.

Cherry, C. (1976). *Creative play for the developing child.* Carthage, Ill.: Fearon.

Curtis, S. R. (1982). *The joy of movement in early childhood.* New York: Teachers College.

Essa, E. (1992). *Introduction to early childhood education.* Albany, N.Y.: Delmar.

Frost, J. L. (1992). *Play and playscapes.* Albany, N.Y.: Delmar.

Gordon, A., & Browne, K. W. (1993). *Beginnings and beyond.* Albany, N.Y.: Delmar.

Isenberg, J. P., & Jalongo, M. R. (1993). *Creative expression and play in the early childhood curriculum.* New York: Merrill.

Pica, R. (1991). On the playground: Bringing movement education outdoors. *Early Childhood News,* 3(3), 1, 13.

Shipley, D. (1993). *Empowering children: Play-based curriculum for lifelong learning.* Scarborough, Ontario: Nelson Canada.

Developmentally Appropriate Practice in Movement Programs For Young Children Ages 3–5

A Position Statement of the National Association for Sport and Physical Education

developed by the

Council on Physical Education for Children (COPEC)

Background

Within the past ten years, the education of young children has become a major focus of public attention. The proliferation of preschools, child development centers, and other child care programs for 3- to 5-year–old children has resulted in increased interest in the education of this age group. Recently this age group has begun to receive more attention from physical educators.

In the mid-1980's, the National Association for the Education of Young Children (NAEYC), the professional association of early childhood educators, published a series of position statements which described developmentally appropriate practice for children from birth through age 8. The Council on Physical Education for Children (COPEC), a division of the National Association for Sport and Physical Education (NASPE), the nation's largest professional association of children's physical education teachers, used the NAEYC model to develop the document *Developmentally Appropriate Physical Education Practices for Children* in 1992. That position statement presented, in a straightforward manner, descriptions of both appropriate and inappropriate practices in physical education programs for children. Since the major responsibility for this instruction has been centered in the schools, it primarily addressed school-based physical education programs.

The purpose of this document is to focus upon developmentally appropriate practices in movement programs for 3- to 5-year-old children. This includes children enrolled in child care centers, private and public preschools, and kindergartens. This document can assist those who educate these children to: (1) make developmentally appropriate decisions about curriculum and content; (2) make appropriate decisions about how content is presented; (3) evaluate existing curriculum and teaching methods; (4) advocate the improvement of existing programs; and (5) more fully integrate movement activities into existing curriculum.

Quality Movement Programs for Young Children

The period of early childhood (which includes 3- to 5-year-olds) is associated with the *Fundamental Movement* phase of motor behavior (Gabbard, 1992; Gallahue, 1989; Wickstrom, 1983). This is a unique period in the lifespan due primarily to the emergence of fundamental movement abilities which establish the foundation upon which more complex movement skills are possible in later phases of development. It is also a crucial time in which positive learning experiences can have a significant influence on establishing a positive attitude and appreciation for a lifetime of participation in regular health-related physical activity.

It is COPEC's strong belief that a general "activity" oriented program consisting primarily of traditional games and dance is not an appropriate process for maximizing children's development. A more appropriate approach for this age group would be to focus on basic motor skills and movement concepts and how these activities can assist in the child's psychological, physical, intellectual, and social development.

COPEC believes that quality, daily movement programs should be available to all children. Quality movement programs are both developmentally and instructionally suitable for the specific children being served. Developmentally appropriate practices in movement programs are those which recognize children's changing capacities to move and those which promote such changes. A developmentally appropriate movement program accommodates a variety of individual characteristics such as developmental status, previous movement experiences, fitness and skill levels, body size, and age. Instructionally appropriate movement programs incorporate the best known practices, derived from both research and experiences teaching children, into a program that maximizes opportunities for learning and success for all children.

The outcome of a developmentally and instructionally appropriate program of physical education is an individual who is "physically educated."

In 1990, NASPE defined a physically educated person as one who:

- HAS learned the skills necessary to perform a variety of physical activities
- DOES participate regularly in physical activity
- IS physically fit
- KNOWS the implications of and the benefits from involvement in physical activities
- VALUES physical activity and its contributions to a healthful lifestyle.

Appropriate movement programs for young children provide an important first step toward becoming a physically educated person.

Premises of Movement Programs for Young Children

In any discussion of movement programs for young children there are five premises that need to be understood.

1. *Three-, 4- and 5-year-old children are different from elementary school-aged children.*

   In terms of motor development, 3- to 5-year-olds are considered to be in the initial and elementary stages of the fundamental movement phase. This is in comparison to 6- to 7-year-olds who are in the mature stage of the fundamental movement phase and 7- to 10-year-olds who are entering the sport-related movement phase of motor development (Gallahue, 1989). Teachers of 3-, 4- and 5-year-old children need to fully understand the continuum of development from toddler through the preschool years as it differs from that of elementary school-aged children. With this knowledge, the focus is on teaching children rather than teaching activities.

2. *Young children learn through interaction with their environment.*

   This well-established concept has been stated in many ways—children learn by doing; children learn through active involvement with people and objects. Developmentally appropriate movement programs for young children are designed so that all children are active participants, not passive listeners or observers.

3. *Teachers of young children are guides or facilitators.*

Since young children learn by doing, it follows that teachers of young children must facilitate the children's active involvement in learning. Teachers construct the environment with specific objectives in mind, then assume the role of guiding the children toward these goals. By carefully observing the children's responses and interests, teachers are able to adapt the learning experiences to best meet the individual child's needs. Children are allowed to make choices and seek creative solutions. They are provided the time and opportunity to explore appropriate responses. Teachers are actively involved in engaging the children in activity and extending their learning. As a result the instruction is "child-centered" rather than "subject-centered."

4. *Young children learn and develop in an integrated fashion.*

Physical, emotional, social, and cognitive development are interrelated. Learning is not compartmentalized. Learning experiences in movement should encompass and interface with all areas of development. Regularly scheduled movement experiences focus upon the development of physical skills while incorporating these experiences in the child's total development. Movement experiences are the primary source for all learning by young children.

5. *Planned movement experiences enhance play experiences.*

A combination of play along with planned movement experiences, specifically designed to help children develop physical skills, would be the most beneficial in assisting young children in their development. A combination of regularly scheduled and appropriately designed movement experiences are enhanced with regularly scheduled indoor and outdoor play experiences giving children an opportunity to freely practice and develop skills.

Intended Audience

This document is written for teachers, parents, school administrators, policymakers, and other individuals who provide educational programs for 3- to 5-year-olds. It is intended to provide specific guidelines that will help them recognize practices in movement programs that are in the best interests of children (appropriate) and those that are counterproductive, or even harmful (inappropriate). The components described in this statement are interrelated. They are separated here only for purposes of clarity and ease of reading. Although these components are not all inclusive, they do represent most of the characteristics of appropriate practice in movement programs for young children.

Integrated Components of Appropriate and Inappropriate Practice in Movement Programs for Young Children Ages 3–5

COMPONENT ONE: CURRICULUM

Appropriate Practice.   The movement curriculum has an obvious scope and sequence based on goals and objectives that are appropriate for all children. In includes a balance of skills and concepts designed to enhance the cognitive, motor, affective, and physical development of every child.

Inappropriate Practice.   The movement curriculum lacks developed goals and objectives and is based primarily on the teacher's interests, preferences, and background rather than those of the children. For example, the curriculum consists primarily of large group games.

COMPONENT TWO: TEACHING STRATEGIES

Appropriate Practice.   Movement exploration, guided discovery and creative problem solving are the predominant teaching strategies employed. Children are provided the opportunity to make choices and actively explore their environment; while teachers serve as facilitators, preparing a stimulating environment and challenging activities.

Inappropriate Practice.   Highly structured, teacher-directed lessons are the most common. Large group instruction is used in which all children are expected to perform the same activities in the same manner. For example, all children are expected to follow verbal cues on recorded music.

COMPONENT THREE: DEVELOPMENT OF MOVEMENT CONCEPTS AND MOTOR SKILLS

Appropriate Practice. Children are provided with frequent and meaningful age appropriate instruction and practice opportunities which enable individuals to develop a functional understanding of movement concepts (body awareness, space awareness, effort and relationships) as an integral part of their total education. These opportunities are meaningful to the child and are within the context of the child's experience.

Inappropriate Practice. Children participate in a limited number of games and activities designed to meet a predetermined standard or which require just one correct answer. The opportunity for individual children to develop basic concepts and motor skills is restricted. For example, children are directed to perform gymnastics skills with "perfect" form.

COMPONENT FOUR: COGNITIVE DEVELOPMENT

Appropriate Practice. Movement activities are designed with both the physical and cognitive development of children in mind. The unique role of movement programs, which allows children to learn to move while also moving to learn, is recognized and explored. For example, teachers ask questions such as, "How can you jump and land quietly?"

Inappropriate Practice. Movement programs are viewed as not contributing to other areas of instruction. Physical development, if addressed at all, is seen as strictly a recreational "play-time" activity, or a means of "burning excess energy" with no relation to the other areas of development. For example, teachers merely "roll out the ball" and intervene only if the situation becomes unsafe.

COMPONENT FIVE: AFFECTIVE DEVELOPMENT

Appropriate Practice. Many opportunities are provided for children to practice age appropriate social skills such as cooperating, taking turns and sharing. Teachers encourage the development of social skills, recognizing that younger children may not be ready to consistently exhibit these skills.

Teachers help all children experience the satisfaction and joy which result from regular participation in physical activity.

Inappropriate Practice. Teachers fail to intentionally enhance the affective development of children when activities which foster the development of cooperation and other social skills are excluded.

Teachers ignore opportunities to help children understand the emotions they feel as a result of participation in physical activity.

COMPONENT SIX: INTEGRATION OF MOVEMENT WITH OTHER CURRICULAR AREAS

Appropriate Practice. The learning environment is structured to permit the inclusion of appropriate movement challenges for all children in a setting that seeks to integrate, whenever possible, the concepts, abilities, and actions that emerge through guided exploration and discovery. For example, colors and sizes are reinforced by using a variety of balloons for striking skills.

Inappropriate Practice. Children's physical development is seen as fragmented from other areas of development. No attempt is made to relate learning in movement programs with other areas.

COMPONENT SEVEN: FITNESS

Appropriate Practice. Teachers recognize the importance of children valuing physical activity as a lifelong habit. Children learn the joy and value of exploring their physical capabilities as a lifetime pursuit. Fitness is considered a byproduct of participation in regular physical activity. For example, after an appropriate period of continuous locomotor movement, children are asked to discuss what is happening to their bodies during exercise.

Inappropriate Practice. Children participate in activities designed specifically to enhance their fitness levels (e.g., running laps, calisthenics, or videotaped aerobic programs).

COMPONENT EIGHT: ASSESSMENT

Appropriate Practice. Systematic assessment is based on knowledge of developmental characteristics and ongoing observations of children as they participate in activities. This information is used to individualize instruction, plan objective-oriented lessons, identify children with special needs, communicate with parents, and evaluate the program's effectiveness.

Inappropriate Practice. Children are assessed solely on the basis of test scores, such as physical skill tests and standardized fitness tests. For example, children's progress is measured by the number of times they can successfully perform a physical skill in an artificial testing situation.

COMPONENT NINE: ACTIVE PARTICIPATION FOR EVERY CHILD

Appropriate Practice. All children are encouraged to be involved in activities which allow them to remain active. Teachers recognize that younger children might need brief rest periods when participating in particularly strenuous activities. Continuous, extended aerobic activity is not expected.

Inappropriate Practice. Activity time is limited because children are waiting in lines for a turn in relay races, to be chosen for a team, or due to limited equipment or playing mostly sedentary games such as "Duck, Duck, Goose." Children are eliminated with no chance to re-enter the activity, or they must sit for long periods of time, as in games such as musical chairs and elimination tag.

COMPONENT TEN: DANCE/RHYTHMICAL EXPERIENCES

Appropriate Practice. The movement program includes a variety of rhythmical and expressive dance experiences designed with the physical, cultural, emotional, and social characteristics of the children in mind. Children are encouraged to use their imaginations and move to the sound of their individual rhythms.

Inappropriate Practice. Dances designed for adults (such as folk or square dances) are taught to the exclusion of other dance forms. Dances are not modified to meet the developmental needs of the children.

COMPONENT ELEVEN: EDUCATIONAL GYMNASTICS

Appropriate Practice. Broad skill areas such as balancing, rolling, jumping and landing, climbing, and weight transfer are presented. Children are given many opportunities to explore these skills in a variety of situations appropriate to their ability and confidence levels.

Inappropriate Practice. All children are expected to perform the same pre-determined stunts, such as forward rolls or cartwheels, regardless of their skill level, body composition and level of confidence.

COMPONENT TWELVE: GAMES

Appropriate Practice. Games are selected, designed, sequenced, and modified by teachers and/or children to maximize the learning and enjoyment of the children.

Inappropriate Practice. Games are taught with no obvious purpose or goal, other than to keep children "busy, happy, and good." Emphasis is placed upon the structure, rules and formations of the games.

COMPONENT THIRTEEN: GENDER DIRECTED ACTIVITIES

Appropriate Practice. Both girls and boys are equally encouraged, supported and socialized toward successful achievement in all realms of movement activities.

Inappropriate Practice. Girls are encouraged to participate in activities which stress traditionally feminine roles (such as rhythmical and expressive movement), whereas boys are encouraged to participate in more aggressive activities.

COMPONENT FOURTEEN: COMPETITION

Appropriate Practice. Activities emphasize self-improvement, participation and cooperation instead of winning and losing.

Inappropriate Practice. Children are required to participate in activities that label children as "winners" and "losers." Comparisons are made between one child's performance and another's.

COMPONENT FIFTEEN: SUCCESS RATE

Appropriate Practice. Children are given the opportunity to practice skills at high rates of success adjusted for their individual skill levels.

When necessary, children are provided an environment in which they can practice skills independently of other children in order to avoid the frustration and anxiety of low skill proficiency. For example, children are able to practice catching a ball which consistently rolls from a chute.

Inappropriate Practice. Children are asked to perform activities which are too easy or too hard, causing frustration, boredom, and/or misbehavior. All children are expected to perform to the same standards without allowing for individual abilities and interests.

Children are placed in small group or partner situations in which their success is limited, resulting in a lack of skill development. For example, when children throw and catch with a partner, more time is spent chasing the ball than practicing the skills of throwing and catching.

COMPONENT SIXTEEN: CLASS SIZE

Appropriate Practice. In order to provide young children with age-appropriate individualized instruction, the group size is limited. No more than 20 children ages 4- to 5-years old are assigned to 2 adults. Younger children require smaller groups (Bredekamp, 1987, p. 57).

Inappropriate Practice. Children participate in physical activities in larger groups than recommended for other activities, thereby necessitating the use of more teacher-directed methods and limiting the opportunities for exploration and guided discovery.

COMPONENT SEVENTEEN: FREQUENCY

Appropriate Practice. Since movement is an integral part of the total educational program, opportunities for daily, quality movement instruction are provided, exclusive of free play sessions.

Inappropriate Practice. Children do not receive scheduled daily instructional movement opportunities.

COMPONENT EIGHTEEN: FACILITIES

Appropriate Practice. Children are provided an environment in which they have adequate space to move freely and safely. Both inside and outside areas are provided.

Inappropriate Practice. Movement activities are restricted due to lack of space and/or appropriate areas.

COMPONENT NINETEEN: EQUIPMENT

Appropriate Practice. Equipment is available so that each child benefits from maximum participation. For example, every child is provided a ball. Minimal time is spent waiting in line to use large apparatus.

Equipment is matched to the size, confidence and skill level of the children so that they are motivated to actively participate. Modified, nontraditional equipment is used where appropriate, such as scarves for catching and balloons for volleying, instead of balls.

Inappropriate Practice. An insufficient amount of equipment is available for the number of children (e.g., one ball for every four children). Children regularly wait in line to use large apparatus (e.g., climbing or balancing equipment).

Regulation or "adult size" equipment is used which may inhibit skill development, injure, or intimidate the children.

COMPONENT TWENTY: MOVEMENT PROGRAMS AND PLAY

Appropriate Practice. Movement programs are a planned and organized part of the total educational program. They are integrated into the curriculum daily. Regularly scheduled indoor and outdoor play experiences enhance these planned movement experiences.

Inappropriate Practice. Children's only physical activity is scheduled as free time or play on the playground. Outdoor play is viewed as recess or a way to get children to use up excess energy; it is characterized by a lack of goals, organization, planning and instruction.

COMPONENT TWENTY-ONE: SAFE ENVIRONMENT

Appropriate Practice. Children are provided a physically and psychologically safe environment in which to explore their capabilities. Opportunities are provided for children to participate in self selected activities that lead to feelings of self-confidence and self-worth. For example, children are allowed to choose whether or not to participate in an activity.

Inappropriate Practice. Each child's readiness to learn is not considered. All children are presented the same tasks without allowing for a range of responses, thereby creating an atmosphere of apprehension and failure. For example, children are shown the "correct" way and encouraged to achieve it.

COMPONENT TWENTY-TWO: INDIVIDUAL AND FREE EXPRESSION

Appropriate Practice. Children are encouraged to use movement as a form of individual expression. They are provided opportunities to ask questions and find individual solutions to problems through movement. They are encouraged to express themselves freely.

Inappropriate Practice. Children are required to move in prescribed ways and to meet set standards of performance. Only relatively quiet, controlled activity is allowed.

COMPONENT TWENTY-THREE: FINE AND GROSS MOTOR ACTIVITIES

Appropriate Practice. Movement programs provide learning experiences with both fine (e.g., finger play activities) and gross (e.g., running, throwing) motor activities.

Inappropriate Practice. Gross motor learning experiences are emphasized to the exclusion of fine motor activities.

COMPONENT TWENTY-FOUR: REPETITION

Appropriate Practice.   Children are provided with a variety of learning experiences throughout the year that emphasize the same motor skill in order that they may develop desired movement patterns.

Inappropriate Practice.   Activities are introduced and practiced only once a year providing little opportunity for children to develop a foundation of motor patterns (e.g., scheduling kicking or throwing and catching activities only one time each year).

COMPONENT TWENTY-FIVE: PARENT-TEACHER COMMUNICATION

Appropriate Practice.   Teachers work in partnership, communicating regularly with parents. Information is provided about the movement curriculum with the intent of promoting parent involvement in children's motor skill development.

Inappropriate Practice.   No communication concerning children's motor skill development is provided to parents.

References

Bredekamp, S., ed. (1987). *Developmentally appropriate practice in early childhood programs serving children from birth through age 8.* Washington, D.C.: National Association for the Education of Young Children.

Gabbard, C. P. (1992). *Lifelong motor development.* Dubuque, Iowa: Wm. C. Brown.

Gallahue, D. L. (1989). *Understanding motor development in children* (2nd ed.). Indianapolis: Benchmark Press.

Wickstrom, R. L. (1983). *Fundamental motor patterns* (3rd ed.). Philadelphia, Penn.: Lea and Febiger.

Sources and Resources

Professional Organizations and Publications

American Alliance for Health, Physical Education, Recreation, and
  Dance (AAHPERD)
1900 Association Drive
Reston, VA 22091
Journal: *Journal of Physical Education, Recreation and Dance*
Associations under AAHPERD umbrella: National Association for
  Sport and Physical Education (NASPE) and National Dance
  Association (NDA)

Association for Childhood Education International (ACEI)
11141 Georgia Avenue, Suite 200
Wheaton, MD 20902
Journal: *Childhood Education*

Music Educators National Conference (MENC)
1902 Association Drive
Reston, VA 22091
Journal: *Music Educators Journal*

National Association for the Education of Young Children (NAEYC)
1509 16th Street, N.W.
Washington, D.C. 20036
Journal: *Young Children*

Relevant Publications

Dance Teacher Now
3101 Poplarwood Court, Suite 310
Raleigh, NC 27604

Early Childhood News
2451 East River Road
Dayton, OH 45439

Early Childhood Today
730 Broadway
New York, NY 10003

*Kids on the Move: The Newsletter Dedicated to Moving & Learning in
    Early Childhood*
6 Fieldcrest Drive
Kennebunk, ME 04043

International Gymnast
P.O. Box 2450
Oceanside, CA 92051

Movement Today
6308 Blair Hill Lane
Baltimore, MD 21209

Parent and preschooler Newsletter
P.O. Box 1167
Cutchogue, NY 11935

Teaching Elementary Physical Education (TEPE)
P.O. Box 5076
Champaign, IL 61825

Movement and Physical Education Book Publishers

AAHPERD
1900 Association Drive
Reston, VA 22091
800/321-0789

Gerstung Publications
6308 Blair Hill Lane
Baltimore, MD 21209
800/922-3575

High/Scope
600 N. River Street
Ypsilanti, MI 48198
313/485-2000

Human Kinetics
P.O. Box 5076
Champaign, IL 61825
800/747-4457

Books on Making Instruments

American Indian Music and Musical Instruments
George S. Fichter
McKay Publishers
New York, NY 10016

Make Your Own Musical Instruments
Muriel Mandell and Robert E. Wood
Sterling Publishing
419 Park Avenue South, New York, NY 10016

Making Music Instruments
Rebecca Anders
Lerner Publications
Minneapolis, MN 55401

Music and Instruments for Children to Make (Book One)
Rhythms, Music and Instruments to Make (Book Two)
John Hawkinson and Martha Faulhaber
Albert Whitman & Co.
560 West Lake Street, Chicago, IL 60606

Shake, Tap, and Play a Merry Tune
Tania K. Cowling
Fearon Teacher Aids
P.O. Box 280, Carthage, IL 62321

Sources for Ordering Instruments

Childcraft
P.O. Box 3081
Edison, NJ 08818
800/631-5652

Constructive Playthings
1227 E. 119th Street
Grandview, MO 64030
800/448-1412

Lakeshore
2695 E. Dominguez Street
Carson, CA 90749
800/428-4414

MMB Music, Inc.
10370 Page Industrial Boulevard
St. Louis, MO 63132
800/543-3771

Peripole-Bergerault, Inc.
2041 State Street
Salem, OR 97301
800/443-3592

Rhythm Band, Inc.
P.O. Box 126
Fort Worth, TX 76101
800/424-4724

Oscar Schmidt
255 Corporate Woods Parkway
Vernon Hills, IL 60061
708/913-5511

Sources for Ordering Recordings

Educational Activities, Inc.
P.O. Box 87
Baldwin, NY 11510
800/645-3739

Educational Record Center
3233 Burnt Mill Drive, Suite 100
Wilmington, NC 28403
800/438-1637

Gerstung
6308 Blair Hill Lane
Baltimore, MD 21209
800/922-3575

High/Scope
600 N. River Street
Ypsilanti, MI 48198
313/485-2000

Kimbo Educational
Dept. T, P.O. Box 477
Long Branch, NJ 07740
800/631-2187

Melody House
819 N.W. 92nd Street
Oklahoma City, OK 73114
800/234-9228

Music for Little People
P.O. Box 1460
Redway, CA 95560
800/727-2233

Pearce-Evetts Productions
P.O. Box 79117
Pittsburgh, PA 15216
800/842-9571

Sources for Ordering Equipment and Props

Bell (Early Childhood Division)
P.O. Box 886
E. Troy, WI 53120
800/543-1458

Childcraft
P.O. Box 3081
Edison, NJ 08818
800/631-5652

Chime Time
2440-C Pleasantdale Road
Atlanta, CA 30340
800/677-5075

Constructive Playthings
1227 E. 119th Street
Grandview, MO 64030
800/448-1412

Flaghouse
150 N. MacQuesten Parkway
Mt. Vernon, NY 10550
800/793-7900

Gerstung
6308 Blair Hill Lane
Baltimore, MD 21209
800/922-3575

J. L. Hammett Co.
P.O. Box 9057
Braintree, MA 02184
800/333-4600

Kaplan
P.O. Box 609
Lewisville, NC 27023
800/334-2014

Lakeshore
2695 E. Dominguez Street
Carson, CA 90749
800/428-4414

Movement Specialists and Workshops

Nancy Conkle
15214 Faubion Trail, Leander, TX 78641
512/259-5125
Terrific Me workshops address the movement needs of children while
extolling movement as a medium for teaching any material in the
curriculum.

Marjorie Corso
INSIGHTS
1933 County Road 782, Woodland Park, CO 80863
719/687-0963
A series of educational videos on the developmental motor skills of
2- to 7-year-old children.

Carol Hammett
61295 Victory Loop, Bend, OR 97702
503/382-9357
Workshops and seminars on developmentally appropriate physical
education curriculum for infants, toddlers, and 3- to 5-year-olds.

Maureen Oosten
Kids on the Move
6 Fieldcrest Drive, Kennebunk, ME 04043
207/985-9234
Movement education classes for children 2 to 12 years old and consult-
ing services, workshops, motor assessment screening, and adapted
physical education services.

Rae Pica
Moving & Learning
178A No. Barnstead Road, Center Barnstead, NH 03225
603/776-7411
Lively participatory movement and music workshops for early childhood and elementary educators. Topics and titles include "Moving
& Learning: Movement and the Young Child"; "Moving & Learning: The Integration of Physical Education and Classroom Curriculums"; and "Music and the Young Child." Workshops tailored to
meet special interests. Keynote addresses, children's performances,
and school residencies also offered.

Janet E. Santopietro
P.E. For Preschools
6592 Benton Circle, Arvada, CO 80003
303/432-2234

Programs designed for children ages $2\frac{1}{2}$ through kindergarten in the preschool setting. Programs focus on fundamental motor skills and related concepts in creative movement, rhythms, simple games, and use of large and small apparatus/equipment.

Phyllis Weikart
High/Scope
600 N. River Street, Ypsilanti, MI 48198
313/485-2000, ext. 211
Offers a variety of training options as well as a Summer Institute program. Workshops include "Teaching Movement—The Young Child"; "Teaching Movement—K-6 Approach"; and "Teaching Movement—The Older Child."

GLOSSARY

Bound flow   Describes movement that is punctuated or halting, such as the movements of a robot.

Creative dance   An art form based on natural movement rather than the stylized movements used in ballet or other forms of theatrical dancing.

Creativity   It is not necessarily related to academic intelligence. The potential for creativity exists in all people, but the greatest chance for its development exists in children between the ages of three- and five-years old. See Creativity and the Young Child in Chapter One for multiple perspectives and definitions of creativity.

Educational gymnastics   A child-oriented, natural progression of the exploration of fundamental movement skills that teaches body management—on the floor and with small and large apparatus—and develops strength, stamina, and flexibility through exploration and discovery. Educational gymnastics are not similar to Olympic gymnastics, where the student's ability to execute stunts determines success or failure.

Elements of movement   Describe *how* a movement is performed. If we liken movement education to the study of grammar, the skills themselves can be considered *verbs,* while the six movement elements (space, shape, time, force, flow, and rhythm) are the *adverbs* modifying them.

Emotional disabilities   They affect a child's ability to learn and are not related to sensory, health or intellectual problems. Such children are often depressed and have difficulties with social relationships and demonstrate inappropriate behavior.

Emotionally handicapped   A term regularly used to describe children with emotional disabilities. Two of the most common behaviors ascribed to emotionally handicapped children are a lack of self-control and a refusal to participate.

Free flow   An uninterrupted movement, such as is visible in ice skating.

General space It is normally limited only by floors, walls, and ceilings. It may also be referred to as shared space.

Hearing impairment Refers to the malfunctioning of the auditory mechanism. Unless there is damage to the semicircular canals, which causes problems with balance, the major challenges for hearing-impaired children in movement programs are related to the use of music and the presentation of instructions.

Individual Family Service Plans (IFSPs) These are required by law for children who qualify for special services and who are under the age of five. Like the Individual Education Plans (IEPs) for school-aged children, the IFSP is developed with input from parents, teachers and service providers. The goal of the plan is to outline short- and long-term goals in one or more developmental areas.

Learning disabled Children who possess average or above-average intelligence but have difficulty in using written or spoken language.

Limited understanding The term as used in this text describes children with learning disabilities as well as those with mild or moderate retardation. Generally, children with limited understanding have a short attention span and tend to become easily discouraged.

Locomotor skills Transport the body as a whole from one point to another. Although it is commonly believed that children acquire and develop locomotor skills automatically, in fact, children are unable to reach a mature stage of development without practice, encouragement and instruction.

Manipulative skills Are defined in this text as any gross motor skill which usually involves an object being manipulated.

Mental retardation Can be defined in many ways. Most commonly, this term refers to below-average intellectual functioning concurrent with an inability to mature personally and socially with age. Mentally retarded children usually are below average in motor development as well, possibly because of cognitive difficulties or a lack of opportunities for physical activity.

Modalities of knowledge acquisition These are divided into four basic groups: visual, auditory, tactile, and kinesthetic.

Movement education Is a success-oriented, child-centered form of physical education emphasizing fundamental movements and the discovery of their variations, which can later be used in games, sports, dance, gymnastics, and life itself.

Nonlocomotor skills   Are movements performed in place, usually while standing, kneeling, sitting, or lying. They involve the axis of the body rotating around a fixed point. Some textbooks describe these as nonmanipulative skills.

Perceptual-motor theorists   Believe that movement is essential to a child's learning process. Unlike cognitive development, which requires children to use and process abstract information (using words and/or numbers), perceptual-motor development relies on the concrete, physical dimensions of the environment.

Personal space   The area immediately surrounding the body. It includes whatever can be reached while remaining in one spot and can be likened to a large bubble surrounding the body.

Physical fitness   According to the American Alliance for Health, Physical Education, Recreation and Dance, is a physical state of well-being that allows people to perform daily activities with vigor, reduce their risk of health problems relative to lack of exercise and establish a fitness base for participation in a variety of physical activities.

Physically challenged   These children are the fastest growing population of children receiving special education services. Among these children are those with disabilities caused by birth defects, accidents, or illness. In one way or another, the mobility of these children is restricted.

Qualities of movement   Are divided into six categories: sustained, suspended, swinging, percussive, vibratory, and collapsing.

Social development   A long and continuous process that begins with self-discovery and results in the ability to interact with others.

Social play   Is divided into six categories: unoccupied behavior, onlooker behavior, solitary play, parallel play, associative play, and cooperative play.

Spectrum of teaching styles   A model of instructional styles based on the premise that the teaching/learning process involves decisions made by the learner before, during, and after learning. Also referred to as Mosston's Spectrum, this model is now accepted and applied throughout the world.

Step-hop   A movement commonly performed in folk dances. Like the skip, it is a combination of a step and a hop; however, unlike the skip, the two movements have the same value and the accent is on the step.

Visually challenged   Those whose visual impairments, even when corrected, adversely affect their learning. With minor modifications, a movement education program can meet the needs of visually impaired children.

INDEX